TORONTO

AND NEARBY ATTRACTIONS

1987

Editor: Gail Chasan
Area Editor: Valerie Ross
Editorial Contributors: Mark Czarnecki, Gloria Hildebrandt, Mechtild Hoppenrath, Helga Loverseed, Paul McGrath, Charles Oberdorf, Pierre Ouimet, Hal Quinn
Illustrations: Ted Burwell
Maps and Plans: Pictograph

FODOR'S TRAVEL GUIDES
New York & London

The following Fodor's Guides are current; most are also available in a British
edition published by Hodder & Stoughton.

Country and Area Guides

Australia, New Zealand
  & the South Pacific
Austria
Bahamas
Belgium & Luxembourg
Bermuda
Brazil
Canada
Canada's Maritime
  Provinces
Caribbean
Central America
Eastern Europe
Egypt
Europe
France
Germany
Great Britain
Greece
Holland
India, Nepal &
  Sri Lanka
Ireland
Israel
Italy
Japan
Jordan & the Holy Land
Kenya
Korea
Mexico
New Zealand
North Africa
People's Republic
  of China
Portugal
Province of Quebec
Scandinavia
Scotland
South America
South Pacific
Southeast Asia
Soviet Union
Spain
Sweden
Switzerland
Turkey
Yugoslavia

City Guides

Amsterdam
Beijing, Guangzhou,
  Shanghai
Boston
Chicago
Dallas & Fort Worth
Greater Miami & the
  Gold Coast
Hong Kong
Houston & Galveston
Lisbon
London
Los Angeles
Madrid
Mexico City &
  Acapulco
Munich
New Orleans
New York City
Paris
Philadelphia
Rome
San Diego
San Francisco
Singapore
Stockholm, Copenhagen,
  Oslo, Helsinki &
  Reykjavik
Sydney
Tokyo
Toronto
Vienna
Washington, D.C.

U.S.A. Guides

Alaska
Arizona
California
Cape Cod
Chesapeake
Colorado
Far West
Florida
Hawaii
I–95: Maine to Miami
New England

New Mexico
New York State
Pacific North Coast
South
Texas
U.S.A.
Virginia

Budget Travel

American Cities (30)
Britain
Canada
Caribbean
Europe
France
Germany
Hawaii
Italy
Japan
London
Mexico
Spain

Fun Guides

Acapulco
Bahamas
Las Vegas
London
Maui
Montreal
New Orleans
New York City
The Orlando Area
Paris
Puerto Rico
Rio
St. Martin/Sint Maarten
San Francisco
Waikiki

Special-Interest Guides

Selected Hotels of Europe
Ski Resorts of North
  America
Views to Dine by around
  the World

CONTENTS

CONTENTS

FOREWORD

Only within the last two decades has Toronto come into its own as one of the most exciting cities in North America. It is also a young city in that so many of its people are either newly arrived (from places such as Italy, Portugal, India, Korea, China, and Middle Europe) or are simply young professional men and women from all over Canada who are bursting with energy. These changes are reflected in the city's ever growing shopping, restaurant, theater (*especially* theater), and night-life scenes. With the possible exceptions of Yorkville and the Eaton Centre enclosed shopping mall, the best places are scattered throughout the city and are not easy to find out. You will need a guide.

Fodor's Toronto is designed to try to describe and explain the city to you, and to help you decide, once you're there, what you want to do and where you want to go. We have therefore concentrated on giving you the broadest **range** of choices the city offers, and within that range to present **selections** that will be safe, solid, and of value to you. The descriptions we provide are just enough for you to make intelligent choices from among our selections, based on your own tastes and pocketbook.

All selections and comments in *Fodor's Toronto* are based on the editors' and contributors' personal experience. We feel that our first responsibililty is to inform and protect you, the reader. Errors are bound to creep into any travel guide, however. We go to press in the summer, and much change can and will occur in Toronto even while we are on press and during the succeeding twelve months or so when this edition is on sale. We cannot, therefore, be responsible for the sudden closing of a restaurant, a change in a museum's days or hours, a shift of chefs (for the worse), and so forth. We sincerely welcome letters from readers on these changes, or from those whose opinions differ from ours, and we are ready to revise our entries for next year's edition when the facts warrant it.

Send your letters to the editors at **Fodor's Travel Guides, 2 Park Avenue, New York, NY 10016.** Continental readers may prefer to write to Fodor's Travel Guides, 9–10 Market Place, London W1N 7AG, England.

Our special thanks to Steve Veale of the Government of Ontario Ministry of Tourism and Recreation in Toronto for his unstinting help during the development of this book.

LANGUAGE/30

For the Business or Vacationing International Traveler

In 30 languages! A basic language course on 2 cassettes and a phrase book ... Only $14.95 ea. + shipping

Nothing flatters people more than to hear visitors try to speak their language and LANGUAGE/30, used by thousands of satisfied travelers, gets you speaking the basics quickly and easily. Each LANGUAGE/30 course offers:

- approximately 1½ hours of guided practice in greetings, asking questions and general conversation
- special section on social customs and etiquette

Order yours today. Languages available: YIDDISH (available fall '86)

ARABIC	INDONESIAN	PORTUGUESE
CHINESE	IRISH	VIETNAMESE
DANISH	ITALIAN	RUSSIAN
DUTCH	TURKISH	SERBO-CROATIAN
FINNISH	JAPANESE	SPANISH
FRENCH	KOREAN	SWAHILI
GERMAN	LATIN	SWEDISH
GREEK	NORWEGIAN	TAGALOG
HEBREW	PERSIAN	THAI
HINDI	POLISH	

To order send $14.95 per course + shipping $2.00 1st course, $1 ea. add. course. In Canada $3 1st course, $2.00 ea. add. course. NY and CA residents add state sales tax. Outside USA and Canada $14.95 (U.S.) + air mail shipping: $8 for 1st course, $5 ea. add. course. MasterCard, VISA and Am. Express card users give brand, account number (all digits), expiration date and signature.
SEND TO: FODOR'S, Dept. LC 760, 2 Park Ave., NY 10016-5677, USA.

FACTS AT YOUR FINGERTIPS

 FACTS AND FIGURES. First settled by French traders in the 1730s, Toronto (or York, as it was known then) has since grown to be Canada's capital of business, finance and anglophone culture.

Today, Metropolitan Toronto is the largest and most populous city in the country, covering an area of 632 square kilometers and the home of more than 2.2 million Torontonians. They are an increasingly mixed lot. Nearly 235,000 Italians make this as large an Italian-speaking city as Florence, Italy. It has the largest Portuguese population in North America, and the continent's second largest conglomeration of Estonians. About 60 percent of the city's population was born somewhere else. Since a remarkable number came to Toronto as refugees—from Hungary, Poland, Latin America, Vietnam, and the Vietnam War-era United States—they have added a sharp edge to the city's traditionally phlegmatic political climate. They have also wrought miracles on Toronto's dining scene.

It is important to note when using this guide that the Municipality of Metropolitan Toronto, established in 1953, includes the cities of North York, Etobicoke, York, and Scarborough, as well as the City of Toronto. Also included in the metropolitan area is the borough of East York. In fact, Toronto was the first community in the Western Hemisphere to give full political recognition to the metropolitan-area concept of urban government.

 WHEN TO GO. You'll enjoy Toronto anytime, but residents may wonder if you arrive in February or March, when the long months of winter are starting to wear on nerves. Yet winter and its lengthy prologue and epilogue are the best times to sample the city's cultural life. Symphony, opera, ballet, and hockey hold their formal seasons between September and May, the city's smaller theaters launch original plays, and the commercial and public galleries open their major shows. The city used to be quieter in the summer, but that difference is growing less marked. As the weather gets warmer, music moves into the parks and the lakeside amphitheater at Ontario Place. Hits of the winter theater season extend throughout summer, gardens unlock their gates, and restaurants open their courtyards and sidewalks to diners. Summer is the time of fairs and festivals. The city's West Indian community throws a huge party named "Caribana," when extravagantly costumed dancers throng the streets. Folk and ethnic festivals park on the lawns of the Toronto Islands, and that hoary old institution, "The Ex"—the Canadian National Exhibition (CNE)—turns West Toronto into a traffic jam and midway.

Today, then, Toronto offers excitement all year long. But whenever you come, prepare for wild variations in temperature. The extremes can make the city look like two different places. In summer, with its long, humid days and

1

warm evenings, crowds stroll the streets until the early morning hours. Winter storms can dump snow a foot high on Toronto and transform city streets into ski tracks. Air-conditioning in summer can give you the chills, and overheated buildings in winter can have you peeling down to your shirtsleeves. A final note of caution: salt on winter streets will ravage leather boots and shoes.

CLIMATE. When you ask Torontonians about their climate, they will invariably grumble about the cold. "Ten months of winter," they say with some exaggeration, "followed by two months of bad skiing."

Fortunately, the city's public works department is efficient and experienced. A prodigious snowfall that would cripple an English or American city on the Eastern Seaboard can be quickly dealt with by a brigade of plows, salt scatterers, and ice chippers. As well, Toronto's intricate network of underground shopping concourses that extends underneath the wind-whipped streets makes it painless to walk for many city blocks, regardless of the weather.

An often brief spring season is followed by three months of hot summer, which sends steamy citizens swarming to poolsides and the shores of Lake Ontario.

The approach of fall can bring a welcome moderation in temperature, and even the most sanguine Torontonians delight in the stunning autumn colors before they start grumbling again about winter.

Average Temperatures

| | Celsius | | Fahrenheit | |
	high	low	high	low
January	−1.1	−7.7	30.1	18.1
April	11.9	3.2	53.4	37.8
July	26.8	16.1	80.3	62.3
October	15.3	7.1	59.6	44.8

PACKING. Winter weather can extend from November to April in Toronto, so bring your warmest coat, hat, scarf, gloves and salt-proof, waterproof boots. Keeping warm and dry in winter is essential for a visitor's enjoyment. Lake Ontario, providing cool relief in summer, can cause winter dampness that seems to get at your bones. You will be more comfortable if you layer your clothing than you will be if you wear just one heavy garment.

Summer temperatures can exceed those of the Caribbean, so pack as you would for the Islands. Light, loose clothing is best. As well, you'll appreciate a hat and sunglasses when out in the glaring sun. Bring a bathing suit. Tuck in a sweater or light jacket in case the nights turn cool.

It's harder to pack for fall, because Indian summer often carries high temperatures into October; heavy fall clothing may be inappropriate at this time.

Clothes and separates that layer well or fit comfortably under a medium jacket are best.

Whenever you come, bring comfortable walking shoes and clothing. Arguably the safest metropolis in North America, Toronto is a city in which to wander. If you plan a lot of walking, a light day pack may be handy for carrying lunches or shopping. Bring rain gear and an umbrella, especially in spring.

If you intend to go to the city's better restaurants or the big, established theaters, you will want appropriate clothes. No *maitre d'* balks at women in pants suits, but men may need jacket and tie. Clean, casual clothes are fine for everything else, although bare chests, exposed midriffs, shorts, and bare feet are usually seen only at parks and beaches. Polyester and leisure suits could earn you a sneer in snootier downtown areas, but the folks in suburbia couldn't care less.

Other items to remember include your camera, guidebooks, and insect repellant if you'll be in wooded areas or heading farther north. Blackflies and mosquitoes can be nasty from May to July.

If you wear prescription lenses, take an extra pair or at least the prescription itself.

 PLANNING YOUR TRIP. The best preparation for your trip is to read up on the area, reserve your hotel and big nights in advance, and check weather reports. Send for publications from Metropolitan Toronto Convention and Visitors Association, Suite 110, 220 Yonge St., Toronto M5B 2H1. Ask a travel agent about package tours to Toronto, because these can be cheaper than arrangements you make yourself. Renting a car can be more bother than help, especially since public transport is good and taxis are plentiful. But, if you plan day trips or jaunts to such suburban attractions as the zoo, a car is undeniably an asset. The Canadian Automobile Association's Ontario Motor League is affiliated with the American Automobile Association. It offers road and weather reports at 925–6341, emergency road services at 966–3000, and technical, legal, and rental information as well. Don't book a suburban hotel if you plan to spend all your time downtown, and vice versa; Toronto sprawls over a wide area, and traveling time can eat up several hours of a day.

Make sure your passport (it's always best to have one) and identification papers are valid. Senior citizens (over 65) and students may be eligible for discounts to many attractions. Bring your major credit cards (American Express, VISA, MasterCard, Diner's Club) and transfer your money into travelers' checks.

Secure your home and your pets, and, if you are driving, make sure your car is mechanically fit. Investigate the cost and benefits of travelers' or health insurance.

```
13.06
534
2400
$230
```

WHAT WILL IT COST? Toronto has one of the highest cost-of-living ratings in Canada, but that does not make it too pricey for tourists. If you know where to look, the city can accommodate champagne appetites and beer pocketbooks. Millionaires and crowned heads of state can pay a premium price for the very best in North American quality and service, but this is really a city of bourgeois delights—decency, cleanliness, good food, safety, and affordability.

Whether luxury or economy are the most important considerations in your trip, it is best to plan and book accommodations before your visit. This will help you estimate your total expenses, as accommodation is usually the largest daily expense. Conversely, it is often better to avoid booking theater tickets in advance; significant discounts on tickets for same-day performances are available at the Five Star Tickets booth (no phone) at the corner of Yonge Street and Dundas.

Nonwinning lottery tickets can sometimes bring discounts to attractions and cultural events. For information, call Public Relations at the Ontario Lottery Corporation, 961–6262, ext. 300.

The relatively high cost of dining out can be limited if you avoid hotel room-service—especially if you are on a budget—and compare the savings if you go out for breakfast to eating it in your hotel. You might shave a third or more off the bill.

Actual prices for accommodations vary widely. As a result, we have estimated costs within a range from $10 per night at the Toronto International Hostel on Church Street (for the backpack and sleeping-bag crowd) to more than $120 for double occupancy at a deluxe hotel. Similarly, a fine dinner can cost $40 a person, not including a bottle of imported wine, while a tasty meal at a delicatessen or ethnic eatery might leave the pair of you beaming over the $15 bill. Specific price ranges and recommendations for food, shopping, and lodging can be found in the *Practical Information* section of this guide.

The following table (in Canadian dollars) provides an indication of the type of daily expenditure that two people might make. Note that many of the tours discussed later in this guide are free of charge.

Typical Daily Budget For Two People

Hotel room–moderate hotel	$65
Breakfast	6
Sightseeing tour	22
Inexpensive lunch	10
Admission to museum or gallery	10
Evening cocktails	10
Dinner at moderate restaurant	35
	$158

TOURIST INFORMATION. The most convenient and complete tourist information can be obtained by writing, calling, or visiting the Metropolitan Toronto Convention & Visitors Association at its office at Toronto Eaton Centre, 220 Yonge St., Box 510, Suite 110, Toronto Ontario M5B 2H1 (416–979 –3143), Monday to Friday, 9:00 A.M. to 5:00 P.M. Guide pamphlets, maps, and a quarterly booklet called *Metro Toronto Happenings* are offered free. In summer, the association also sets up distinctive red-and-white visitors' information booths in many high-traffic street locations.

Other sources of information of interest to visitors include the entertainment sections of Toronto's three daily papers: *The Globe & Mail, The Toronto Star,* and the *Toronto Sun. Now* is a weekly entertainment newspaper listing pop and underground cultural events; it is available free at many midtown restaurants, cafés, and shops. Some monthly publications, such as *Toronto Life* magazine, carry restaurant reviews and upcoming events, as well as annual features on where to get inexpensive merchandise. Teleguide terminals offer free information on all aspects of Toronto, and are located in hotels, shopping malls, attractions, and other public places.

 TIPS FOR BRITISH VISITORS. Passports. Visas are not required to enter Canada, but you must of course have a valid passport (British Visitor's Passports are also valid for entry into Canada). Passports are valid for ten years and fee is £15; British Visitor's Passports are valid only 1 year, cost £7.50. No health certificates are required for entry.

Customs. If you are 18 or older, you may import duty-free: 200 cigarettes and 50 cigars and 2 lb. tobacco; plus, 1 bottle (40 fl. oz.) liquor or 24 pints of beer; plus, a small amount of perfume; plus other goods to the value of $40. Do not take in meats, seeds, plants, or fruits, etc.

Insurance. We heartily recommend you insure yourself, to cover health and motoring mishaps, with *Europ Assistance,* 252 High St., Croydon, Surrey CRO INF (01–680 1234). Their excellent service is all the more valuable when you consider the possible costs of health care in Canada.

Travel Agents. When planning a holiday, a good travel agent is probably the traveler's best friend as they can set you up with any of a vast array of travel arrangements, from simple flight reservations to land and air package tours. There is no charge for using an agent as they simply get a percentage of the booking cost, paid for by the tour operator or airline.

Tour Operators. The following handle Canadian tours:

Thomas Cook, Ltd., P.O. Box 36, Thorpe Wood, Peterborough, PE3 6SB.

Jetsave, Sussex House, London Rd., East Grinstead RH19 1LD.

Speedbird, Alta House, 152 King St., London W.6.

Trekamerica Ltd., Trek House, The Bullring, Deddington, Oxford, Oxon OX5 4TT.

Air Fares. We suggest that you explore the current scene for budget flight possibilities. Unfortunately, there is no longer any standby service on any of the major airlines; but do check their APEX and other fares at a considerable saving over the full price. Quite frankly, only business travelers who don't have to watch the price of their tickets fly full-price these days—and find themselves sitting right beside an APEX passenger!

VISAS AND CUSTOMS. Although Canada has had long-standing political and cultural ties with Great Britain, the bulk of the country's tourists come from the United States. Because of the close ties between Canada and the United States during the last century, customs regulations between the two countries are generally liberal. Citizens and legal residents of the United States do not require passports or visas to enter Canada. Some form of proof of birth or citizenship is, however, advisable. Permanent U.S. residents who are not citizens require an alien registration ("green card") receipt.

Canada Customs allows visitors to bring boats, trailers, hunting rifles, shotguns, and 200 rounds of ammunition without paying any duty. As visiting British rock stars have discovered, the smuggling of narcotics and other contraband items is frowned upon and may lead to an extended visit in the province's penal system. There are limits on tobacco, and handguns and automatic weapons are strictly prohibited. If you are driving a rented car, be sure to retain the contract. While cats may enter freely, dogs must be brought in with proof of a veterinary inspection to ensure they are free of communicable diseases. Finally, any plant material must be declared and inspected.

CURRENCY. The monetary unit in Canada is the dollar (all prices in this guide refer to Canadian dollars unless otherwise indicated), which floats in the world's currency exchange market. After paper currency, the smaller units include the quarter ($.25), the dime ($.10), the nickel ($.05), and the penny ($.01).

U.S. currency is accepted at most larger shops, stores, and restaurants, but it is advisable to exchange any foreign currency at a bank or exchange firm, which usually offer rates 5 percent to 10 percent higher than those given by retail establishments. The current official exchange rate is about $.70 U.S. to the Canadian dollar, but banks and firms usually exchange at a premium above this rate.

Any Canadian bank or trust company will exchange U.S. or British currency. But banking hours generally run Monday to Thursday, 10:00 A.M. to 3:00 P.M. and Friday 10:00 A.M. to 6:00 P.M. (some suburban banks are open Saturdays). So it may be wise to exchange currency at one of the three Toronto locations of Deak-Perera Ltd., which have longer hours and exchange all kinds of currency: 10 King St. E., 863–1611, the Sheraton Centre, 862–8677, or the ManuLife Centre, 961–9822. For full listings of bank branches and exchange firms see the Yellow Pages.

HINTS TO THE MOTORIST. The Toronto Transit Commission (TTC) urges citizens to use public transit to avoid traffic congestion in the downtown core. And public transit is fast, safe, and cheap. Still, many tourists may find it more comfortable to get around Toronto's large urban area in the comfort of their own cars. For such visitors, there are a number of useful hints that will make motoring in the city more pleasant and less stressful.

The use of seat belts is mandatory in Ontario. Infants must be strapped into infant car seats; holding your child on your lap is illegal. Motorcyclists must wear helmets and always drive with their headlights on.

Speed limits are 50 kilometers per hour (approximately 30 m.p.h.) unless otherwise posted. If your speedometer only shows m.p.h., remember also that 40 k./hr. is approximately 25 m.p.h., and the highway speed limits of 80, 90 and 100 k./hr. roughly correspond to 50, 55 and 60 m.p.h. As well, pedestrian crosswalks are marked with overhead signs and large painted Xs, right turns on red lights are allowed, and there is usually no parking, stopping, or standing on main streets during the rush hours of 7:00 A.M. to 9:00 A.M. and 4:00 P.M. to 6:00 P.M.

Many main streets in the downtown area have streetcar service, which may pose problems to the uninitiated driver. Remember to wait behind the rear doors of a streetcar when it has stopped to take on or let off passengers.

When visiting in winter, make sure your car is equipped with a good set of all-weather or snow tires, as snowy and slushy road conditions are common. The use of studs on tires is not allowed in Ontario.

HOTELS AND MOTELS. Consider your plans carefully when choosing accommodations. A suburban hotel with moderate rates is not a good choice if you have to travel downtown every day. But, if you're just stopping over on your way through town, don't go to a plush downtown hotel. There are hotels near the airport and motels along Highway 401.

Be sure to reserve ahead, because conventions and peak seasons can crowd hotels. Accommodation Toronto is a service of the Hotel Association of Toronto and can help you find the accommodation you want at the price you want. Call (416) 596–7117.

DINING OUT. There is an impressive range of restaurants in Toronto. The cuisines of Peru, the Middle East, Vietnam, Japan, Portugal, and Greece, in addition to the familiar French, Italian, Chinese, and North American menus, are available here. There are places to suit the most particular palates: vegetarians, raw-seafood lovers, meat-and-potato traditionalists, and children. The prices range widely as well.

You are advised to make reservations for lunch or dinner at the more expensive places, but if you forgot to, don't be afraid to drop in and ask if there's a free table. Casual places don't require reservations, but if they are popular there may be lines of people waiting for a table. Most restaurants are open from Tuesday to Saturday; some close on Sunday, some on Monday. So, check ahead unless you are eating in hotel dining rooms, which are open weeklong.

TIPPING. Tipping, the cause of as many headaches as any other element of traveling, is supposed to be a voluntary expression of appreciation for good service, but one usually does it out of habit or shame. These days, it seems that everyone expects money for often barely adequate service. How much, when, and to whom are questions that visitors should not have to ask. But they do, so here are some rules of thumb.

Taxi drivers are used to getting 10 to 15 percent and won't get out to open the door for you. Bellhops get $.50 a bag, while sundry other hotel service people expect $1. Hairdressers, bartenders, waiters, and waitresses all anticipate 15 percent of the total bill. For one-night stays in hotels you leave nothing. But for longer stays, or particularly arduous clean-ups after wild hotel-room parties, leave $1 to $2 per person per week.

Many of these people rely on tips for part of their income and are supposed to work for this by providing good service. When someone has been particularly prompt or thoughtful, a good tip is clearly in order. When service has been surly or inconsiderate, a small tip or none at all is supposed to communicate your displeasure. All too often, this is simply misunderstood. If restaurant service spoiled your meal, write on the bill that because of your dissatisfaction, you are not leaving a tip. If you can be precise about the reason, do so. You'll feel good that you stood up for yourself.

DRINKING LAWS. The legal drinking age in Ontario is 19. Lately, Toronto has become very conscious of the dangers of drunken driving. If motorists are found to have over 0.08% of alcohol in their blood levels, they may lose their licenses, their cars for a night, or spend a few hours behind bars of a different kind. For this reason, walking, public transit, or taxis are in order for anyone planning to spend an alcoholic night on the town.

All licensed bars, taverns, and restaurants are open from noon to 1:00 A.M., when Ontario's "Blue Laws" state they must close. Many taverns and restaurants serving food are also licensed to serve liquor on Sundays, and these usually remain open till 11:00 P.M.

Beer, wine, and liquor are not sold in grocery stores but are regulated by the provincial government and distributed through government-run outlets. Beer may be purchased at any Brewer's Retail store, open weekdays from 10:00 A.M. to 10:00 P.M. and Saturday from 10:00 A.M. to 8:00 P.M. Liquor, wine and some beer may be bought at the Liquor Control Board of Ontario (LCBO) locations listed in the phone books. These are open for business Monday, Tuesday, Wednesday and Saturday from 10:00 A.M. to 6:00 P.M., Thursday and Friday to 9:00 P.M. It's handy to know that a few LCBOs, such as the one at Yonge and Summerhill subway and others in plazas, are open until 10:00 P.M. on week nights. Domestic wines may also be obtained in retail outlets owned by the various wine-producing companies.

 BUSINESS HOURS, HOLIDAYS, AND LOCAL TIME. The first thing the visitor should do when arriving in Toronto is to adjust his or her watch to local time. Metropolitan Toronto and all of central and eastern Ontario uses Eastern Standard Time, which means if you are from Montreal, New York, or Bogota, Colombia, you won't gain or lose an hour of sleep. Visitors from London will have to set back their watches five hours, and those from Vancouver or Los Angeles must adjust ahead by three hours.

Business hours in the city can vary, but generally retail stores are open Monday through Saturday, 10:00 A.M. to 6:00 P.M. Many of the large department stores and shopping malls are open longer, to 9:00 or 9:30 P.M., particularly on Thursday and Friday nights. Because of Toronto's Lord's Day Act, the only retail stores that are permitted to open on Sundays are those in designated tourist areas, such as Markham Village, Chinatown, and Queen's Quay at Harbourfront. The continued applicability of this act is being fought in the courts, and Toronto may soon give retailers the option to carry on business on Sunday. Most restaurants and convenience stores (Becker's, Mac's Milk, 7–11) are open on Sundays. Most streetcars and some buses run around the clock, but subways operate only between 6:00 A.M. (9:00 A.M. on Sundays) and 1:30 A.M. After that, you take a night bus.

Banks in the city, traditionally open Monday through Thursday from 10:00 A.M. to 3:00 P.M. and Friday from 10:00 A.M. to 6:00 P.M., have been experimenting with extended hours. Access to funds has been made even more convenient with the proliferation of automated teller machines across the city. Bank branch locations can be found in the Yellow Pages.

The main civic and national holidays observed in Toronto are:

New Year's Day, January 1; Good Friday, Friday before Easter; Easter Monday, Monday after Easter; Victoria Day, fourth Monday in May; Dominion Day, July 1; Civic Holiday, first Monday in August; Labour Day, first Monday in September; Thanksgiving, second Monday in October; Remembrance Day, November 11; Christmas Day, December 25; Boxing Day, December 26. Note that Remembrance Day, November 11, is not a legal holiday, and only government offices and schools are likely to be closed. It should also be noted that when a holiday falls on a weekend, the following Monday is taken as the holiday.

SEASONAL EVENTS. There is something different happening every month in Toronto, although the weather dictates the kind of activity.

To get help in planning your visit, write ahead to the Metropolitan Toronto Convention & Visitors Association (see the *Tourist Information* section above) and ask for information on upcoming special events. Once in town, check the newspapers, magazines, and Teleguide terminals for theater, dance, music productions, other happenings.

The major winter events are skating at City Hall Square, cross-country skiing at the Metro Zoo, and sleigh riding at Black Creek Pioneer Village. The International Boat Show comes to town in January and the Sportsman's Show takes place in March. June brings a quickening of the city's festivities. There's the Toronto International Festival (music and dance), Caravan (a celebration of the city's ethnic communities), and the opening of the Stratford and Shaw theater festivals. Caribana in July is a kind of mardi gras put on by the city's West Indian communities. The Canadian National Exhibition (CNE) opens in August. In September, cinematographers flock to town for the Festival of Festivals (a film fête). November brings the Royal Winter Fair and Horse Show. For more detailed information on seasonal events, see *Practical Information.*

PARTICIPANT SPORTS. "Participaction" is a high-profile Federal Government program that for the past decade has urged Canadians to improve their slothful habits. The boom in health and fitness awareness has led to a growth of facilities in and around the Metro area, and visitors to Toronto now have a wide choice of ways in which to exercise year-round.

Favorite summer activities include sailing on Lake Ontario, jogging and cycling alongside it, and swimming—but only the brave swim in it. Most people prefer Toronto's many free—and cleaner—public pools. Swimming can also be a year-round affair, as there are fourteen indoor pools within the City of Toronto alone. Phone 392–7259 for more aquatic information.

One of the newest watersports, boardsailing, is also growing in popularity, and lessons and board rentals can be arranged at High Park and at the Beaches area rental shops and sailing clubs. You can fish, fly, hike, and horseback ride within Metropolitan Toronto's city limits.

Golf lovers will be pleased to know that there are over thirty-two private and public golf courses in the Toronto area. Information on public courses may be obtained by phoning City Parks at 392–7291. For private clubs offering pay-as-you-play deals, consult the Yellow Pages.

Tennis is also available at the numerous free public courts. For the one nearest you, phone City Parks at 392–7291.

Winter shouldn't limit your exercise as there are many indoor and outdoor skating rinks, which are generally open from December through the end of February. The large rink in front of City Hall is a favorite. Skaters also glide on rinks in the middle of Yorkville's Hazelton Lanes shopping complex and at College Park (between Yonge, Bay, and College streets).

Although there is little consensus on the most thrilling tobogganing hill in the city, some prime locations include Christie Pits, High Park, and golf courses in the Don Valley and Riverdale Park just east of Cabbagetown.

Canadians love to ski as much as they love hockey, and the visitor will find several skiing resorts within a 90-minute drive from Toronto; see the *Nearby Attractions* chapters.

CAMPING. Although camping may not be the most comfortable way to experience Toronto's cosmopolitan pleasures, there are a few locations convenient enough for the real enthusiast or the budget-minded. Many private campgrounds in southern Ontario are close enough to the city to make commuting possible. A list of these licensed and inspected private campgrounds and trailer parks may be had from Travel Information, Ministry of Industry and Tourism, Third Floor, Hearst Block, Queen's Park, Toronto M7A 2E5.

A list of provincial parks and recreation and conservation areas is available from Provincial Parks Information, Whitney Block, Queen's Park, Toronto M7A 1W3.

The only location offering tent and trailer camping within Metropolitan Toronto is in the 25-acre Glen Rouge Park in the city's northeast end. The park offers nature trails, horseback riding, and proximity to Metro's renowned zoo.

 HUNTING. The only shooting that the visitor is likely to be doing within the Metropolitan Toronto area is with a camera in front of City Hall. You usually have to drive a few hours out of town to do any hunting, although as deer become increasingly pesky gourmets of suburban shrubbery, some townships just west of Toronto are experimenting with a controlled hunt. Deer, moose, and black bear seasons are in the fall. Waterfowl season goes from fall to winter and in the spring the Ministry of Natural Resources permits spring bear and small game seasons. Handguns are, of course, prohibited, and bag limits depend on environmental considerations. Be sure to obey all "No Hunting" or "No Trespassing" signs. Licenses are available at The Wildlife Branch, Ministry of Natural Resources, Queen's Park, Toronto M7A 1W3, or at most sporting goods stores.

Information on game, seasons, and restrictions can be obtained by writing the Ministry's Wildlife Branch or calling them at 416–965–4251. Additional information is available from the Ontario Federation of Anglers and Hunters, P.O. Box 1269, Campbellford, Ontario.

 FISHING. One of Ontario's greatest natural resources, the lakes and rivers that cover a large portion of the province, provide the fisherman with boundless opportunities for freshwater fishing of trout, perch, bass, walleye, salmon, muskies, pike, and whitefish.

There are many waterways within relatively easy driving distance of Toronto. For locations, seasonal information, and restrictions, write to The Wildlife Branch, Ministry of Natural Resources, Queen's Park, Toronto M7A 1W3; 416–965–4251. Check with the Ministry if you intend to eat your catch, as many species may contain contaminants.

Within Metro Toronto, fishing is permitted in the well-stocked depths of the trout pond at Hanlon's Point on Toronto Islands and Grenadier Pond in High Park. An interesting fishing event takes place right off the Toronto shoreline.

The annual "Great Salmon Derby," sponsored by *The Toronto Star,* is held every summer. Substantial prizes are awarded for the biggest salmon caught, and a $1 million cash prize is offered to the fisherman who reels in the specially tagged "million-dollar salmon."

 NATIONAL AND PROVINCIAL PARKS. Parks Canada operates four national parks in Ontario, only two of which are located close enough to Toronto to be of interest to the visitor.

Georgian Bay Islands National Park is situated on forty islands covering 5.4 square miles in the Georgian Bay of Lake Huron. Features include excellent fishing, wildlife, scuba diving around sunken wrecks, and the rock formations of Flowerpot Island (access point is Tobermory on the Bruce Peninsula). Admission is free and camping for up to 14 days is permitted. It takes about two hours to drive the approximately 210 kilometers (130 miles) from Toronto to Honey Harbour, the park's main access point.

The six square miles of *Point Pelee National Park* are a mecca for bird watchers during the spring and fall migratory seasons. Situated on the southernmost peninsula in Canada (at the same latitude as Northern California), Point Pelee makes a worthwhile weekend trip for the naturalist. No family camping. Drive approximately 325 kilometers (200 miles) from the city, southwest toward Windsor.

General information on these national parks can be obtained by writing or calling Parks Canada–Ontario Region, P.O. Box 1359, Cornwall, Ontario. K6H 5V4; 613–938–5866.

The Province of Ontario operates 128 parks around the province. Most of these have full camping facilities, and many have some water, electric power, and sanitation facilities to service trailer campers.

While there are many provincial parks of varying sizes to the north and east of the city, none is as large as Algonquin Provincial Park, Ontario's second largest park. Algonquin's 2,955 square miles of dense forest, crystalline lakes, and meandering rivers are easily accessible from Highway 60. The lion's share—black bear's share, actually—of the park is not accessible by any road and visitors must be prepared to backpack or canoe into the heart of this wilderness. There are admission charges, and camping and fishing are permitted only during the late spring to late fall season. More detailed information can be obtained from the Superintendent, Algonquin Provincial Park, Algonquin P.O., Ontario. The park is approximately 270 kilometers (167 miles) from Toronto.

A complete list of parks, campsites, and picnic grounds in the Toronto vicinity is available from Provincial Parks Information, Whitney Block, Queen's Park, Toronto M7A 1W3.

HINTS TO HANDICAPPED TRAVELERS. Toronto has made some attempts in recent years to address the needs of the handicapped or disabled. Most downtown buildings have been equipped with facilities for the handicapped, parking spaces with easy access have been designated close to store and shopping-mall entrances, and special splay ramps are replacing high curbs on city street corners.

For information on social and health services and facilities for the handicapped visiting Toronto, phone the Community Information Centre at 863–0505.

The Advocacy Resource Centre for the Handicapped (ARCH) at 482–8255 is a legal resource center that takes on cases concerning the rights of the physically and mentally handicapped. Its address is 40 Orchard View Blvd. Its TTY number for the hearing impaired is 482–1254.

The hearing impaired have access to information on city services, functions and events, by calling the TTY-TDD telephone number, 392–8069.

The City Parks and Recreation Department offers integrated summer programs for the disabled at community centers that are fully accessible. For information on the activities, call 392–7251.

The Toronto Transit Commission operates Wheel-Trans, a service for people (and their escorts) unable to use regular public transit due to physical disability. Handicapped visitors can apply for a temporary pass by calling 393–4111 or writing Wheel-Trans at 1910 Yonge St., Toronto, and asking Registration to mail an application. The TDD line is 393–4555.

POSTAGE. Postal rates are $.34 for letters and postcards (under 30 grams) mailed to destinations within Canada. Postcards and letters mailed to the United States are $.37 for the first 30 grams. Airmail to all other countries is $.64 for first 20 grams; $.99 to 50 grams; $1.54 to 100 grams.

Mailboxes, painted red, are located near many street corners. Many small stores (drugstores, hardware, and smoke shops) have a small Post Office inside. These stores display a special Canada Post emblem in the front window.

TELEPHONES AND EMERGENCY TELEPHONE NUMBERS. Pay telephones, distributed widely around city streets and buildings, cost $.25 per call. The Toronto area code is 416. Some calls made within the 416 area are nonetheless long distance and callers must dial "1" before the seven-digit number. For long-distance calling beyond the 416 area, dial "1," then the area code, then the seven-digit number.

Operator assistance on any call may be obtained by dialing "0." Directory assistance (information) is reached by dialing 411. All emergency assistance (police, fire, ambulance) can quickly be reached by dialing 911. The Rape Crisis Centre's 24-hour number is 964–8080. There are two Distress Centre numbers for the troubled and suicidal; anonymity is guaranteed. Call 598–1121 or 486–

CONVERTING METRIC TO U.S. MEASUREMENTS

Multiply:	by:	to find:
Length		
millimeters (mm)	.039	inches (in)
meters (m)	3.28	feet (ft)
meters	1.09	yards (yd)
kilometers (km)	.62	miles (mi)
Area		
hectare (ha)	2.47	acres
Capacity		
liters (L)	1.06	quarts (qt)
liters	.26	gallons (gal)
liters	2.11	pints (pt)
Weight		
gram (g)	.04	ounce (oz)
kilogram (kg)	2.20	pounds (lb)
metric ton (MT)	.98	tons (t)
Power		
kilowatt (kw)	1.34	horsepower (hp)
Temperature		
degrees Celsius	9/5 (then add 32)	degrees Fahrenheit

CONVERTING U.S. TO METRIC MEASUREMENTS

Multiply:	by:	to find:
Length		
inches (in)	25.40	millimeters (mm)
feet (ft)	.30	meters (m)
yards (yd)	.91	meters
miles (mi)	1.61	kilometers (km)
Area		
acres	.40	hectares (ha)
Capacity		
pints (pt)	.47	liters (L)
quarts (qt)	.95	liters
gallons (gal)	3.79	liters
Weight		
ounces (oz)	28.35	grams (g)
pounds (lb)	.45	kilograms (kg)
tons (t)	1.11	metric tons (MT)
Power		
horsepower (hp)	.75	kilowatts
Temperature		
degrees Fahrenheit	5/9 (after subtracting 32)	degrees Celsius

1456. Sick Children's Hospital runs an information and poison-control service: 598–5900.

 LEAVING CANADA. Visitors from the United States. For most flights out of Toronto to the United States, passengers will be subject to U.S. customs at Toronto airport before the flight leaves, so extra time should be allowed for that before flight time.

Each U.S. resident visiting Canada for at least 48 hours is allowed to return home with Canadian goods with a retail value of up to U.S. $300.

It is recommended that all purchases made in Canada should accompany travelers on their return home, as most parcels shipped or mailed to home addresses are subject to duty charges.

In order to avoid lengthy and embarrassing delays at customs, try to keep all purchases in one piece of luggage and all purchase receipts close at hand (not in the bottom of a piece of luggage). Note, however, that customs officers use their own practiced estimates of the retail value of goods, not what you claim was the purchase price of an item. These officials are rarely fooled, so avoid unnecessary risks.

Remember that family members can pool their exemptions, as even the tiniest tot is entitled to a $300 exemption.

Travelers are permitted to mail gifts home to friends and relatives duty-free, but these must be under $25 in value, may not contain liquor, tobacco, or perfume, and must be marked on the outside with the nature and value of the contents.

Visitors from the United Kingdom. Visitors from the United Kingdom returning home from Toronto are allowed to bring back the following goods without paying duty:

Tobacco—250 grams, or 200 cigarettes, or 100 cigarillos, or 50 cigars.

Alcohol—2 liters of wine and 2 liters of sparkling wine, or 2 liters of alcohol not more than 38.8% proof, or 1 liter of alcohol more than 38.8% proof.

Perfume—50 grams plus ¼ liter of toilet water plus other goods to a maximum value of £28.

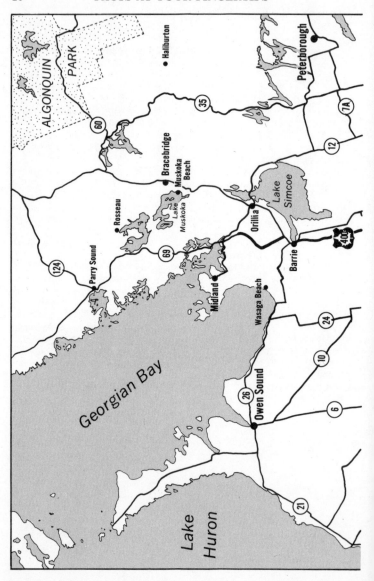

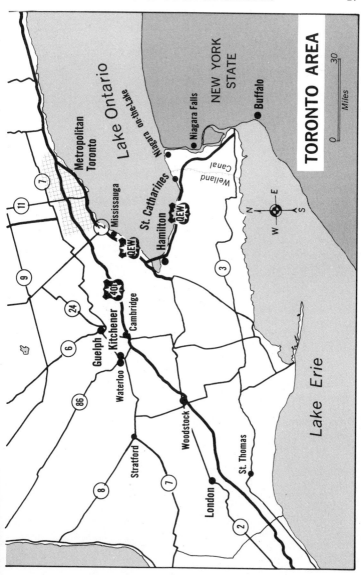

INTRODUCTION TO TORONTO

by
VALERIE ROSS

Valerie Ross has been a writer and is an editor for Maclean's *magazine, the foremost Canadian national news magazine. She has written for most major Canadian magazines and many other publications, including* Playboy, *and for CBC–TV. She is a long-time resident of Toronto.*

When they are not calling their home town "Hogtown," native Torontonians pronounce Toronto "Tirana," like the capital city of Albania. Indeed, until recently, the two towns had a similar image. Both were grey, boring, rule-bound, and definitely off the tourist track.

But since American urbanologist Jane Jacobs *(Life and Death of the Great American Cities)* moved here at the end of the 1960s declaring "Here is the most hopeful and healthy city in North America," the world has had only good things to say about Canada's largest metropolis. The U.S. Committee on Economic Development has urged American cities to be guided by "the Toronto experience"; *Fortune* magazine has pronounced the place "North America's newest great city."

As for the rest of Canada, it still loathes Toronto for being the single largest concentration of power, privilege, media, and money in the country. But now its hatred is tinged by envy rather than disdain. Montreal, arguably the most exciting city in Canada, has lost so many citizens and head offices to Toronto that Toronto can now support a French-language weekly paper *(l'Express)* and Francophone theater. And on March 6, 1984, when 20,000 Torontonians jammed Nathan Phillips Square in front of City Hall defying subzero weather to celebrate the city's 150th birthday, the rest of the country sent its congratulations, and admitted that Toronto was at last becoming loveable.

The admiring attention is certainly due in part to the massive social changes Toronto has undergone since World War II. A quarter of all immigrants to Canada since that time have settled here, bringing with them their cooking and their cultures. At present there are more Italians in Toronto than in Florence. There are more West Indians here than on the island of Grenada. And there are large and vibrant communities of Jews, Chinese, Germans, Portuguese, Ukrainians, and even enough Albanians to support a men-only Muslim café, Tirana-style.

But Toronto's metamorphosis does not entirely explain the world's change of heart. What has happened is simply that the world's definition of a civilized city has caught up with Toronto. No one laughs any more at its middle-class, small-town virtues of decency and orderliness —no one except perhaps *New York Times* columnist Russell Baker, who recently complained, "There is a disturbing distaste for vandalism in Toronto which will make it hard for the city to wholeheartedly enter into the vigor of the late Twentieth Century." (He also found the subways unnervingly clean.) But for most travelers, "civilized" has come to mean a city where you can take a solitary stroll in the park and return home with your wallet; where the streets are clear of trash and the walls are not covered with rude commands; and where your fellow citizens do not eye you with fear and mistrust—unless of course you are littering, still a very unnatural pastime in Toronto.

Toronto the Good: that label used to be a swipe at the city's dullness, but is now a recognition that it is a well-functioning, pleasant, sane place to be. Appropriately, the city's mascot, adopted for its sesquicentennial celebrations in 1984, is the amiable, industrious, nut-gathering rodent that populates the city's parks: the black squirrel. Equally appropriately, the city's busy, smug, well-meaning motto is "Industry, Intelligence, Integrity."

Some outsiders are bound to find Toronto's approach to life rather quaint, similar to expressing faith in Smokey the Bear or the United Nations. The *New Yorker* magazine, which reprints bizarre items from the world press, recently noted with surprise that the trustees of the Toronto Board of Education had just gone on record as opposing "racism, pollution, sexism, militarism and bad taste in all its forms." Yet that vision of a sensible Utopia is the wellspring of Toronto's charm.

In many respects, this city of 2.1 million is just a collection of small towns. Toronto contains neighborhoods where wine grapevines decorate the walls of *boccie* ball courts; slum neighborhoods that have successfully fought off well-meaning urban developers; neighborhoods where no English is spoken and the residents take to the streets on a saint's day or to celebrate a soccer victory, snarling all crosstown traffic; and neighborhoods that keep the dour Methodist spirit of Prohibition alive by refusing to allow in licensed bars and restaurants. There is even a neighborhood that claims to have seceded from the rest of Canada, establishing its own tiny perfect state, "The Republic of Rathnelly," financed by frequent street fairs.

The neighborhoods thrive under an efficient local government. Toronto pioneered the two-tiered metropolitan form of city government back in 1953, by uniting all suburbs under a Metro Council and giving Metro the job of integrating such services as police, health, tax assessment, and traffic planning. Each of the five suburbs and the city share with Metro the power to run schools, parks, libraries, and parking, and each elects its own local council, which in turn sends senior members on to Metro. The chairman of Metro Council is appointed by the province.

The metro system worked very smoothly indeed in its earliest days. But by the mid 1960s dissent developed over the question of just what a modern city should be and do. Simply put, the split—which continues to this day—cuts between the progress-minded technocrats and the urban guerilla conservationists, who would rather renovate and restore than redevelop. What makes Toronto different from other North American cities is that the technocrats have not always predominated. While new developments such as the glass-galleried Eaton Centre bear testament to the city's vitality, at the same time people have successfully fought off attempts to raze downtown communities. As a result, Toronto has never experienced the same flight of money and the middle classes to the suburbs as so many of its American counterparts have done.

Toronto staked out a new direction for itself in the late 1960s, when the residents of Cabbagetown—an area described by novelist Hugh Garner as "North America's largest Anglo-Saxon slum"—first organized behind a leather-jacketed, hell-raising lawyer named John Sewell. Together they opposed a planned high-rise development that would have destroyed their community, and eventually they won the right to participate in a more creative redevelopment scheme of mixed public housing and infill housing. Today you can see the results as you stroll down Sherbourne Street south of Dundas: there are modern projects behind the seedy mansions-turned-roominghouses, and the old piles themselves are undergoing a sandblasting and a sprucing-up.

The combative Sewell went on to become mayor of Toronto and the technocrats' favorite antagonist. Championing gay rights and police reform, Sewell was the most controversial mayor since William Lyon Mackenzie, who 150 years ago led a rebellion down Yonge Street to overthrow the colonial government. More on Mackenzie soon; the important thing about Toronto's second "rebellion," in part led by Sewell, in part by another Mayor, "Tiny Perfect" David Crombie, was that it changed the face of city planning. While other Canadian cities were slashing their downtowns open in an orgy of construction pits and steel girders, Toronto slapped a two-year moratorium on buildings over 45 feet high. Inner-city housing here grew faster than other cities' skylines, and stockbrokers, Latin-American refugees, and welfare mothers began to live side by side. For proof, simply visit Crombie Park, the red-brick mixed-income housing project adjacent to the St. Lawrence Market.

There have been many other battles over Toronto planning. Folk songs and children's nonsense verse—The Day We Stopped Spadina, by poet Dennis Lee—celebrate one triumph of ratepayers who successfully opposed a proposed expressway that would have bisected their neighborhoods. Late in the 1970s there was another planning controversy when residents of Toronto Islands physically tussled with officials from the Sheriff's Office who were trying to evict them to turn their end of the islands into public parks. But what all these small, separate battles add up to is a city whose citizens have forced it to serve their needs first.

Local passions are fueled by a vigorous local media. And it helps that Toronto is North America's most competitive newspaper town, with three lively dailies competing for readers' attention. The *Globe and Mail* is Canada's *New York Times* and, indeed, often carries its stories. *The Globe,* the closest Canada comes to a national newspaper, also boasts excellent foreign coverage in certain areas, notably China and Latin America. Its arts coverage is quirky and high-brow—you may find a long discourse on an obscure magazine of French semiotics or a scholarly discussion of *Heavy Metal* comics—but it is never dull.

Toronto's other morning paper is *The Toronto Sun* (*The Toronto Star* also prints an A.M. edition, but that's a competitive marketing tactic rather than a matter of when the material gets reported). In the *Sun,* bikinis wrestle for space with sex crimes, sports and hi-fi ads, while columnists from William F. Buckley to his attractive Canadian counterpart Barbara Amiel routinely denounce the world's drift into the arms of Communism. Ironically, *The Sun's* founding editor, a saturnine, sneakers-wearing right-winger named Peter Worthington, was himself several times investigated by the Mounties for leaking government secrets in his paper. Worthington is now an outspoken radio and newspaper columnist.

The Toronto Star, a weekly tabloid, is a tourist's best source of entertainment listings and the country's largest-circulation newspaper. *The Star* has been immortalized both in Ernest Hemingway's memoirs (he worked there, unhappily, in the 1920s) and by a man named Joe Shuster, the cartoonist who created Superman—and yes, in its earliest panels, Clark Kent worked at the *Daily Star.* Perry White may have been *The Star's* founder, a man named "Holy Joe" Atkinson. Atkinson led so many crusades for social reform that the *Star's* conservative competitors dubbed it *The Toronto Daily Pravda.* Today *The Star* is blander, but bigger than ever.

In addition to the papers, Toronto celebrates itself in the glossy well-written pages of a monthly consumer magazine, *Toronto Life.* As well, there's a dizzying array of 24 local TV channels to choose from. Of particular interest is CITY-TV, the independent channel 57 that serves up a frothy diet of rock video, sports, talk shows, and cheeky low-budget newscasts; CITY is also the model for the satirical comedy series SCTV.

Overstimulated certainly; overpraised, perhaps; but Toronto is still not overconfident about its attraction. Its cosmopolitanism is as new as the world's praise; both seem to natives a thin veneer over an essentially dour, Scottish, protestant soul. Scots names still dominate the downtown's gilded office towers. The high point of the city's social season is not a gala cultural event but the annual November Royal Winter Fair, when the city's true bluebloods emerge, dowdily resplendent in kilts and mothy mink, to observe the Fair's horse show. You can still find plenty of bars in the city's older districts with separate Ladies and Gents entrances, so sexually segregated people can sit in the dark, plagued by guilt over the very act of drinking. Anti-Catholic bigotry is stronger here than are most other forms of prejudice. The Orange Day parade brings out the local Reverend Ian Paisley-style Irish, who stay conspicuously sober on St. Patrick's Day. Significantly, the voters of Toronto have over the years elected two Jewish mayors—and even had a black deputy mayor back at the turn of the century—before ever seeing a Catholic hold the top office.

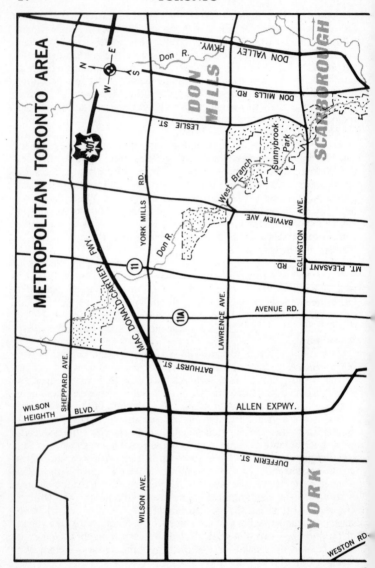

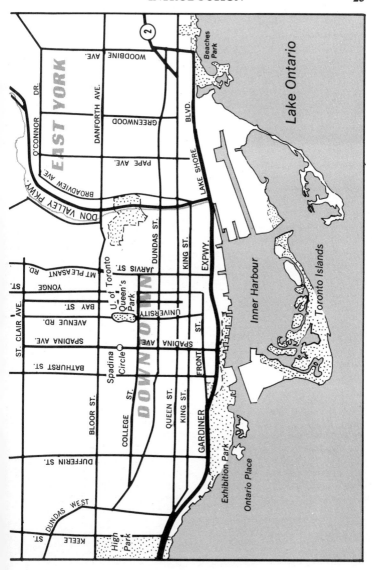

It is ironic, then, that the first European inhabitant of this most WASP of towns was a Catholic Frenchman named Etienne Brûlé. In 1615, Brûlé arrived at a settlement along the marshy shores of Lake Ontario, a place the local Huron Indians called Tarantou, or meeting place. He lived among the Indians, traded furs with them, and cuckolded them. Exasperated, the Indians finally killed Brûlé and ate him.

Perhaps as a result, Toronto's poor reputation among people of sophisticated tastes persisted through its early days. It became a French trading post, then an English fort, and finally the capital of the British colony of Upper Canada, but never, in those days, a place people wanted to call home. Known as Muddy York, the town was so crudely constructed that local jokesters said if you found a hat in the mud on the street, there was probably a horse and rider beneath it. One early resident, Mrs. Anna Jamieson, summed up the glum impression the place created on most visitors: "A little, ill-built town, on low land, at the bottom of a frozen bay . . . some buildings in staring red brick in the most vulgar style imaginable . . . I did not expect much, but for this I was not prepared." A hundred years later, another visitor, the English poet Rupert Brooke, wrote, "The depressing thing about Toronto is that it will always be the same, only bigger."

And yet from the beginning the town had a hidden spirit its chroniclers failed to appreciate. It gallantly resisted an invasion by 1,700 American soldiers in the War of 1812; the British and Canadian defenders of Fort York finally torched their powder kegs rather than let the fort fall into Yankee hands. In retaliation for the burning of York, the British put Washington to the flame; this forced Americans doing the cleanup to paint the president's house white—hence the White House.

In 1837, the city exploded again—this time in rebellion, under William Lyon Mackenzie. He was a journalist whose hackles were raised by the arrogant rule of a clique of English-colonial administrators and their hangers-on, whom his newspaper dubbed "The Family Compact." For its part, the Compact referred to Mackenzie as "Five foot nothing and very like a baboon," and dumped his printing presses in Toronto Harbour. Yet, perversely, local voters elected Mackenzie first mayor of the renamed city of Toronto in 1835. Two years later, and out of office, Mackenzie led a rag-tag band of farmers armed with pitchforks down Yonge Street in a doomed attempt to overthrow what he called "a wicked and tyranical government." The group was routed, two of its members hung, and Mackenzie had to flee to the United States for ten years before returning home.

The Family Compact eventually crumbled and survives today only in the minds of a few dwellers of Rosedale and graduates of the fashionable Bishop Strachan School (named after the Compact's favorite priest). Indeed, the Compact was already on its way out in Mackenzie's lifetime, with the advent of representational government. Over the past century the provincial government, headquartered in Toronto at Queen's Park, developed a peculiarly responsive, paternalistic but effective style that somehow hypnotized Ontario voters into returning the heirs of the Compact, the Progressive Conservative Party, to power year after year. The Conservatives held power without break from 1943 to the spring of 1985, making them one of the longest serving political parties in power outside the Communist Bloc. Toronto has had its flirtations with other kinds of politics of course; it once elected a Communist to the provincial government, and the feminist anarchist Emma Goldman (celebrated in E. L. Doctorow's novel *Ragtime*) died here, above Switzer's Deli on Spadina Avenue. But you cannot understand Toronto's character without remembering that it is, at bottom, Tory Toronto.

And indeed, one of the crucial factors behind Toronto's present state of health may be the stability and pragmatic conservatism from which the city has sprung. What is special about Toronto is a fragile sensibility that could vanish in another decade. Already, the city's only claims to beauty are endangered. Its ravines are shrinking to housing divisions, and its lakeshore is polluted. Its rich ethnic mix could turn volatile if ignited by the resentments of continued unemployment. The city's odd spirit of creative conservation could vanish under a gung-ho, pro-development city government. Whether Toronto has the wisdom or the luck to remain an enviable city remains to be seen. But at present, it is perversely charming, fun but safe, clean but exciting—unstable combinations, true; but ones that make it a city like no other.

EXPLORING TORONTO

by
MECHTILD HOPPENRATH and CHARLES OBERDORF

Mechtild Hoppenrath and Charles Oberdorf have been travel columnists for Homemaker's, Saturday Night *and* The Financial Post Magazine. *Charles Oberdorf is Senior Editor of* City and Country Home *and a member of the Society of American Travel Writers.*

Most first-time visitors to Toronto get the same initial impression of the city. From a distance, it seems to be almost a mirage above an otherwise uneventful landscape. But driving in from any direction, including the airport, calls for at least a few final kilometers on a highway called the Gardiner Expressway. It's this last elevated stretch of the Gardiner that makes it real.

As you pop up onto it from the Don Valley Parkway to the east or from the sunken roadway next to the Canadian National Exhibition grounds to the west, the sudden soaring towers of the financial district announce the town like a fanfare of massed trumpets. It's a bold and modern Big Town skyline, if a little irrational amid surroundings of so much low-rise construction and open land.

European cities have cathedrals; Toronto has banks. Each of the Big Five Canadian chartered banks controls more capital than all but a small handful of their U.S. counterparts, and about fifteen years ago some of them got into a skyscraping competition with new headquarters buildings at the Toronto intersection of King and Bay streets.

The first skyscraper to go up was the matte black 54-story tower of the Toronto-Dominion Bank, designed by the great German-American architect Ludwig Mies van der Rohe. This was the tallest building in the British Commonwealth until, just across Bay Street, the silvery-mirrored Bank of Commerce tower, designed by I. M. Pei, shot a couple of stories higher. The marble-clad monolith that the American-American architect Edward Durrell Stone designed for the Bank of Montreal came some years later and is just *that* much higher still.

Ironically, the real show-stopper turned out to be not very high at all. It is a couple of blocks south of the other monoliths and was designed by a local chap, Boris Zerafa, for the Royal Bank. This is the one that really catches the eye, especially in late afternoon, when you drive in from the west, as most people do. The glass curtain-walls of its many-faceted façades are mirrored against the sun with a translucent film of real gold—about 2,500 ounces in all—so that people living or working west of the Royal and within sight of it get double sunsets, the one reflecting off the bank often being the more dramatic.

There is another skyscraper, or sky-pricker, that soars far above the banks from a distance but actually shrinks by comparison from the nearness of the Gardiner Expressway. The CN Tower, as you will hear and read until you're sick of the fact, bills itself as "the world's tallest free-standing structure." "Free-standing" means that it has no guy wires, or no stabilizing cables, as do other radio transmitter masts. Well, that, as some Torontonians would put it, is a bit of a crock. The three finlike buttresses that sweep out at its base have cables hidden inside them, providing both tension and compression at once.

Still, it is one high tower all right, at 1,815 feet (553 meters), and the obligatory revolving restaurant at the 1,150-foot level (351 meters) makes a perfect place to get the lay of the land.

Do not go for lunch or dinner at the Tower's restaurant if you value your palate or your purse. Instead, reserve a table for the late afternoon cocktail hour. The price of the drinks won't seem quite so extortionate when you factor in the elevator ride, which is free for drinkers but not for others. And once you're up there—provided you aren't above a layer of cloud, as sometimes happens—look down.

The following compass points won't be dead accurate, but they're close enough for tourists, and for Torontonians too, in day-to-day conversation. Consider Lake Ontario, just at the tower's base, on one side, to be south. The city's main axis, Yonge Street, a couple of long blocks east of the tower, runs north. (And north, and north, for more than 200 miles.) The major cross streets—Front, King, Queen, Dundas, College, Bloor—all go (more or less) east-west, with street numbers getting higher in each direction according to distance from Yonge Street. The landscape tilts—slowly, slowly—up and away from the lake.

The economist John Kenneth Galbraith, in recalling another part of southern Ontario where he grew up, once wrote downheartedly that "the only available hill could be climbed in a matter of four or five minutes." Toronto kids have the same problem. The city actually does have topographical features, though they are virtually invisible from the CN Tower and far too neglected by the locals. A sort of reverse topography, they are Toronto's lovely hidden and wooded ravines. On the whole, though, you're looking at an uneventful midwestern landscape.

The first cross street north of the tower—you'll have to look way, wa-a-a-ay down—is called Front Street, because it once marked the city's waterfront. All the land south of Front is fill. (Loosen the grip on your gin-and-tonic; the tower's foundations go down to bedrock.) There's a lot to see on that fill, as soon as you've finished your drink, but first it's worth looking off in the other directions.

Looking east, west, and north from the tower, the city's street plan makes an almost unvarying rectangular grid—like the grids of most North American cities, including San Francisco, where a grid makes a lot less sense than in flat Toronto.

Clusters of towers seen at regular intervals off in the distance almost always mark major subway stations. They indicate, too, that the property taxes generated by subways go a long way toward paying back the subways' capital costs; Toronto's Bloor Street subway—the string of towers paralleling the lake about two miles (three kilometers) north of it—didn't open until 1966.

The city's other important grid, which is invisible, would look, if you could see it, like a cartoonist's version of a sunset, with a half-disc (the downtown core) at the middle of the bottom edge and broad rays shooting out from it. This would be a map of Toronto's ethnic populations with, for example, the local Italian community still holding on to its oldest neighborhood, at College and Clinton streets, but stretching

CENTRAL TORONTO

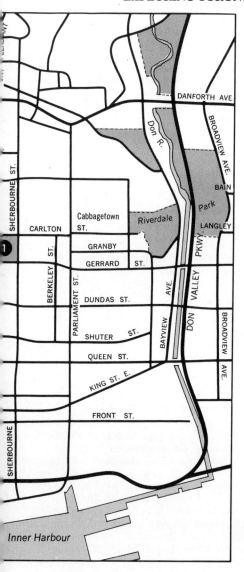

Points of Interest

1) Allan Gardens
2) The Annex
3) Chinatown
4) City Hall
5) CN Tower
6) Grange Park and Art Gallery of Ontario
7) Nathan Phillips Square
8) Parliament Bldgs.
9) Royal Bank Plaza
10) Toronto General Hospital
11) Union Station

far to the northwest and dominating ever longer strips of storefronts along each major east-west thoroughfare it crosses.

Toronto really does have such easily identifiable population pie slices —one Jewish, a slim Portuguese one, and so on—formed as succeeding generations of immigrant families amassed more wealth and moved, until recently, ever outward but in the same directions in which their parents settled.

To see that Toronto, though, you'll have to get back down to street level. Don't forget to chuckle when the tower's elevator operator says, "Thank you for flying CN." The CN company, which built the tower for its telecommunications arm, is best known as Canada's national railway.

The Waterfront

Getting to the Lake Ontario waterfront from the CN Tower—or from just about anywhere else downtown, for that matter—can be a slight problem. Only three of the city center's major north-to-south streets—York, Bay, and Jarvis—go right down to the lake. Others have obstacles in the way: railway lines and marshalling yards, the Gardiner Expressway and its ramps, or its ground-level equivalent, called Lakeshore Boulevard. And it hasn't been very long since there were more impediments. On the very first map of Toronto, drawn in 1793 by Governor Simcoe's surveyor, a man named Aitken, the downtown waterfront was clearly designated "Reserved." Very shortly after, though, and for more than a century-and-a-half, the city fathers gave over the shoreline to goods, not people. The area south of Lakeshore Boulevard became mostly warehouses, grain silos, and malodorous malting towers for the local distillers and brewers.

About ten years ago, all four levels of government—city, Metro, Ontario, and federal—began working mightily to re-humanize the lakeshore. The work is far from finished. In fact, the area will probably be pockmarked with construction sites for at least another decade. But improvements to date have already made the waterfront one of Toronto's most popular districts, especially on weekends.

The area worth visiting begins just west of the base of Jarvis Street and continues westward. The first stop is at the northwest corner of Cooper Street and Queen's Quay (pronounced "key" here), where a low warehouse set in a large parking lot welcomes thirsty shoppers. This is the all-brands store of the provincial government's liquor monopoly, the Liquor Control Board of Ontario, which always stocks everything on the Board's lists, and then some. The prices are outrageous, but the selection, it must be admitted, is vast. Of special interest to collectors is the LCBO's Rare Wines and Spirits department, at the

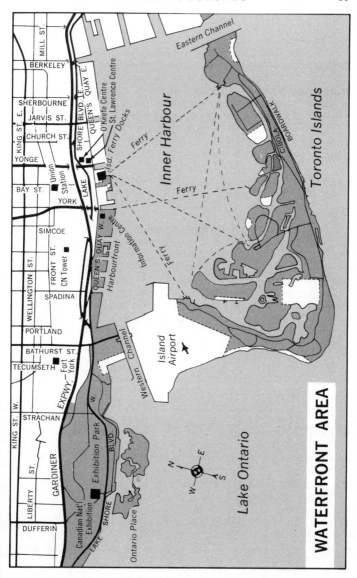

MILL ST.
BERKELEY
SHERBOURNE
JARVIS ST.
CHURCH ST.
YONGE
KING ST. E.
SHORE BLVD. E.
QUEEN'S QUAY E.
O'Keefe Centre
St. Lawrence Centre
Isd. Ferry Docks

Eastern Channel
Inner Harbour
Ferry
Ferry

Toronto Islands
CIBOLA
BOARDWALK

Union Station
BAY ST.
YORK
SIMCOE
FRONT ST.
CN Tower
WELLINGTON ST.
SPADINA
PORTLAND
BATHURST ST.
TECUMSETH
KING ST. W.
STRACHAN
GARDINER
LIBERTY
ST.
DUFFERIN

LAKE
QUEEN'S QUAY W.
Harbourfront
Information Centre
Ferry

Fort York
EXPWY.
Western Channel
Island Airport

Exhibition Park
Canadian Nat'l Exhibition
LAKE SHORE BLVD.
Ontario Place

Lake Ontario

N
E
S
W

WATERFRONT AREA

back of the store. Here the Board sells products of too-minor interest to get into its catalogue. Rare, in those terms, usually means expensive, but not always.

Next door, heading west, is the home of *The Toronto Star,* a mammoth newspaper popular with almost everyone except former staffers and regular freelancers. It may not be true that this rather new building began listing ominously into the fill beneath it when the presses were installed, but a lot of writers got a good smirk out of the rumor.

Just across Queen's Quay in the next block is the Toronto Hilton Harbour Castle hotel and its companion tower of condominium apartments, the two effectively screening from view the embarkation point for ferry boats to the Toronto Islands (about which more later).

At York Street, the next stoplight west, begins Harbourfront, a 1¼-mile-long, 91-acre federal-government project in which old warehouses and silos were bought up and either converted or torn down to make way for residential and cultural developments and parks, many of the buildings still to come.

The most dramatic conversion was the old Terminal Warehouse building, the first massive structure by the water, which was renamed Queen's Quay Terminal and now has two levels of restaurants and glitzy boutiques, a theater devoted almost solely to dance, and a new superstructure of pricey condominiums.

The next conspicuous building by the water, a rambling one-story affair called York Quay Centre, houses a film theater, two restaurants, open crafts studios, a fine crafts boutique, and a community art gallery. A second exhibition space, Harbourfront Gallery, often outperforms the Art Gallery of Ontario at organizing shows of serious contemporary work, and with a fraction of the AGO's budget. An adjacent gallery, a single wall controlled by a local photographers' co-op, has for several years mounted the most consistently interesting photo exhibits in Canada.

Across the street, another low concrete block shed is a market for antique dealers, open all week but with many more dealers and traders on hand at the weekend for special antique and flea markets.

Harbourfront has lots more to see, including a fine winter skating rink, a busy summer marina, and frequent outdoor festivals. The westernmost quays of the project, though, are mostly construction sites now, where some of Canada's finest architects have been commissioned to design new residential complexes.

Farther west, past Bathurst Street, come three sites—Fort York, the grounds of the Canadian National Exhibition (CNE), and Ontario Place—all described at length elsewhere in this book. Visitors to the Ex, as the exhibition grounds are known, can spend a pleasant and very uncrowded hour in the Marine Museum out there, one of Toronto's least-known such institutions. They should also have at least a drive past the very festive Victorian exhibition buildings at the west end of the grounds, some of them recently given last-minute reprieves from demolition and long-overdue facelifts.

The nightly summer concerts in the Forum at Ontario Place, free with admission to the grounds, represent one of the great entertainment buys in town. And the Children's Village at Ontario Place may just be the best-designed playground in North America, worth a look even for grownups visiting without kids. One day a year, just before the Ontario Place summer season, a few adults receive special permission to play in the Children's Village. The invitation is one of the city's most sought-after.

West of the Ex grounds, along the lakeshore, a recently restored old public swimming pool and a 1930s-style dance hall, Palais Royale, recall the pre-expressway days when the surrounding area, called Sunnyside, was a popular amusement park. There's still a beach here, a jogger's track, snack stands and, in summer, sunbathers. But at present swimming in the lake is not recommended.

Toronto Islands

Those ferries that depart from a dock behind the Harbour Castle Hilton chug to the city's loveliest breath of fresh air, the 600-acre park on the Toronto Islands. The islands, bridge-linked to each other but not to the mainland, have beaches galore (some gay and some nude) and yacht clubs. As well, there are tennis courts, canoes and paddleboats for exploring the lagoons, rental bicycles, a sailing school, a very low-pressure amusement park, a petting farm, a small craft airport, even—at the easternmost end—a tiny (and, since 1974, embattled) residential area. And no cars.

The few eating places cannot be recommended. The best plan is to take a picnic basket and a bike (or rent the bike once you are there), pedal around for a couple of hours, then settle down on the landward side, where you can enjoy your meal in the bliss of looking back at the looming city across the harbor.

Culture Centre I

Immediately northeast of the CN Tower, on King Street just west of University Avenue, stands the new home of the Toronto Symphony orchestra, Roy Thomson Hall, named for Lord Thomson of Fleet, the Canadian-born, longtime owner of *The Times* of London. Concert-hall-acoustics buffs argue over the merits of the hall's interior. Certainly the mirrored swoops of its outer shell typify the work of Canada's best-known architect, Arthur Erickson of Vancouver. The building is a gem of a sort, but it might as well lie on black velvet for all it has to do with the city around it.

More fitting to the streetscape is the Royal Alexandra Theatre just across the way, a charming Edwardian place, its interiors all red plush and gilded baroque. The owner, a flamboyant discount retailer named Ed Mirvish, recently became the toast of London by restoring the Old Vic Theatre, too, to a grandeur it probably didn't even have when it was new. An evening at the Royal Alex can be a treat regardless of what's on stage, just for the sake of the hall itself.

Between them, the two auditoria have created a sort of critical mass that has generated all sorts of new, small eating places nearby, though the most conspicuous ones, Ed's Warehouse (roast beef) and Old Ed's (discount dining) were Mirvish profit centers when only the theater brought them business.

Culture Centre II

A five-minute walk east along Front Street brings you to Toronto's other pair of bookend playhouses: the mammoth 3,000-seat O'Keefe Centre, at Yonge and Front streets (operas, musicals, big ballets) and the two-theater St. Lawrence Centre (two repertory companies, small concerts) just half a block east. Around these, too, you can find many places to eat, some of them good, all tending to almost empty at curtain time.

There is another theater about three blocks up Yonge Street, which has just been restored to its 1920s elegance. The Winter Garden stood empty for half a century before the restorers got to it, trapped in a kind of time warp from the days when a theater with its name would naturally have a proscenium arch and auditorium walls decorated with trellises and lacy leaves.

In an unlikely looking Adelaide Street building, about halfway between the Winter Garden and the others, the Adelaide Court Theatre provides a home for small but ambitious local stage productions. And the Young People's Theatre, a couple of blocks east of the St. Lawrence Centre on Front Street, generates not only children's productions but Shakespeare and modern classics, too, which many adults find perfectly to their tastes.

St. Lawrence Market and the Old Town of York

At Front and Jarvis streets, between the Young People's Theatre and the others, Toronto's very first (1844) City Hall continues to serve the citizenry, though now as a food market. The cavernous south market is open Tuesday through Saturday, and it's a great place to put together a first-rate—and cheap—lunch if you're in the area. (Rudolf Scheffler's delicatessen along the east wall, for example, sells a fine ham-and-cheese-on-a-kaiser.) At the north end of the building, the city archive runs a small exhibition room on the second floor, where it frequently mounts fascinating shows about Toronto's history.

The nondescript modern building across Front Street is only open on Saturday, when it becomes a splendid farmer's market, which is particularly bountiful between June and November.

Just north of that, on the south side of King Street, stands Toronto's second City Hall (the city has four), built in 1850, restored in 1967, and now called St. Lawrence Hall. A ground-floor bank and restaurant are painstakingly Victorian (except, alas, for the restaurant's menu). Upstairs there's a noble auditorium where Jenny Lind sang and P. T. Barnum introduced the midget General Tom Thumb. Much of the rest of the building is now home to the National Ballet of Canada.

Although they're slightly outside the mainstream today, the St. Lawrence Hall and Market were clearly at the center of things 150 years ago, when Toronto first changed its name from the Town of York and incorporated itself as a city. The blocks around them, just emerging from decades of neglect, contain some of the city's oldest buildings. Renovations are still spotty, but if you want to see what will be a very classy neighborhood ten years from now, look around.

Union Station to Old City Hall

The boulevard of real power in Toronto (and Canada) these days is Bay Street between Union Station and Old City Hall (number three, built in 1899). Bay Street is the Wall Street of Canada—equally scrutinized, equally loathed. Canada's major financial institutions are all genuinely on Bay, or were until 1983, when the Stock Exchange moved one block off it.

Union Station, at the base of the street, was opened in 1927 by the Prince of Wales, one of whose party reportedly remarked, "You build railway stations like palaces out here." Union Station is indeed more palatial than any of its London counterparts, with a neoclassic façade of 22 limestone columns 40 feet tall, and a soaring, 88-foot-high ticket lobby with ceilings of Italian tile. The railways wanted to tear their palace down a few years back, but public sentiment squelched that idea.

Across Front Street, the even loftier glass-clad atrium of the Royal Bank Plaza deserves a peek inside. It's quite as spectacular as the building's gilded exterior. Just across Wellington Street from there, facing Bay, stands the old Stock Exchange, built in 1937 and one of the city's best art-deco buildings. (Its replacement should only have been so accomplished, architecturally.) With the trading floor gone, it's unlikely visitors will be able to see the handsome interiors. In fact, the building itself may soon disappear, Torontonians being less sentimental about finance than about transportation.

The next cross street to the north, King Street, brings the remaining head offices of Canada's Big Five chartered banks (the fifth being the Royal), whose branches can be found on every street corner from Newfoundland to Vancouver Island to the Arctic Circle. The complex of black towers just past the old Stock Exchange is Mies van der Rohe's aforementioned Toronto-Dominion Centre. The towers themselves are pretty boring once you get over the blackness, but the one-story banking pavilion at the corner is one of the finest Mies buildings anywhere—his style suited banks—and someone at T-D obviously takes care to maintain its purity.

I. M. Pei's Commerce Court complex, on the east side of Bay, for the Canadian Imperial Bank of Commerce, works less well, but the old Bank of Commerce building, just east of the silver tower, has handsome ground-floor banking rooms where the employees don't seem to mind gawkers. (Toronto really *does* build banks the way European cities have cathedrals, and visitors should look around them in the same way.)

Just north of the Commerce, the Bank of Nova Scotia's 1929 headquarters branch, with a scrumptious interior, gives a sense of what this intersection was like before the building boom of the 1960s.

From King to Queen Street, Bay becomes a narrower—and perpetually traffic-jammed—corridor of lower buildings chock-a-block with trust companies and lawyers' and brokers' offices. The National Club, at number 303, is just as exclusive an Establishment as it looks. Nonmembers can't go in there, but they should peek into the ground-floor restaurant at number 336, across the street. Here the developer had the wit to salvage and reconstruct the façade of the building he replaced. The old place was called the Savarin Tavern, and its pseudo-Spanish Provincial front, in this setting, always looked somewhat like a blossoming magnolia tree in a grove of oaks.

The clock tower at the head of Bay Street belongs to the Old City Hall, now given over mostly to courtrooms. The architect of this one was E.J. (Edward James) Lennox, the titan of his field in Victorian Toronto—also responsible for making something coherent out of Sir Henry Pellatt's instructions for Casa Loma. Against orders, Lennox signed his name to the City Hall, in widely spaced letters hidden in the stone ornament near the eaves. Some of the gargoyles are said to resemble obstreperous city politicians of the time.

But now we must go back to Union Station again, where we started, because there's an altogether different way to get from there to here.

The Labyrinth

Most of the buildings just mentioned, plus many more, are linked together by a system of underground concourses and tunnels that, in foul weather year round and for most of the winter, become major pedestrian thoroughfares. These are not blank-walled mole tunnels, either, like the subway concourses of New York, London, or Paris. They're clean, well-lit and lined with all manner of retail shops, eating places, even two live theaters.

The labyrinth evolved with almost no help from government planners. Pairs of adjoining developers simply agreed to align their underground passageways as nearly as possible, then enlisted the city's help with the connecting links under the streets that separated them.

At this writing, the system reaches from Union Station to the New City Hall, but it will shortly link up, through Simpson's department store, to the Eaton Centre, and so north to Dundas Street. Three major hotels—the Royal York, the Westin, and the Sheraton Centre—have direct access to the labyrinth.

And a labyrinth it really is, with many secondary passages leading off to east and west and with still no really good map to explain it in terms of the streets above. To get from one end to the other most directly, follow the signs from the train station to the Royal Bank Plaza to the Toronto-Dominion Centre to First Canadian Place (a.k.a. Bank of Montreal) to the new Stock Exchange to the Richmond-Adelaide Centre to the Sheraton Centre. Here the path divides, going north through a gigantic underground parking garage to the New City Hall (number four) or east through the Thomson Building to Bay Street. Along the way will be one or two indoor "sidewalk" sales, temporary art exhibits, possibly some street musicians, certainly some nice fountains and light wells—favorite rendezvous spots—and, during rush hours in inclement weather, a virtual stampede of two- and three-piece suits.

Experts in such things say Toronto's is the largest such pedestrian network in the world. Certainly it's a part of the city that few people, even those who use it daily, have ever explored in its entirety. The ethic of it may be a little dubious (Why should cars get the air and sunlight and people not?) but during long, hard Toronto winters that question doesn't get asked a lot.

The Eaton Centre, between Queen and Dundas streets, will make an enormous addition to the labyrinth when it is connected to the system. And there are similar, though much smaller, underground retail concourses between Yonge and Bay streets on College Street, and on Bloor Street between Church and Bellair.

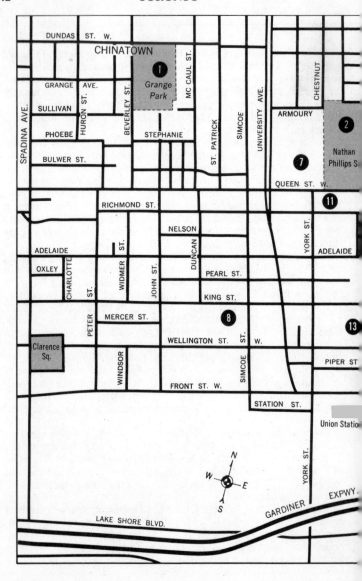

Points of Interest

1) Art Gallery of Ontario
2) City Hall
3) Commerce Court Complex
4) Eaton Centre
5) O'Keefe Centre
6) Old City Hall
7) Osgoode Hall
8) Roy Thomson Hall
9) Royal Bank Plaza
10) St. Lawrence Centre
11) Sheraton Centre
12) Simpson's Dept. Store
13) Toronto-Dominion Centre

The Beaches

And now, after the catacombs, a breath of fresh air. To many American commentators, Toronto works as a city in large part because it never quite lost its prim middle-class residential districts to wholesale apartment developments or to the suburbs. Several of these neighborhoods are still within easy walking distance of the core.

One of the most charming, however, is far off to the east, at the end of the 501 (Queen Street) streetcar line. The district is most often called The Beaches (although longtime residents refer to it as The Beach). Much of its charm certainly derives from its mile or more of boardwalk along Lake Ontario and the spacious sand beaches and grassy parks on either side of the boardwalk. But there's something sweetly small-town about the Queen Street shopping strip and the quiet streets running off it, many of whose houses were once summer cottages for downtowners, though all have long since become permanent homes.

The boardwalk is a favorite with mature European immigrants, who've made it their venue for traditional long strolls. The residential streets—as the Queen Street shops and eateries imply—have recently become fashionable among upwardly mobile professionals with young families.

Ride east to the end of the 501 line, to the "Neville Park Loop." Spare a minute to admire the Beaux-Arts-style façade of the R. C. Harris Filtration Plant just up the hill. (There are tours of the inside, frequent on weekends, less so through the week, and interesting enough if you like waterworks.) Now find your way down to the lake and walk west, toward the city, until you either get bored or run out of boardwalk. Then, if your feet and curiosity are still with you, head back up to Queen and back toward the waterworks, window-shopping, maybe stopping for an incomparable Italian ice cream cone at The Boardwalk Café (2 Wheeler Ave., just off Queen), and, when you've had enough of small-town, catch the 501 car westbound back into the big city.

More Queen Street

A two-week visitor to Toronto might well consider one of the city's more arcane tours, a ride to the western terminus of the 501 streetcar at Queen and Roncesvalles, the heart of Toronto's Little Poland. The ride is about as much urban mileage as you can buy anywhere these days for $1 and will uncover an interesting cross-section of the city, especially if you have a knowledgeable native with you who can point out the sights. Visitors with less time should at least get to the first few blocks of Queen west of the two City Halls.

Immediately west of the New City Hall, also on the north side of the street, stands Osgoode Hall, headquarters since the 1830s for the "trade union" of Ontario's barristers and solicitors, the Law Society of Upper Canada. Tours are available by telephoned pre-arrangement, and the glorious stained-glass-windowed Great Library on the second floor lives up to its title. The cast-iron fence around Osgoode Hall is one of Toronto's sacred cows: the strange entryways are called "cow gates." They were installed in the Hall's early days to keep wandering livestock from grazing on the Law Society's well-tended lawns.

Cross University Avenue: The old brick building on the right was once the home of an early nineteenth-century Chief Justice of Upper Canada. It was moved to this site—very slowly, very carefully—in 1972, has been thoroughly restored, and is open for tours, except on weekdays at lunchtime, when it becomes the private club for the lawyer members of The Advocates' Society.

Just behind that house, looking like something out of the imagination of George Orwell, is the headquarters for the Canada Life Assurance Company. It has a tower at its top that predicts the weather. When the cube of light at the tip of the tower flashes white, snow is coming. Flashing red means rain; steady red, cloudy; steady green, clear. When the lights below blink upwards, the temperature is rising, and vice versa. Now try to find one Toronto native who knows the whole code without looking it up.

Beginning about two streets west of University Avenue and continuing to slightly beyond Spadina, Queen Street West becomes a particularly lively shopping strip full of New-Wave fashions (Leighton Barrett), antique dealers (The Artisans and others), trendy decorator accessories (Zephyr), bohemian eating places (The Queen Mother Café), and a virtual community of bookstores. Bakka sells only science fiction; One Man's Meat has books about hobbies and collectibles; Abelard, About Books and David Mason Books deal in antiquarian material; and there are more. The flagship is Edward's Books and Art, with out-of-print art books, serious current releases, always an art exhibit toward the back, and a wonderful selection of publishers' remainders at wonderful prices, especially on Saturday and Sunday.

Three factors contributed to the arrival of these places on Queen Street West. About ten years ago the Art Gallery of Ontario, a long block north on Dundas Street, began a vast expansion of both its exhibition space and its local cultural importance. About the same time, students from the Ontario College of Art, between the AGO and Queen Street on McCaul, began to take more interest in the area around the school, spurred to a large degree by a splendid local character, Charles Pachter. A first-rate painter and graphic artist (his witty Queen and Moose prints are locally famous), Pachter got frustrated by the economics of the art market. So he turned part of his formidable talent to real estate, especially Queen Street West real estate. He foresaw, invested in, and helped create the transformations of its seedy old storefronts into the city's most vital new commercial strip.

Chinatown

The next commercial district north of Queen Street West—Dundas Street from Bay to Spadina Avenue, Spadina from Dundas to College Street, and many of the smaller side streets—has undergone a similar dramatic change.

The change really began in the mid-1950s, when the clearing of land for the New City Hall displaced part of Toronto's old Chinatown, which for many years was confined to the blocks immediately behind the hall. Even after the new hall was completed, Chinese businesses remained primarily on that short stretch of Dundas Street for another decade.

Relaxed immigration laws of the late 1960s, however, brought Toronto a sudden surge of new Chinese immigrants, mainly from Hong Kong. They were better-educated than their predecessors, and in many cases already experienced entrepreneurs. They quickly expanded the old Chinatown along Dundas Street past the Art Gallery and then up Spadina, into storefronts that had been more or less abandoned by a diminishing garment industry. (Torontonians still speak of the easternmost blocks of Dundas Street as Old Chinatown and the rest as New Chinatown. In fact, the two areas have become a seamless whole, and there are a couple of newer New Chinatowns farther from the core.)

There are times, wandering this district, when it's hard to remember what continent you're on. The police precinct house on Dundas Street identifies itself with Chinese characters, as do street signs, phone booths, and bank branches. And because the district is so new, its denizens so much closer to their roots, it is possible to boast that the shops and restaurants here beat those in San Francisco's celebrated Chinatown hands down.

Kensington Market

In the early 1970s a man who seemed to be a creature from another age showed up in Kensington Market, that warren of narrow streets just west of Spadina Avenue between Dundas and College Streets. His name was Anton, and he looked about 60 years old. A Jew, he had just immigrated from Russia when he turned up in the market selling his wife's wonderful loaves of homemade marzipan from a table he set up on the sidewalk every day, winter and summer.

Within a year, Anton and Mrs. Anton had scraped together enough capital to rent a storefront, expand their line, and put up two or three tables for shoppers who wanted a coffee with their sweet. Five years later, Anton had relocated to elegant Eglinton Avenue.

Anton sometimes referred to himself jokingly as "the last Jew in the Market." Not quite true, but he was probably the last to follow a pattern that had swept through the district fifty or sixty years earlier. In those days, Kensington was called The Jewish Market, but a half-dozen immigrant groups have since used its streets to establish a foothold in the North American economy. Just now the market is Portuguese-turning-to-West Indian.

And at any given moment over the past two decades, though, its been possible to find something like 100 different nationalities of first-generation immigrants in the market's streets, all haggling. Kensington makes a wonderful antidote for those visitors who think Toronto is all neat and tidy and full of polite people who queue to get on the bus. It may not be the prettiest part of town, but it sure isn't WASP.

University Avenue

Toronto's ceremonial boulevard, complete with fountains and flowerbeds in the median strip, is very WASP indeed, lined on either side with insurance companies and hospitals. It is the most boring walk in the city, so see it by car if at all.

Just north of College Street, University divides and becomes an enormous one-way traffic circle around Queen's Park. The Victorian pile of stone near the south end of the park is the provincial legislature, where, from the visitors' gallery, you can witness the smug antics of Ontario's rulers (when the House is sitting).

Along the west side of the park, the Sigmund Samuel Canadiana Museum, a branch of the Royal Ontario Museum, displays fine Canadian antiques and usually has some special exhibition of local historic interest. In a city as heritage-nutty as Toronto has become, this quiet museum attracts fewer visitors than it should.

A little north from the Sigmund Samuel Museum, the Edward Johnson Building—home of the University of Toronto's music faculty—regularly presents concerts and operas of remarkable quality. Regulars remember a recent *Don Giovanni* from which all the lead singers, then students, have gone on to become bright new lights of professional troupes in Canada, New York, and Paris.

Just north of that, easily identifiable by its domed roofline, the McLaughlin Planetarium presents the now customary mix of astronomy lectures and psychedelic sound-and-light shows.

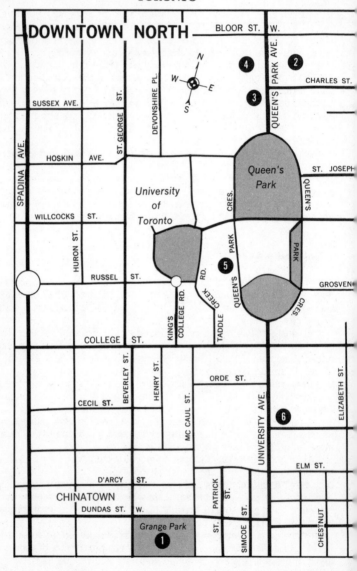

BLOOR ST. E.

CHARLES ST.

ST. MARYS ST.

ST. NICHOLAS

ISABELLA ST.

GLOUCESTER ST.

ST.

DUNDONALD ST.

WELLESLEY ST.

MAITLAND ST.

ST.

ALEXANDER ST.

YONGE ST.

CHURCH ST.

JARVIS ST.

CARLTON ST.

GRANBY ST.

GERRARD ST.

ST.

MUTUAL ST.

ELM ST.

GOULD ST.

OWARD ST.

VICTORIA

BOND ST.

DUNDAS ST. E.

Points of Interest

1) Art Gallery of Ontario
2) Gardiner Museum of
   Ceramic Art
3) McLaughlin Planetarium
4) Royal Ontario Museum
5) Sigmund Samuel
   Canadiana Museum
6) Toronto General
   Hospital

Finally, at the corner of University and Bloor Street, the Royal Ontario Museum—called "The ROM" by many locals—is a treasure house for natural-history and antiquities buffs. Recently reopened after prolonged renovations, The ROM remains an odd mix of dinosaur bones and Roman vases, butterfly collections and Egyptian wall paintings. It should really be two museums, maybe three, since its Chinese holdings, among the world's finest, could easily fill a building of their own.

Just across University Avenue, the newly opened Gardiner Museum of Ceramic Art—built, filled, and endowed by a still-living Torontonian—stands as a vivid example of the sort of accessible institution the ROM would do well to emulate. Its 2,000-piece collection of pre-Colombian pottery, Italian Maiolica, and German porcelain makes Toronto one of the world's leading scholarly centers for ceramics.

The Yonge Street Strip

Parallel to University Avenue and two blocks east, the stretch of Yonge Street between Dundas and Bloor streets could hardly make a livelier contrast to University's chilly streetscape. Some visitors find this the most alluring part of Toronto and return to the strip night after night.

Locals who long for Toronto the Good, as the city used to be called, hold a different view. They tend to bridle at the Times Square raunchiness below Gerrard Street, the striptease bars, the streetwalkers, and the visiting conventioneers out for a toot. To their annoyance, two restaurants especially popular with the local Establishment, Barberian's and Bangkok Garden, are just steps from the seediness, on Elm Street, and one of the best-stocked record shops on the continent—Sam the Record Man—stays open late in the very heart of the sleaze.

North along Yonge, especially between College and Wellesley streets, the action in the bars and in the shadows becomes more furtive and (largely) homosexual. One of Prime Minister Trudeau's very first pronouncements in office was that "The state has no business in the bedrooms of the nation." Even before he said that, Toronto took about as liberal an attitude toward homosexuality as New York or San Francisco. The local cops stage an crackdown at Halloween—to keep up statistics, apparently—and as well, once made a massive raid on gay bathhouses. But other than that, gays can comport themselves about as openly as they'd like here.

North of Wellesley, Yonge Street becomes progressively less tawdry, more like the next major cross street, Bloor.

The Real Boulevard

It seems almost silly to describe Bloor Street between Yonge and University to visitors, since they almost all spend hours there anyway, discovering far more than can be itemized here.

Those two long blocks represent Toronto's version of, say, Fifth Avenue near Saks in New York, Bond Street or Regent Street in London, Königsallee in Düsseldorf, or Rodeo Drive in Beverly Hills. All the right names are on Bloor—Cartier, Louis Vuitton, Guy Laroche—plus some local stores of interest to compulsive and well-heeled shoppers: Creed's (ladies' wear), Holt Renfrew (more ladies' wear, with smaller departments for men and kids, and a food shop), William Ashley (fine china at great discounts), David's (top-name shoes at full price).

Many of Toronto's first-run cinemas are on or very near this part of Bloor. Out-of-towners should also remember that in foul weather a shop-lined subterranean corridor between the Hudson's Bay Company department store and the Bellair subway entrance links most of the shops. At some point it will also connect to the ManuLife Centre, with more shops and eating places, on the south side of the street.

The Windsor Arms Hotel, south of Bloor on a quiet side street called St. Thomas, has one of the coziest cocktail lounges in the city and a first-class coffee shop—though that's far too inadequate a description for it—called the Courtyard Café. Both are ideal places to collapse after too much window-shopping. On Bloor Street itself, the trendy bar side of Bemelmans' restaurant is one of the few spots in town where gays and straights both gather without any evident tension.

Yorkville

The little pocket of low-rise buildings just north of Bloor Street—mostly old Victorian townhouses now gussied up with storefronts, on Bellair, Cumberland, Yorkville, Hazelton, Scollard, and Berryman—once constituted a separate community outside the city limits, which ended at Bloor. The Yorkville coat of arms, still displayed on the façade of the firehall at 34 Yorkville Ave., depicts the trades of the village's founding fathers.

In its own way, Yorkville remains a village apart, though these days it's populated by some of the city's top art dealers, couturiers, interior decorators, restaurateurs, and the beautiful people who support them in clearly lavish style. All this has happened in not much more than ten years. Prior to that, and especially in the hallucinogenic late 1960s, Yorkville was better known as Toronto's equivalent to San Francisco's

Haight-Ashbury; it was the epicenter of the Canadian drug scene. Ironically, many of its habitués are still the same people. Toronto's flower children simply grew up, cut their hair, and began purchasing less grass and more Italian shoes.

Two spots visitors might miss, and shouldn't, are Cumberland Court and Hazelton Lanes. The former, with entries from both Yorkville and Cumberland Street, is a small mall of shops, notable chiefly for a place called The Coffee Mill, which comes as close as Toronto gets to a Viennese café—great for a light lunch or a mid-afternoon coffee and cake. Hazelton Lanes, another mall, is more conspicuous from its Avenue Road side but is hidden by a row of houses on Hazelton Avenue. Inside are two stories of shops lining corridors that must have been designed by a sadist determined to disorient anyone entering the place. Ah, but such shops: Davidoff cigars, arguably the finest in the world; Turnbull & Asser shirts and ties from London; Hermès silks and leathers. Makes you almost wish you were rich.

For those with historical interests who'd like to see what the neighborhood was like before chic, even before psychedelia, the small lane called Scollard Street preserves some of the Victorian rowhouse feeling; Berryman Street, the next street north and even narrower, preserves more.

The Annex and Bloor Street West

Just west of University Avenue (or Queen's Park, as it's called just south of Bloor; or Avenue Road, as it's called north of Bloor), Bloor street passes rather tediously through the institutional precincts of the University of Toronto—a great school but not a very neighborly neighbor. Sightseers would have a better time picking a path through the carefully guarded residential streets just north of Bloor: Prince Arthur or Elgin or Boswell, Bedford Road or Admiral Road, or Lowther Avenue. This quarter, with its solid old homes, is what city planners mean when they describe Toronto's almost miraculous preservation of comfortable streets for living in the heart of downtown. The home of academics, lawyers, rooming-house tenants, and frat boys, the area is called The Annex. The name dates to about a century ago when the area was newly annexed within the city limits.

On Austin Terrace, near Spadina and Davenport, looms the Casa Loma, a fantastical 98-room mansion built between 1909 and 1913 by financier Sir Henry Pellatt. Now run by the Kiwanis Club, this top Toronto landmark is open to the public.

Just west of Spadina Road (called Spadina Avenue south of Bloor), Bloor Street suddenly picks up again, with an odd mix of Eastern European delis and bakeries, student-oriented pubs, coffeehouses and bookstores, and a growing clutch of Korean-owned shops and eating places.

Just past Bathurst Street, on the south side of Bloor, stands the outrageously schlocky discount house called Honest Ed's. This is the font of the fortunes of Ed Mirvish, now owner of Toronto's Royal Alexandra Theatre and London's Old Vic. Consider its gaudy paint job, its shrieking, punning signs: is it any wonder that theater lovers in both cities felt apprehensive about him before he dispelled their fears?

Mirvish also owns virtually all of the buildings in the first block of Markham Street south of Bloor, now a charming assembly of antique shops, good bookstores, and multi-cultural eating places. Markham Street may well be where Ed "got religion." He'd planned to tear down all the Victorian houses to make a parking lot for Honest Ed's. The city wouldn't let him. His wife convinced him to convert all the ground floors into commercial spaces and the upstairs rooms into artists' studios. He's been crying his way to the bank ever since. Ed personally put together the old-fashioned ice cream parlor at the Bloor Street corner. His son David, who now runs Honest Ed's, once had an internationally renowned art gallery on Markham Street and still runs an excellent art book shop there.

High Park and Beyond

Still farther west, past Greek, Italian, and West Indian neighborhoods, Bloor Street eventually defines the northern limit of High Park. The park's 400 acres, along with the Toronto Islands, constitute the city's green "lungs." A bustling place in summer, High Park has a public swimming pool, tennis courts, playgrounds, soccer and baseball fields, flower gardens, paddocks of wild North American animals, a sizable pond for ducks and boating, and a summer tour train to help orient strangers to the place.

What Torontonians don't like to talk about is this: The man who gave the city all this acreage, although generous and civilized in other ways, was also a resolute Orangeman, a fervent anti-Catholic. He gave the park to the city, but only so long as a Roman Catholic was not mayor. Through circumstances that had nothing to do with the proviso, a Roman Catholic was never actually elected Mayor until the present occupant won the seat. So far, no one has stepped forward to take High Park back from the city.

Just east of High Park, a long north-south street, Roncesvalles Avenue, is the commercial heart of Toronto's Polish community, with one butcher shop after another selling homemade Polish sausages (great to grill in the park). West of High Park, at Runnymede Road, Bloor Street takes on a European, primarily Germanic and Ukrainian, flavor, with some excellent food, clothing, and home-accessories shops.

Cabbagetown

And where are Toronto's legendary White Anglo-Saxon Protestants? you might well be asking about now. Back in the center of the city, actually, or just slightly east of that, in two distinctive residential districts, one north of Bloor Street, one south of that great divide.

South first. Specifically, to the many little streets bounded by Bloor, the Don River, Gerrard Street on the south, and Parliament Street on the west.

Those are fairly arbitrary limits to what is now called Cabbagetown —especially to the west and south, where the character of the neighborhood frequently spills over.

Pedants of Toronto lore would argue, too, that we've put the whole district a few blocks too far north, but the area we've described is what most people call Cabbagetown today.

Hugh Garner, a tough-guy novelist, now dead, who grew up in Cabbagetown, once called it "the world's largest Anglo-Saxon slum." A bit of an exaggeration, perhaps, but not that much of one. Certainly the area got its name from the cooking odor that permeated its streets for decades.

All that has changed since the early 1970s, when upwardly mobile young professionals began buying the old Victorian working-class houses of the district, cleaning up their brick fronts, knocking out walls, punching skylights in the roofs, and moving in macramé plant holders and stripped pine antiques. Harry Bruce, a Canadian journalist, coined the term "white-painters" for these people, and the term has caught on far beyond Toronto, as other cities undergo the same unorganized, individual initiatives in one-house-at-a-time urban renewal.

Hugh Garner wouldn't recognize the Cabbagetown of his youth any more. Houses that sold for $35,000 or less in 1965 now bring upwards of $150,000, and sport stained glass, stone dogs in the front yards, and Mercedes-Benzes in the drives. Today's white-painters are trying to work the same magic all around the fringes of the district.

Parliament Street, Cabbagetown's main shopping street, mingles old and new Cabbagetowns haphazardly, with precious Japanese antiques being sold next door to deep-discount Formica kitchen sets, designer originals rubbing shoulders with shops that advertise "Welfare Cheques Accepted," and the liquor store doing about equal trade in rotgut sherry and crème de Cassis. A stroll along Parliament Street is never boring.

Cabbagetown's secret treat is the park at the east end of Carlton Street, where the pens of what was once Toronto's minuscule zoo have been transformed into a downtown farm, complete with draft horses, breeding sows and, in spring, dozens of lambs, foals, calves, kids, chicks, and ducklings. It is said that the civil-servant farmer even sells the freshest eggs in town to his very fortunate neighbors. A shop at the corner of Winchester Street overlooking both the zoo and the adjacent Toronto Necropolis sells great ice cream.

Rosedale

North of Bloor Street, roughly between Mount Pleasant Road and the Don River, and south of the Canadian Pacific Railway line, Toronto's wealthiest still maintain their enormous mansions, some of them, astoundingly, within ten minutes' walk of the Yonge-Bloor subway station.

Rosedale, as the district is called, has meandering streets understood by almost no one who doesn't live there. It is the sort of privileged enclave almost never found in the heart of any city anywhere anymore. Actress Gina Lollobrigida has lived here (on Inglewood Drive), as does novelist Morley Callaghan, an old boxing mate of Ernest Hemingway's. Cabbagetown may (and does) have a tour of renovated houses each year, but outsiders get into Rosedale homes only by specific invitation. Visitors can, and should, drive freely through the streets, but they should also take along a good map. The district is not really made for walking, though, and the one TTC bus that serves it, and the tour buses that pass through it, don't get to the best parts. To see some of those, look for Beaumont Road, a cul-de-sac called Old George Place, and—best of all—a little park called Craigleigh Gardens. Now try to find your way out again.

Beyond Downtown

Toronto has several other residential districts that are only slightly less prestigious than Rosedale, including the Kingsway, along the Humber River in the west end of the city; the Bridle Path, just north of the York University Glendon Campus, east off Bayview Avenue; and, far to the north-northwest, the gentlemen-farmers' estates of Maple and King City.

Rosedale's nearest downtown rival for prestige is the area called Old Forest Hill, north of St. Clair Avenue between Spadina Road and Avenue Road. A number of foreign governments maintain homes for diplomats in Old Forest Hill (a.k.a. Forest Hill Village) and the population is far less Anglo-Saxon than Rosedale's. Country singer Anne

Murray lives here among WASP and Jewish upper-middle-class neighbors. The area's wealth shows immediately in the quality of shopping, the kosher delis, and the good Chinese restaurants along Eglinton from Avenue Road to well beyond Bathurst Street.

The city's next ethnic slice begins far downtown, at about College and Clinton Streets, and extends all the way to Downsview Airport—home of DeHavilland Aircraft, makers of commuter planes—and beyond. This huge wedge is home for most of Toronto's immense Italian population, which, by itself, constitutes one of the largest Italian cities outside Italy. The streets are never dull in this part of town. When Italy won the soccer World Cup in 1982, more than a half-million Italian Torontonians and their friends poured out onto the roadways spontaneously, tying up traffic for miles and erupting in a Sunday whoop-up now immortalized in photos on local restaurant walls.

The city's German immigrants are harder to find. There are those families mentioned earlier, along Bloor Street West at Runnymede and on Roncesvalles. A much larger settlement seems to have happened in Scarborough, at the eastern end of the city, to judge from some businesses and restaurants out there, but that suburb is too dispersed and too mixed for them to have had much impact.

West Indians cluster on Bloor Street West around Christie Street and in a couple of other small neighborhoods, though you can now find snack bars selling *roti*—spicy Jamaican pasties—in almost any part of town. Indians from the subcontinent are equally dispersed, although there's one very concentrated strip of Indian shops, restaurants, and dramatically advertised movie houses along Gerrard Street East near Greenwood Avenue.

Danforth Avenue (or, more commonly, The Danforth), as Bloor Street is called east of the Don River, is so Greek that the street signs are printed in two alphabets. On warm summer nights, when the restaurants along the Danforth are still doing a thriving business in souvlaki and stewed lamb after midnight and the air hums with bouzouki music from open doors and windows, you can easily think you've tripped into some particularly orderly part of the *plaka* in Athens. Indeed, Greece's socialist prime minister Andreas Papandreou, who visited town a few years ago, lived in this area during the days of the colonels' regime, just another Toronto Greek exile.

Many things about Toronto may appeal to visitors—the disproportionate number of performing arts groups, for instance (because Torontonians have to do *something* with those long winter nights), the very clean streets (because the snowplow operators have to do something, too, when there isn't any snow), and the evident livability of the city's downtown neighborhoods. (This may be a result of early amalgamation of the suburbs into the metropolitan government, so that suburbanites had to bear equal financial responsibility for the city's schools and services, and many middle-class people simply never left the core.) What Torontonians probably like best about the place, though, are some of those things just mentioned. We do live in a safe, fairly prosperous, midwestern North American city, yes. But we can also eat souvlaki at 1:00 A.M. if we've a mind to, or the best spaghetti-and-cuttlefish this side of Trieste, if we've got a hankering for that pungent treat. Some of our neighbors show up at the ballet looking perfectly appropriate in the most amazing silk saris or kimono. At least one local newspaper and one radio station routinely cover international cricket in their sports reports. And about 20 percent of our fellow citizens go completely around the bend when Italy wins the World Cup.

If visitors to Toronto can get off the Bloor Street-Harbourfront-Eaton Centre circuit for at least a little while, and into one or two of those other Torontos, they'll get a lot closer to the real pulse of this remarkably humane metropolis. No other city anywhere has managed the easy mix of races, languages, religions, and colors that coexist so happily here, in what outsiders tend to regard as a bastion of Anglo-Saxonism.

SIGHTSEEING CHECKLIST. The following list is just a sketch of attractions in Toronto and the surrounding area that the authors of this guide think you should see if you are near them. They are described in greater detail in *Facts at Your Fingertips* or other sections of this guide.

Algonquin Park. Three hours' drive north of Toronto lies this magnificent 2,900-square-mile tract of genuine Canadian wilderness. The park marks the northernmost boundary of white-tailed deer, the southernmost of moose. You may see both here, as well as members of the park's bear population. Most of the park is accessible only by canoe—there are 1,600 miles of charted canoe routes—but there are roadside campgrounds and three splendid lodges for more civilized exploration.

Bloor St.–Yorkville. Toronto's most glittering shopping area also boasts some of its best restaurants, bars, bookshops, and five museums: the Royal Ontario, the Roy Gardiner Ceramic Museum, the Planetarium, the Sigmund Samuel Museum of Canadiana, and the Museum of the History of Medicine.

Casa Loma. With 98 rooms, secret passageways, turrets, and grand balconies, this early twentieth-century folly of a flashy financier, Sir Henry Pellatt, dominates the hill above Spadina Road. Built between 1909 and 1913 by stone masons imported from Scotland, it is now open for unguided visits by the general public. The entrance fee goes to Kiwanis Club charities.

City Hall Square. Not much to see here really, other than the "Great Gray Clam," City Hall itself, designed by Finnish architect Viljo Revell, and Torontonians themselves skating (in winter), sunbathing (in summer), protesting, displaying art, and listening to itinerant musicians. Come to think of it, that's a lot. Renowned British sculptor Henry Moore's "The Archer" dominates the northwest corner of the square. To the east stands the old City Hall, with gargoyles and clock tower; to the west, Osgoode Hall, the neoclassical (1830s) headquarters of the Law Society of Upper Canada. To the north, Chinatown and the Eaton Centre.

CN Tower. At press time, this is still the world's largest free-standing structure: 1,815-feet, 5-inches, or 553.33-meters, tall. Four elevators whisk you skyward at a rate of 1,200 feet per minute—the same rate as a jet takeoff. The Skypod, two-thirds of the way up the tower, contains a revolving restaurant and observation deck. Above it, at 1,465 feet is the world's highest public observation gallery. On a clear day you can see forever—or at least for 100 miles.

George R. Gardiner Museum of Ceramic Art. 111 Queen's Park. Housed in a beautiful two-story pink granite jewel box of a building, this museum contains world-class examples of pre-Columbian pottery and European and Oriental ceramics. Information, 593–9300.

Guelph Spring Festival. This cultural event in an old college town 50 miles west of Toronto highlights jazz and classical music, dance, and art exhibitions from the end of April through the middle of May, and attracts world-class talent. Call (519) 821–7570.

Harbourfront. Between the Harbour, Castle Hilton, and the CN Tower, Toronto's waterfront has been turned into a pedestrian's paradise; island ferry docks; Queen's Quay Terminal building's glittery boutiques; boat slips; free concerts; craft shops and art shows; weekend antique flea markets and lakeside benches.

Historic Huronia/Martyrs' Shrine. About 70 miles north of Toronto is a settlement where six of North America's eight saints died in the seventeenth century—French missionaries tortured to death by the Iroquois. Today their memory is preserved in many ways: at the Catholic pilgrimage of Martyrs' Shrine; at Ste. Marie Among the Hurons, a reconstruction of the Jesuit missionaries' seventeenth-century mission; at the reconstructed Huron Indian Village, a palisaded village with medicinal smoke house; and at the Huronia Museum and Gallery in Midland's Little Lake Park.

Hockey. The Hockey Hall of Fame, a museum in Exhibition Park, is a memorabilia collection where the Stanley Cup is housed. Today NHL teams vie for possession of the cup at Maple Leaf Gardens. And you'll see hockey throughout the winter wherever three children play together on the street.

McMichael Canadian Collection. At Kleinburg, just north of Toronto, a large art gallery made of logs and timbers houses a large and very popular collection of landscapes by Canada's Group of Seven School of painters, plus native Indian and Inuit art.

Niagara Falls. One of the world's great wonders, this 186-foot-high falls is surrounded by 25 miles of parks and gardens and a heavy concentration of tourist traps, both honky tonk and genuine attractions. Nearby are Marineland (a dolphin and whale show and children's amusement park) and the Shaw Theatre Festival at Niagara-on-the-Lake.

Oktoberfest. In Kitchener-Waterloo, 62 miles west of Toronto in the center of Ontario's "Dutch" (Mennonite) and German Country, from the first Friday in October until the second Saturday, some 600,000 visitors arrive annually to eat, drink, and dance at the many tents and beerhalls. Call (519) 576–0571.

Ontario Place and Forum. It's a modern, 96-acre park of manmade islands with food stands and games; futuristic buildings with high-tech displays; a spectacular 70-mm. domed movie screen; lawns for picnics; a marina; and The Forum—an amphitheatre featuring first-rate pop, rock, and classical concerts all summer long.

Ontario Science Centre. This place is a child and adult's wonderland of biology, technology and physics made comprehensible. Simple engines, computers, lasers, genetics, and meteorology are explained in demonstrations, displays, and games.

Royal Ontario Museum. Canada's largest public museum contains an unsurpassed Chinese section with a sculpture garden from a Ming Tomb. After a recent $60-million renovation, new galleries contain imaginative displays of dinosaurs, geology, reptiles, and North American native culture. Important temporary exhibitions are held here, too.

Stratford Shakespearean Festival. Since it began in 1953, the Stratford has become a major attraction in world theater. The summer-long festival also features pop and classical music, original Canadian and rep theater, and the quiet charm of a pretty village just three hours' drive west of Toronto.

Zoo. Opened in 1974, this 710-acre park keeps its human visitors on paths and in aisles while animals roam freely in re-creations of their native geographic habitats. These are re-created in both outdoor pastures and huge pavilions. *The New York Times* ranks the Metro Zoo as one of the ten best zoos in the world.

PRACTICAL INFORMATION FOR TORONTO

 HOW TO GET THERE. By air. Nearly every major and minor airline serves Toronto's two terminals that make up the Lester B. Pearson International Airport. More fondly referred to by its old name, the Toronto International Airport officially assumed its new name in January, 1984, to honor the late Nobel Peace Prize-winning Prime Minister.

The airport is about 32 kilometers (18 miles) northwest of Toronto, a half hour's drive. Special airport buses connect to Yorkdale and York Mills subway stops, and taxis or limousines are always available. (See also *How to Get Around,* below.)

Buttonville Airport serves military and private aircraft only. Toronto Island Airport also serves the public, flying short distances within Ontario. No international or charter jets land there. Lester B. Pearson International Airport also has facilities for private planes.

By train. *Via Rail* reaches downtown Toronto's grand old Union Station from eastern and western Canada, and *Ontario Northland* connects the north to Toronto. Once a day, an *Amtrak* train staffed by *Via* personnel arrives from New York and another comes from Chicago. *GO* trains offer commuters rush-hour transit from neighboring southern Ontario towns, with a convenient connection to Union subway station located beneath the train station. Union Station has one cathedral-like hall where tickets are sold, but the low-ceilinged departures area is dreary.

By bus. The old Toronto Bus Terminal at 610 Bay St., and the newer Elizabeth St. Terminal connected to it on the west side, are downtown depots for buses from all over North America. The terminals are within walking distance of subway lines.

In the United States, Buffalo and Detroit are transfer points for passengers going to Toronto, while Montreal links passengers from some eastern states. Most major bus lines reach Toronto, including *Greyhound, Gray Coach, Voyageur* (serving Quebec and eastern provinces), *Travelways* (from western Ontario), *Canada Coach,* and *Eastern Canadian. GO* buses use the Elizabeth St. Terminal. *Trailways* connects with *Greyhound* to serve U.S. points.

By car. *Highway 401,* also known as the *Macdonald-Cartier Freeway,* connects Montreal in the east and Windsor in the southwest with northern metropolitan Toronto. Travelers from Buffalo and Niagara Falls, New York, can take the *Queen Elizabeth Way* along the shore of Lake Ontario into Toronto, where the highway becomes the *Gardiner Expressway,* going right downtown.

Highway 400 brings northern Ontario travelers to the city. *Highway 11* in the north eventually turns into Yonge Street, the longest street in the world.

TELEPHONES. The area code for all of Toronto and many surrounding towns is 416. You do not need to dial the area code if it is the same as the one from which you are calling. Some towns using area code 416 are nevertheless long distance from Toronto; when dialing these, dial number "1" before the seven-digit number. When dialing long distance beyond the 416 area, you must dial "1", the area code, and the seven-digit number. Dial "0" for an operator to assist you with person-to-person, billing to third number, collect calls, and other special calls.

Toronto pay phones cost $.25 (American quarters are fine) and are located on subway platforms, streets, in shopping malls, and other usual places. Although you will hear a dial tone as soon as you lift the receiver, your call won't be completed unless you pay first. The number for directory assistance (information) is 411, and 911 is the number for all types of emergency assistance. There is no charge for 411, 911, and 0 calls made from pay phones.

HOTELS AND MOTELS in Toronto range from a couple of world-class showcases, at fabulous prices, to countless small but clean mom-and-pop operations along the roadsides in older suburban areas. We've put together only a small selection, perhaps over-represented a bit at the top end, but deliberately so since some of these deserve to be singled out for their dining rooms as well as their bedrooms. Except as noted, rates are based on high-season (summer and fall) double occupancy. The list is alphabetical within each price category, with airport hotels listed separately. *Super Deluxe* prices run upwards of $150 per night; *Deluxe* prices begin at $99; *Expensive* begins at $80; *Moderate* begins at $65; *Inexpensive* begins at $49; and *Basic Budget* prices are less than $49. Please note that these prices do not include Ontario's 5 percent provincial sales tax. (All prices are quoted in Canadian dollars.) Many hotels accept at least some major credit cards, but it is always wise to check *before* making plans.

SUPER DELUXE

Four Seasons Toronto. 21 Avenue Rd., M5R 2G1; 416–964–0411. When *Institutional Investor* magazine polled its readers—the traveling captains of finance—about their favorite hotels in the world, at least four high scorers were owned or managed by Toronto's Four Seasons chain. If any hotel in such a chain can be called a flagship, the Four Seasons Toronto, also a bankers' favorite, is it. Elizabeth Taylor, in for a lengthy stay during filming, wanted windows that opened. She got them—within 48 hours. All 379 rooms were renovated recently at a cost of $3.5 million. Indoor pool, non-smokers floors. Special family and weekend rates.

King Edward Hotel. 37 King St. E., M5C 1E9; 416–863–9700. After too many years of neglect, this Edwardian classic was finally purchased and thoroughly renovated a few years back by a group of local investors. Some of the restorations were less than sensitive; the kitschy platform with pergola in the Victorian Dining Room desecrates one of Toronto's great interiors. And the management, the British Trusthouse Forte group, has a few glitches yet. Still, it's a treat to have this splendid structure restored to pink-marble grandeur, once again attracting the well-heeled clientele it so manifestly deserves. 318 rooms. 24-hour room service. Non-smokers' floors. Family and weekend rates.

Sutton Place. 955 Bay St., M5S 2A2; 416–924–9221. This 33-story tower, located conveniently close to the various ministries of the Ontario provincial government, is a favorite with lobbyists, corporate lawyers, and the like. Service is more personal than you'd think, since the place isn't as big as it looks—many of the floors house apartments, not hotel rooms. The Sansoucci restaurant is first rate. Facilities include pool, health club, 24-hour room service, and special floors for executives and non-smokers. Family, off-season, and weekend rates are available.

DELUXE

Hotel Plaza II. 90 Bloor St. E., M4W 1A7; 416–961–8000. This one is a small, 256-room hotel Torontonians tend to forget. It's perched, along with some apartments, atop the Hudson's Bay Company's department store near the busy intersection of Yonge and Bloor streets. Pool, saunas. Off-season and weekend rates.

Park Plaza. 4 Avenue Rd., M5R 2E8; 416–924–5471. With only 350 rooms in the hotel, the Park Plaza's five restaurants have long had to reach outside the hotel for business. The Prince Arthur Dining Room, at the north end of the ground floor, has served Sunday dinners to local Establishment families for generations. The rooftop bar has been a meeting place for journalists (including Ernest Hemingway) for almost as long. The hotel is very convenient to Yorkville and the university. Its rooms seem to coast by on their old-shoe familiarity to regular Toronto visitors who've been staying in them since the days when there was much less choice.

Royal York Hotel. 100 Front St. W. M5J 1E3; 416–368–2511. It may still be—as it was for decades—the "largest hotel in the British Commonwealth." At 1,600 rooms and 13 restaurants, it's unarguably a monster of a place. The service is necessarily impersonal, room service not outstanding, and there's always a convention of some sort going on. Still, it's venerable, comfortable, close to the financial core of the city, and rarely booked solid.

Sheraton Centre. 123 Queen St. W. M5H 2M9; 416–361–1000. A 1,430-room conventioneers' tower just across Queen Street from the New City Hall. The below-ground level is part of Toronto's labyrinth of shop-lined corridors, and there are more shops on the ground floor and second floor. The restaurants' reach seems to exceed their grasp, but the Long Bar, overlooking Nathan Phillips Square, is a great place to meet friends for a drink. 24-hour room service. Non-smokers' floors. All sorts of special rates and packages.

Toronto Hilton Harbour Castle. 1 Harbour Sq. M5J 1A6; 416–869–1600. A favorite with convention organizers, this modern, 976-room tower by the lake is part of the Hilton International chain, the group that operates Vista hotels in the United States but is no longer associated with the less prestigious Hilton Hotels of America. A little inconvenient to the city's amenities except for those directly on the lakeshore, the Hilton does, however, have many amenities of its own, including pool, health club, four restaurants, non-smokers' floors, family, off-season and weekend rates. Ferries to the Toronto Islands depart from directly behind the hotel.

The Westin. 145 Richmond St. W. M5H 3M6; 416–869–3456. It's a credit to the Westin group that this 601-room financial-district hotel never gives you the feeling that it has twice as many rooms as Sutton Place or the King Edward. The Westin has a comparatively low profile with Torontonians, perhaps because its dining rooms don't get—and don't seem to want—much local trade. Its reputation is better with the people who stay here. Family plan and weekend rates.

EXPENSIVE

Holiday Inn–Don Valley. 1250 Eglinton Ave. E. M3C 1J3; 416–449–4111. A Holiday Inn is a Holiday Inn. Ontario links in the chain tend to be fairly well maintained. This one attracts some locals to its restaurants and bars.

Holiday Inn–Downtown. 89 Chestnut St. M5G 1R1; 416–977–0707. Toronto politicians squelched a plan to put a huge sign high on the south wall, since it would have shone forever above Nathan Phillips Square and probably would have deceived some outsiders into thinking that the New City Hall was part of the chain where "the best surprise is no surprise." The only surprise about this link is its central location.

Holiday Inn–Yorkdale. 3450 Dufferin St. M6A 2V1; 416–789–5161. Just off Highway 401, this 373-room high-rise has a pool, saunas, one restaurant, conference rooms, and special rates for families, weekends and off season. Convenient to Yorkdale Shopping Centre, Canada's first and still one of its best malls.

Loew's Westbury Hotel. 475 Yonge St. M4Y 1X7; 416–924–0611. Thirty years ago, when Toronto deserved to be called Hogtown, the Westbury was *the* place to stay—thanks largely to its dining room, which was years ahead of its time in bringing superb food to a gastronomic wasteland. Times change. These days the Westbury's chief advantage is proximity to the CBC network studios and Maple Leaf Gardens. The dining room, now called Creighton's, is still pretty good, but it's not what it was and the competition is a lot stiffer. Non-smokers' floors. Family and weekend rates.

Windsor Arms. 22 St. Thomas St. M5S 2B9; 416–979–2341. Katharine Hepburn, Peter Ustinov, the Rolling Stones, and scores of other celebrities patronize this very small 81-room inn that nestles behind its ivy on a quiet, outdoor-café-lined side street just steps from the high-ticket shops of Bloor Street. One of the three Canadian members in the prestigious French *Relais et Châteaux* association, the Windsor Arms is also one of the few downtown hotels anywhere to meet that group's standards for "calm, comfort, and cuisine." No pool. No conference facilities. Just a superb kitchen (patronized by thousands of Torontonians who enjoy the hotel's four restaurants) and rooms fit for a country inn, including a handful of very reasonable single rooms.

MODERATE

Brownstone Hotel. 15 Charles St. E. M4Y 1S1; 416–924–7381. 115 rooms with TV. You could not be closer to the center of town and still get a quiet night's sleep.

Carlton Inn. 30 Carlton St. M5B 2E9; 416–977–6655. 535 reasonably priced rooms right next door to Maple Leaf Gardens and convenient to the Carlton/College subway stop. A favorite with budget travelers and salesmen with tight expense accounts. Pool, saunas.

Delta Chelsea Inn. 33 Gerrard St. W. M5G 1Z4; 416–595–1975. The big wall of 995 rooms on the south side of Gerrard Street began as a "budget" hotel. Prices have crept up, although they're still reasonable by downtown standards. The Chelsea is much-favored by tour organizers, and the elevators, which were meant to serve the apartment building this was originally meant to be, can be hard to catch when all the buses are leaving at once. Some rooms with kitchenettes. Non-smokers' floors. Pool, sauna, 24-hour room service.

Hampton Court. 415 Jarvis St. M4Y 2G8; 416–924–6631. In summer, quite a few of the ground-floor rooms with doors that open directly onto the courtyard pool area rent by the day to downtowners who are looking for a quiet place to swim and sunbathe. The closest motel-style accommodations to the heart of town.

Holiday Inn–Toronto East. 22 Metropolitan Rd. Scarborough, M1R 2T6; 416–293–8171. Special rooms for executives. No in-room TV movies, but the hotel has VCR machines available if you want to bring your own tapes. 193 rooms, one restaurant.

Howard Johnson's, Oakville. 590 Argus Rd. L6J 3J3; 416–842–4780. A smallish, 147-room, two-restaurant hotel just outside the city in a suburb along the Lake Ontario shoreline that had, until two years ago, the highest per-capita income of any community in Canada. Oakville has convenient commuter-train service into Toronto, good shopping, and better-than-average restaurants. The hotel has a pool, saunas, conference facilities, and special floors for executives and non-smokers.

Lakeshore Inn. 2000 Lakeshore Blvd. W. M6S 1A2; 416–763–4521. One of the pleasanter possibilities in the strand of hotels strung along Lake Ontario just outside the city. 143 rooms, three restaurants. Pool, special TV movies. Family, off-season, and weekend rates.

Roehampton Hotel. 808 Mt. Pleasant Rd. M4P 2L2; 416–487–5101. A quiet, 112-room hotel, including 20 rooms with kitchenettes, Roehampton Hotel costs less than many other hotels due to its location slightly outside the downtown core, near Eglinton Avenue. Conference facilities, American pay-TV, pool.

INEXPENSIVE

Bond Place. 65 Dundas St. E. M5B 2G8; 416–362–6061. 285 clean, budget-priced rooms conveniently located just one block from the Eaton Centre. At these prices, you don't get many amenities. No pool; just one, strictly utilitarian, restaurant. But the rooms are fine. At least one fussy Swiss banker presently working in Toronto puts his visiting family and friends here. For non-working visitors, it's about the best deal going.

Executive Motor Hotel. 621 King St. W. M5V 1M5; 416–362–7441. A friendly, inexpensive motel-style facility in an unlikely location convenient primarily to the garment district. Like many downtown motels, this one is much favored by salesmen with lots of samples and others who like their vehicles close to their rooms.

Journey's End Motel–North York. 66 Norfinch Dr., Downsview M3N 1X1; 416–736–4700. Hwy. 400, exit 25; Finch Ave. east to Norfinch. Clean and spartan. 145 rooms have air-conditioning and TV. Only 8 minutes from Canada's Wonderland amusement park.

Seahorse Motel. 2095 Lakeshore Blvd. W. M8V 1A1; 416–255–4433. A small, slightly tatty, 80-room motel about 15 minutes' drive from downtown along the Lakeshore, the Seahorse is best-known to Torontonians for the blaring billboards it used to have up around town announcing the availability of "ooo-ooo! waterbeds!"

BASIC BUDGET

Metro Inn. 2121 Kingston Rd. M1N 1T5; 416–267–1141. Newly renovated, 10 minutes from downtown. Wheelchair access. Plenty of free parking.

Neill-Wycik College Hotel. 96 Gerrard St. E. M5B 1G7; 416–977–2320. In summer this residence for students at Ryerson Polytechnic becomes a budget hotel, ten minutes' walk from the Eaton Centre, with full, country-style natural-foods breakfasts served in the café, non-temperance beverages at a sidewalk patio, and a student-travel agency on the premises.

Toronto Bed and Breakfast. P.O. Box 74, Station M, Toronto, Ontario M6S 4T2. 416–233–3887 or 233–4041 evenings and weekends. An answering machine gives information through the week. A $3 booklet from this address lists at least 30 homes in the city where singles pay about $35 per night, couples about $45 per night, for a room and breakfast.

Toronto International Hostel. 223 Church St. M5B 1Z1; 416–368–0207. The very central Toronto hostel has 96 beds, in nine bedrooms, but no other facilities to speak of. $9 to $15 per person. Three nights maximum.

AIRPORT HOTELS

Very few of Toronto's airport-strip hotels offer much more than standard, middle-of-the-road rooms and meals. Except for the few exceptions, these hotels are primarily for visitors arriving on late flights or leaving on early ones.

All of the following have pools, conference facilities, pay TV or special movies, and weekend rates. Other features are noted by hotel.

Deluxe

Bristol Place. 950 Dixon Rd. M9W 5N4; 416–675–9444. The classiest of the "strip" hotels, Bristol Place is represented internationally by HRI–the Leading Hotels of the World, a pretty selective group. Bristol Place and the Constellation are the only airport hotels whose kitchens have both the ambition and means to transcend the ordinary. 287 rooms, three restaurants. Saunas. 24-hour room service. Off-season rates but no family plans.

Expensive

Constellation. 900 Dixon Rd. M9W 1J7; 416–675–1500. The Constellation's main dining room has long attracted business from outside the hotel. Staff turnover is exceptionally low, so service tends to be smooth and confident. Members of Parliament from Ottawa stay here when they're in town just for the night. 840 rooms, five restaurants. Saunas. 24-hour room service. Special floors for executives and non-smokers. Family and off-season rates.

Moderate

Airport Hilton. 5875 Airport Rd. L4V 1N1; 416–677–9900. 263 rooms, four restaurants. Pool. Sauna. 24-hour room service.

The Ascot Inn. 534 Rexdale Blvd. M9W 1S2; 416–675–3101. Convenient to Woodbine Race Track and slightly off the "strip," this small, 93-room hotel has been around much longer than the others.

Cambridge Motor Hotel. 600 Dixon Rd. M9W 1J4; 416–249–7671. 175 rooms. Two restaurants. Off-season rates but no family plan.

Cara Inn. 6257 Airport Rd. L4V 1E4; 416–678–1400. 200 rooms. Health club and saunas. Family and off-season rates. Children under 18 free.

Carlingview Airport Inn. 221 Carlingview Dr. M9W 5E8; 416–675–3303. 112 rooms. One restaurant.

Holiday Inn–West Toronto. 2 Holiday Dr. M9C 2Z7; 416–621–2121. The Holiday Inn overlooks scenic Highway 427, on the way to the center of the city. Pool. Two restaurants. Conference facilities. Off-season and weekend rates.

Howard Johnson's–Airport. 801 Dixon Rd. M9W 1J5; 416–675–6100. 242 rooms. Two restaurants. Saunas. Special floor for executives. Family plan, off-season rates, honeymoon packages.

Valhalla Inn. 1 Valhalla Inn Rd. M9B 1S9; 416–239–2391. 242 rooms. Four restaurants, including one that serves Scandinavian specialties. Saunas and an adjacent squash club. Executive floors and special "Lady Executive Suites." Free TV movies. Family plan. A longer drive from the airport than most, in the direction of downtown.

HOW TO GET AROUND. By subway, bus, and street-car. While Toronto residents complain about the fares, schedules, and overcrowding of the public transit system, they really have it pretty good. The Toronto Transit Commission (TTC) keeps winning international awards for operating one of the cleanest, safest, and most convenient systems in the world.

Subway trains cross Toronto from east to west and loop north and south on the Yonge and Spadina-University lines. Tokens and tickets can be purchased in subway stations and convenience stores on bus and streetcar routes. Surface vehicles will only accept tickets, tokens, and exact fares. Be sure to get a free transfer where you pay your fare, so you can make connections without paying again.

For information on public transit, call 393–INFO between 7:00 A.M. and 11:30 P.M. daily. Single adult cash fare is $1. You spend less per token if you buy five for $4.00 or 25 for $20. The Holiday/Sunday pass, good for one day, is a bargain at $3.25 for unlimited rides for two adults and up to three children below age 16. If you're staying a month, consider a "Metropass," a photo-identity card that lets you ride as often as you want. It costs $41.50.

By automobile. The Toronto Transit Commission has an ongoing campaign to convince motorists that transit is "the better way." But driving in Toronto is not bad at all. Of course, downtown is usually congested and rush hours are a drag all over town, but you can still get around.

There is usually no parking on main streets during the busy hours of 7:00–9:00 A.M. and 4:00–6:00 P.M. Signs designating downtown areas as towaway zones mean just that: park here and you can lose your car to a tow truck. There are plenty of parking lots. Municipal ones are cheaper than private ones.

The Canadian Automobile Association's local branch, the Ontario Motor League, is affiliated with the American Automobile Association. It offers road and weather reports (925–6341), emergency services (966–3000), legal and technical information, and even car inspection.

It might help you to know about a few highways and major streets. Highway 401 goes east-west through northern Toronto. From it, the 427 runs south in the west end, and the Don Valley Parkway winds south in the east. Lake Ontario lies to the south of Toronto. Two major arteries run east-west along its shore: the Gardiner Expressway and the slower Lakeshore Boulevard. Yonge Street, the longest street in the world, runs north-south through the heart of the city, and Bloor-Danforth cuts through from west to east.

There are a few other things to note. The law requires you to wear a seat belt. Drivers of cars whose passengers do not buckle up can be prosecuted. Infants must be strapped into infant car seats. It is illegal to hold them on your lap. Motorcyclists must wear helmets and ride with headlights on. Canada has converted to metric, and distances, speed, and gas are measured in kilometers and litres. Handicapped parking is designated by a blue-and-white symbol of a wheelchair within a square. Curbs and street sections painted with yellow lines indicate that no parking is allowed. Pedestrians may cross streets at crosswalks marked by "X"s. Watch out; not all people look both ways and wait for you to stop. They still have the right of way. You can make a right turn on a red light unless otherwise indicated.

It makes sense to give the right of way to TTC surface vehicles, because if the TTC provides good service, fewer people will use their cars, and this means easier driving (so says the TTC). Cars are expected to stop behind the rear doors of a streetcar when it lets off passengers at a TTC stop.

When locating street numbers, it's helpful to remember that even numbers are on the west or north side of a street, and odd numbers are on the east or south side. Numbering for east-west streets begins at Yonge Street, and street numbers go higher the farther east or west you go. North-south streets start numbering at the south, lakeside.

From the airport. Since the airport is about 32 kilometers (18 miles) northwest of the city, buses will be a lot cheaper than taxis. Gray Coach operates express buses that link the airport to three subway stops. The fare to York Mills on the Yonge line is $4.75, while for $4.00 you can go to Yorkdale on the Spadina-University line, or for $3.75 to Islington on the Bloor line. Buses go from around 8:00 A.M. to 11:30 P.M. Call 979–3511 for exact times.

Gray Coach also runs a bus right downtown to the Royal York Hotel, seven days a week. The ride costs $7.00, takes 35 minutes, and is available at 20-minute intervals from roughly 7:00 A.M. to midnight. Again, call 979–3511 for information.

If you'd rather go by limousine, get one at the arrivals level. Getting downtown will cost you $25 or so.

By taxi. Fares start at $1.20 and increase by $.20 every fifth of a mile (cabs seem to resist metric measurement). Remember the speed of inflation; these rates may go up at any time. All marked taxis provide reasonable service, but some of the bigger companies are Co-op (364–8161), Diamond (366–6868), and Metro (363–5611).

By rental car. The Yellow Pages list all the companies under "Automobile Renting," but the most familiar ones are Avis, Budget, Hertz, and Tilden. Cars can easily be rented at the airport and other parts of town; reservations aren't usually necessary. Limousines line up at the arrivals level of the airport. The Yellow Pages describe the features of several companies, if you're interested in special service. The Canadian Automobile Association's Ontario Motor League is affiliated with the American Automobile Association. It offers rental information at 964–3145 for domestic and foreign cars, as well as road and weather reports (925–6341) and emergency services (966–3000).

By bicycle. Toronto has several long bicycle paths, some of which go through the city core. Maps of the routes are available from the Visitors Association at Yonge and Dundas.

On foot. Walking gives you the best sense of any city, and Toronto has several areas that should only be explored on foot, including Kensington Market, Yorkville, Queen Street West, the Beaches, Bloor West Village, High Park, and the University of Toronto campus. The Toronto Islands parks bear signs inviting you to "Please walk on the grass."

It's difficult to get lost in most of Toronto because of its grid street design. But residential areas such as Rosedale are notoriously labyrinthine. Generally, downtown streets are safe at night, but beware of empty suburban streets and underground parking lots.

TOURIST INFORMATION. The *Metropolitan Toronto Convention & Visitors Association* maintains a permanent office in the Eaton Centre, 220 Yonge St. Instead of being at street level, the office is one floor above in The Mews. It is easy to get lost in the huge mall as you search for Suite 110 in the Galleria Offices. Take the escalator up one floor to the elevator that goes to the Galleria Offices. Or take the elevator for just one floor. Don't despair if you can't find the main office; the Association has a year-round information booth just outside the Eaton Centre, on the southwest corner of Dundas and Yonge streets. The booth has plenty of helpful booklets, including the quarterly *Metro Toronto Happenings,* a guide map, and a discovery guide, all free. Trained counselors are on duty.

You can write for Toronto information to Metropolitan Toronto Convention & Visitors Association, Toronto Eaton Centre, 220 Yonge St., Box 510, Suite 110, Toronto Ontario M5B 2H1. Or call the visitor information line, 979–3143, from 9:00 A.M. to 5:00 P.M. Monday through Friday, year round.

From late May to Labour Day there are red-and-white visitors' booths in many popular street locations, including Nathan Phillips Square, the corner of Bloor and Yonge, down by the Ferry Docks, and the Metro Zoo.

Five Star Tickets shares booth space with the Visitors Association at Yonge and Dundas. Here you can buy half-price tickets to same-day performances at theaters that don't expect to sell out that day. As well, you can buy advance tickets at full price. There's no telephone, so come in person Monday through Saturday, noon to 7:30 P.M., Sundays 11:00 A.M. to 3:00 P.M., and be prepared to pay cash.

Publications that carry information of interest to visitors are the monthly magazines *Toronto Life* (at newsstands) and *Key to Toronto* (in hotels) and the entertainment sections of the daily papers: *The Globe and Mail, The Toronto Star,* and the *Toronto Sun. NOW* is a free-spirited weekly entertainment newspaper available for free at most restaurants, bars, and theaters.

Teleguide computer terminals are found in hotel rooms and lobbys, malls, and public places to provide free tourist information at the push of a button.

SEASONAL EVENTS. January. The New Year is greeted by crowds of people in Nathan Phillips Square. Some of them might even be skating, which is free at City Hall all winter. When snow conditions permit, cross-country skiers begin to plow through parks and the Metro Zoo. Black Creek Pioneer Village offers weekend horse-and-sleigh rides. The *International Boat Show,* at the Coliseum in Exhibition Place, is a sailor's dream.

February. The *Farm Show* comes to the Coliseum.

March. The Exhibition's Coliseum houses the *Canadian National Sportsmen's Show,* as well as *Quarterama,* an enormous horse show with a quarter-million dollars in prize money.

April. The cruelest month is marked by the *Winter's End Craft Show,* and the *National Home Show.*

May. History comes to life at the annual *Fort York Festival.* Firework displays still celebrate *Queen Victoria's Birthday* on the May 24th weekend, but since Torontonians get a day off because of it, who's complaining? The B'nai B'rith *Bazaar* draws bargain hunters to Exhibition Place.

June. *Metro International Caravan* is an exciting way to sample the drinking, dining, and folklore of Toronto's ethnic communities in a nine-day festival. The *Toronto International Festival* brings the best of the world's musicians, plus dancers—classical, avant-garde and traditional—to a week-long, mid-month extravaganza. *Mariposa Folk Festival* is a celebration of folk music, mime, puppetry, and sun bathing held an hour's drive from Toronto in Barrie. The thoroughbred race for the Queen's Plate is the oldest race in North America.

July 1st marks *Canada Day,* with citywide celebrations. *Caribana* is the West Indian community's festival, with floats, parades, limbo dancing, and reggae. CHIN radio station sponsors an *International Picnic,* a free, several-days-long event of eating contests, a beauty pageant, and ethnic music. It's listed in the *Guinness Book of World Records* as "the world's biggest free picnic." The Toronto *Outdoor Art Exhibition* brings craft sellers, art buyers, and browsers to Nathan Phillips Square.

August. The grandfather of Canadian fairs, the *Canadian National Exhibition,* draws hundreds of thousands of visitors and residents every year to a midway, livestock and high-tech exhibits, gardens, concerts, an air show, and fireworks displays every night.

September. The *Festival of Festivals* lures film critics and film lovers to what is becoming one of the world's major film festivals.

October. Check out the Hadassah *Bazaar* at Exhibition Place if you want to bring home hard-to-find treasures.

November. The *Royal Winter Fair,* displaying livestock, horses, produce, and even butter sculpture is a favorite among school children and adults. Its horse shows are *the* social event of local gentry. Santa pops into town for the Metro *Santa Claus Parade,* held before snow is on the ground. The *Ice Capades* glitter each year at Maple Leaf Gardens.

December. Along with crowds of shoppers, the Christmas season is marked by special events at Black Creek Pioneer Village, the National Ballet's *The Nutcracker* at the O'Keefe Centre, and the *Christmas Treats Walk* on December 26 at the Metro Zoo, where the animals are given their favorite food.

 FREE EVENTS. Summer offers the most free activities and events, although some continue all year. *Harbourfront,* a federally funded waterfront complex, is the most ambitious and diverse free show going, offering everything from puppet films, theater workshops, a "kaleidoscope" (crafts and games) program for kids, jazz concerts, and vocal performances to lectures and a weekly antique market. In summer the entertainment expands outdoors and late into the night, when people dance to live music and watch the boats in the harbor.

Riverdale Farm is for city children and adults who want to escape the city. Tucked into downtown Cabbagetown at the corner of Sumach and Winchester, it's a farm garden with horses, pigs, goats, sheep, rabbits, cows, chickens, crows.

To see still more animals, go to the *High Park Zoo.* This zoo is small, with deer, sheep, llamas, yaks, and bison, but if you're looking for things to do with children, it offers a nice diversion.

The *Metro Library* occasionally hosts free readings or lectures; call 928–5313 to find out if anything's on. On the main floor of the library there's a gallery that displays a variety of artistic, literary, and historical exhibits.

Also free are tours of Queen's Park (965–4028), City Hall (392–7341), Ecology House (967–0577), Toronto Stock Exchange (947–4676), and University of Toronto (leaving Hart House in the summer).

Local television stations sometimes cry for audiences to attend their tapings. It's best to call them and find out whether you can take part: CBC (975–3311); CFTO of the CTV channel (299–2000); and Global (446–5311). Watch the newspapers for occasional free concerts in the city's churches and at Hart House at the University of Toronto.

Summer is the time when Torontonians move outside and enjoy free activities —such as swimming off Lake Ontario's beaches (when they haven't been closed for health reasons) and in the city's many free outdoor pools.

Canada Day celebrations are held all over town on the July 1st weekend. Later that month, the CHIN radio station's *International Picnic,* billed in the *Guinness Book of World Records* as the world's biggest free picnic, carries on in various locations for several days, and local artists show their works at the Toronto *Outdoor Art Exhibition* at Nathan Phillips Square, City Hall.

Throughout the summer, you can enjoy the trout pond, beaches, canals, and parklands of the *Toronto Islands* for free, once you've paid for the ferry. The Forum features top acts, which are free once you've paid admission to Ontario Place. There are magnificent floral gardens at High Park, Edwards Gardens, Allan Gardens, and the city's cemeteries—which invite the public to come and enjoy the grounds.

Ask at Five Star Tickets on the corner of Yonge and Dundas about free summer theater. A few companies undertake productions of Shakespeare-in-the-park (High Park), which is a lovely way to spend a summer's eve.

While you can spend a lot of money at the *Canadian National Exhibition,* there are two associated events that are free: the opening day parade and the air show. Ask the Visitors Association (979–3143) about the CNE parade route. And watch the annual *Air Show* anywhere down by the lake or from a skyscraper. If you're in the CN Tower, the planes will zip by at eye level.

Late summer or fall is the time for the *Cabbagetown Cultural Festival,* when Parliament Street between Wellesley and Gerrard hangs out its cabbage banners and people wander around sipping Kool-Aid and rummaging for bargains. In

November, the Metro *Santa Claus Parade* gives children a chance to scream at clowns walking on their hands and to wave at the jolly old man.

In winter, there is free skating everywhere, including Nathan Phillips Square, Ryerson Polytechnical Institute, Hazelton Lanes, and Scarborough and North York civic centers. Some of these locations occasionally offer free refreshments. Cross-country skiing is popular in the large parks, ravines, and golf courses. Some of the free places to cross-country ski are: the Don Valley, High Park, and the Beaches. Get more information from the Visitors Association at Yonge and Dundas. On New Year's Day, metropolitan Toronto's various mayors and the Lieutenant Governor of Ontario host "levees"—festive official, receptions for the general public—serving everything from Christmas cake to (if you're early and lucky) an occasional glass of sherry.

TOURS. *Happy Day Tours* at 30 Carlton (593–6220) run half-day tours of Toronto for $19.95 per person. Admission to Black Creek Pioneer Village is included. After stepping back in time you'll visit Forest Hills, Casa Loma, Chinatown, Queen's Park, Yorkville, and Harbourfront. Tours run every day except Christmas. Book at least a day ahead.

Gray Line Sightseeing Bus Tours of Toronto & Casa Loma, Bus Terminal, 610 Bay St. at Dundas; 979–3511. Tours start daily at 2:00 P.M. from the Elizabeth St. Terminal and major hotels, and take in the Eaton Centre, both City Halls, Queen's Park, University of Toronto, Yorkville, Ontario Place, and Casa Loma, where you spend an hour. The 1½-hour tour will cost $13.75 for adults and $8.50 for children under 12.

Toronto by Trolley Car, 134 Jarvis; 869–1372. For $11.95 adults, $7.50 children, you can ride a 60-year-old restored trolley car on weekends. Board at the Sheraton Centre.

Boat Tours International at 5 Queen's Quay W. (364–2412) takes people on a glass-enclosed boat tour of Toronto Harbor and the Islands. Departures are hourly from late April through late October and cost $7.95 for adults and $3.95 for children 4 to 11. Children under 4 are free. Lunch and dinner package tours are also available.

Central Airways at the Toronto Island Airport offer tours of Toronto by air. Up to three passengers can experience a Cessna 174 for $105 an hour (half-hour minimum). A ferry from the foot of Bathurst St. takes you to the Island Airport. Reserve a couple of days in advance.

SPECIAL-INTEREST SIGHTSEEING. *City Hall,* at 100 Queen St. W., invites you to free tours Monday to Friday at 3:15 P.M. Tours take about 40 minutes. Groups are asked to book ahead by calling 392–7341.

The *Ontario Parliament Buildings* in Queen's Park at College and University also offer free tours of the legislature every hour on the hour on summer weekends. During the week you should book ahead. For information, call 965–4028.

Catch the action of the *Toronto Stock Exchange,* Monday through Friday at 2:00 P.M. Call 947–4676 for information on these free tours.

Molson's Brewery at 640 Fleet St. W. allows the public to go on free tours of the plant a couple of times a day during the summer. Call ahead to 869–1396. Visitors must be over age 19.

Inspect the architectural, acoustical, and interior-design features of stunning *Roy Thomson Hall,* 60 Simcoe St.; 593–4822. Tours begin at 12:30 P.M. Monday through Saturday, last about 45 minutes, and cost $2 for adults, $1 for students and seniors. Phone ahead to make sure the tour is on.

From May to September, the *Ontario Jockey Club* takes horse lovers through Greenwood and Woodbine race tracks on Wednesday and Thursday mornings. For free thoroughbred tours, call 675–6110; for the standard-breed tours, call 698–3131.

For free guided walking tours of *University of Toronto's* colleges, grounds, and gargoyles, call 978–2105 or 978–5000. Tours take place in June, July, and August.

The *Toronto Field Naturalists* organize *nature walks* through parks and ravines. They may be energetic hikes or slower walks devoted to bird-watching, botany, or astronomy. Call 488–7304 to find out what's planned.

Ecology House is open to the public Wednesday through Sunday, noon to 5:00 P.M. On Sunday there is an hour-long tour starting at 2:00 P.M. Groups of at least ten people can arrange for a guided tour at $2 each by calling ahead to 967–0577. Ecology House, run by Pollution Probe, shows examples of conservation and energy-efficient domestic technology. The address is 12 Madison Ave., north of Bloor, just east of Spadina.

PARKS. Toronto is a city with parks and "parkettes" just about everywhere. Most neighborhoods have them within easy walking distance. Where there are ravines and valleys, Toronto has wisely chosen to create parks and let them remain relatively untended. That's why the raccoons often check out the garbage cans of downtown houses, and deer have been spotted in suburban backyards.

The City Parks and Recreation Department looks after 325 parks, courts, rinks, and playing fields, and Metro Toronto Parks and Property Department is responsible for many others. It's impossible to name them all here, so we'll mention only the biggest and best-known ones.

High Park is the largest and most famous. It covers 399 acres from the southwest corner of Bloor Street West and Keele Street. There are nature trails and fitness trails through forests, fields for playing and picnics, a small zoo, the Grenadier Pond, formal gardens and bicycle paths.

Queen's Park is the central downtown park at University Avenue between Bloor and College. The provincial legislature is housed at the south end, the Royal Ontario Museum is just to the north, and the University of Toronto almost surrounds it. On the morning of Remembrance Day the park is unbearable because of ceremonial cannon fire, but the rest of the time it's a haven for students, office workers having lunch, joggers, and squirrels.

Also within walking distance of downtown and midtown Toronto is the *Sir Winston Churchill Park* and reservoir at St. Clair and Spadina Road (St. Clair W. subway). Tennis courts on a grassy plateau overlook a wooded ravine that stretches northwest for several miles.

Downtown, the Cabbagetown neighborhood boasts *Riverdale Park and Farm* at Sumach and Winchester, east of Parliament. Toddlers and dogs romp in the little park while whole families explore the nineteenth-century model farm and its landscaped pond, barns, and farm animals.

Just behind the Old Mill subway stop, west of Jane Street and north of Bloor, the Humber River flows past a ruined mill in Etienne Brûlé Park. Optimistic anglers fish here, and bridal parties take their wedding photos. There are tennis courts, too.

For breathtaking scenery of 90-foot-high lakeside cliffs, go to *"The Bluffs"* in Scarborough. Bluffers Park and Cathedral Bluffs Park can be hazardous, however; the bluff is crumbling and in winter you risk being blown into the lake.

Sherwood Park, a bit north of Mt. Pleasant and Eglinton, is a charming park with big hills, a ragged ravine, a children's playground, and large wading pool.

Wilket Creek Park and Edwards Gardens (Leslie Street between Eglinton and Lawrence) is a serpentine ravine linking the Ontario Science Centre to the magnificent pools and streams of Edwards Gardens. In between, the ravine passes Sunnybrook Park riding stables.

Leave Toronto behind when you visit the *Toronto Islands.* Just a short ferry ride across from downtown, the 552 acres of park and beaches seem to be a world away, although it might look like the world goes to Centre Island on summer weekends. Centreville has a little amusement park and a petting zoo.

East of the Islands and connected to the mainland is the Leslie Street Spit, the accidental product of dredging projects and dumping. Nature has created wild parkland out of man's debris, and ducks, geese, and gulls make The Spit an urban bird-watcher and naturalist's paradise.

ZOOS. Torontonians love the **Metro Zoo.** Early in 1984, when a Bengal tiger a little too long in the tooth was threatened with being put to sleep, there was an uproar from citizens and local politicians that made the headlines. The tiger received a stay of execution, and everyone slept better at night.

The New York Times' rating of the Metro Zoo as one of the ten best in the world is no surprise. Over 710 acres and five climate-controlled pavilions have been turned over to more than 3,000 animals that wander nearly unrestricted. The pavilions are dedicated to six geographic regions, painstakingly constructed in an attempt to duplicate the animals' natural habitat. The animals appreciate it, as, for example, the presence of a third generation of orangutans testifies.

Springtime provides educational opportunities when the animals get frisky, although there may be more going on than you care to explain to the kids.

Boxing Day (December 26) is the time for the annual Christmas Treats Walk, when the animals are fed their favorite snacks. As well, people cross-country ski at the Zoo throughout winter.

The Zoo is located at Highway 401 East at Meadowvale Road. Parking costs $2 in the busy summer season, and admission prices are: $5 adults, $2.50 seniors and youths 12 to 17, $1 children 5 to 11, while the younger ones get in for free. The zoo is open from 9:30 A.M. daily. For people not up to walking over the vast acreage, there is an electric train and a "zoomobile" that provide thorough tours.

High Park has a tiny zoo containing sheep, deer, llamas, yaks, and bison in small fenced-in fields, but they seem happy enough. As part of an exploration of the huge park, the zoo is fun to see, especially for young children who never see such animals.

Riverdale Farm is located on the old site of the Riverdale Zoo. Now a nineteenth-century model farm, Riverdale (in Cabbagetown at Sumach and Winchester) has cows, goats, chickens, horses, pigs, rabbits, and other animals.

Very young children will be thrilled with the *petting zoo* in Centreville on Centre Island. Take the ferry across the harbor (in warm weather) and let your children pet some tranquil farm animals.

Two commercial animal attractions are within easy driving distance of Toronto. The *African Lion Safari* at Rockton (take the Queen Elizabeth Way and Highway 403 west to Highway 8) is a 500-acre drive-through park in which lions, tigers, monkeys, and giraffes roam free. Open daily, April to October. For information, call 1–519–623–2620. *Marineland,* near Niagara Falls, is a 1,000-acre complex. One admission price ($11.95 adults; $6.95 children under 10 and seniors 60 and over. Children under 4 free when accompanied by an adult paying full price) covers all its attractions: the killer whale show, the dolphin show, elephant rides, and a huge roller coaster. Call 1–356–8250 for further information. Open all year.

 GARDENS. Perhaps it's the fault of the climate, Toronto is not noted for its public gardens. However, there are a handful of beautiful, established gardens in the city.

Allen Gardens is a park on Sherbourne Street between Carlton and Gerrard. It contains a 70-year-old greenhouse that is said to be Toronto's oldest botanical garden. Inside are over 800 species of tropical plants and flowers that are particularly lovely in winter. Admission is free; open daily from 10:00 A.M. to 5:00 P.M.

Every weekend in fine weather there are wedding parties having their pictures taken in *Edwards Gardens.* These lovely 34 acres are situated at Lawrence Avenue E. and Leslie Street, with a tributary of the Don River flowing through. The gardens are set among pools and hillsides. Overlooking the gardens are the Civic Garden Centre, Gift and Book Shop, and a Specialist Horticultural Library.

High Park has impressive formal gardens just east of Grenadier Pond. Another formal garden is located in *James Gardens* east of Royal York Rd. in the west end.

In nearby Hamilton (one hour's drive west of Toronto along the Queen Elizabeth Way) the *Royal Botanical Gardens* are a much more impressive floral display than anything Toronto has to offer. Here, in 2,000 acres, is an internationally renowned lilac garden and arboretum, a rose garden, and a marsh and wildlife sanctuary.

 BEACHES. Nowhere are Toronto's extremes of temperature more evident than at the beaches. In August the coarse sand can blister your bare feet, and in winter the frozen shore seems as chilling as the Arctic. Yet in any season the beaches are a splendid place for a soulful walk. But lately, to Toronto's shame, most mainland (but not island) beaches have been deemed too polluted for safe swimming. Call the city of Toronto's public health department at 392–7450 or the Visitors Information Service at 979–3143 for up-to-date information.

Beaches Park in the east end south of Queen Street east of Coxwell is the most popular beach area. A boardwalk that lines the stretch of sand is heavily used by joggers and people walking their dogs. In summer lifeguards keep watch and the snack bars and the local canoe club open for business. Close by are public washrooms, tennis courts, and a lawn-bowling green. A bit to the west are two other areas perfect for boat watching and sun bathing: Woodbine Beach Park and Ashbridges Bay Park. Parking will be your main concern on weekends.

"The Beaches," including the strip of Queen Street E. just to the north, is one of the trendiest neighborhoods in Toronto. The skyscrapers of downtown are just a streetcar ride away but the clapboard houses and sprawling verandahs make it feel like cottage country. Only the unusual specialty stores and stylish restaurants show an urban influence.

Cherry Beach at the foot of Cherry Street is quieter than the east-end Beaches because, being surrounded by industries, it is more remote. Parking is easier here, and the facilities include washrooms and a small snack bar. Just don't count on these always being open. Cherry Beach is at the Eastern Gap to Toronto Harbor, directly east of the Islands.

To really feel as if you're getting away from it all, visit the beaches on the *Toronto Islands.* The south side of Centre Island is very popular, while the southeast part of Ward's Island and the west side of Hanlan's Point are less crowded. There are free washrooms near all beaches.

On the lakeshore to the west, due south of High Park, is *Sunnyside Beach.* Here you'll find a pool, snack bar, jungle gym, washrooms, and crowds in good weather. This is not the easiest beach to get to by public transit, and taking a car on weekends can give you a parking headache. Still, plenty of residents pack up the whole family and head west from Bathurst Street along Lakeshore Boulevard.

Wasaga, the world's largest freshwater beach, is only an hour's drive from Toronto, due north on Highway 400, then west on Highway 26.

THEME PARKS AND AMUSEMENT CENTERS. Every August until Labour Day, Exhibition Place draws hundreds of thousands of visitors to the **Canadian National Exhibition.** Children want to visit the Midway, a huge carnival of deafening rock music, lightning rides, games of chance, and junk food. Happily, there are other reasons to go to "the Ex." They include the Food Building, full of promotional displays, cooking demonstrations, free food samples and inexpensive meals; the Horse Colosseum, where prize animals go through their paces; and the other technical exhibits, fashion, furniture and craft shows, and band-shell performances. The prices seem to climb every year (in 1983 adult admission was $4) and midway rides cost more than a dollar each.

Because teenagers can't seem to get enough of a bad thing, a local radio station, CHUM, sponsors the *CHUM Midway,* which previews the Ex's midway in spring. Hundreds of teens congregate daily in front of the ride playing the loudest, trashiest rock music, standing in tight groups of friends, smoking cigarettes, and checking each other out.

Ontario Place is a huge waterfront park devoted to technological exhibits, films, bars, and boat slips. The chief attraction is The Cinesphere, an enormous dome that houses a six-story-high wraparound screen capable of showing 70-mm. films. The Forum is a permanent tent-covered revolving stage where such world-class performers as Ray Charles, the Toronto Symphony, and Anne Murray appear free to those who have already paid admission to Ontario Place. Children's Village is open only to little people, who get to romp in an unusual playground of tube slides, bins, and a water-play area. Ontario Place is open from mid-May to mid-September. When the CNE is on, one admission price covers the Ex and Ontario Place.

Canada's Wonderland is the newest addition to Toronto's theme parks. Just north of the city, on Highway 400 at Rutherford Road, it has six live shows, 30 thrill rides, Hanna-Barbera Land for children, "international" shopping, and restaurants. Wonderland, which charges $16.95 for a one-day passport, opens in spring, is busiest through the summer, and remains open on weekends through early October.

Centreville is a small amusement center for children on Centre Island. It's open during the warm months and admission is free. There are small carnival rides, a few nineteenth-century-style buildings, and a petting farm full of barnyard animals.

Black Creek Pioneer Village is a careful re-creation of a nineteenth-century Ontario village. Men and women in authentic costumes go about their daily business of grinding flour, baking bread, dipping candles, making soap, blacksmithing, farming, and shearing. Special activities warm up Christmas, and winter weekends are devoted to tobogganing, skating, and one-horse-open-sleigh rides.

The **African Lion Safari** at Rockton (take the Queen Elizabeth Way and Highway 403 west to Highway 8) is a 500-acre, drive-through park in which lions, tigers, and giraffes roam free. Open daily, April to October. For information, call 1–519–623–2620.

Marineland, near Niagara Falls, is a 1,000-acre complex. One admission price covers all its attractions: a killer-whale and dolphin show, elephant rides, a huge roller coaster, and more. Open all year. Call 1–356–8250 for further information.

 FISHING AND CHARTER BOATS. It follows that a province that is a cartographer's nightmare is also a fisherman's dream. The Ontario Ministry of Tourism and Recreation candidly admits that the province has so many lakes that they are "uncountable." Innumerable too are the stories of anglers from around the world who have tangled with the legendary Ontario muskie (maskinonge or muskellunge). Muskies have been known to weigh in at over 50 pounds. For those too timid or not quite ready for a muskie, Toronto provides a jumping-off spot for a wide variety of freshwater fishing. As well, it is home port to several Great Lakes fishing charters.

Throughout the lakes and rivers of both the southern and northern parts of the province, anglers can vie for one of North America's great sports fish, the northern pike. Or they can go after walleyes (yellow pickerels), smallmouth and largemouth bass, lake trout, rainbow trout (steelhead), and brown and brook (speckled) trout. The Ministry of Natural Resources (416–965–7883) will provide information on seasons, transportation, and fishing lodges.

For those interested in a morning, afternoon, or overnight fishing expedition on the Great Lakes, charter boats are available from docks in nearby Mississauga and Port Credit. Sport fishing on the Lakes has enjoyed a renaissance since New York State began stocking Lake Ontario with Pacific salmon in the 1960s. Ontario has been stocking the lake with coho salmon since 1969, with chinook salmon since 1973, and has continuously stocked the lake with rainbow trout and lake trout. The charter fleet on Lake Ontario now exceeds 100 boats, whose captains charge about $50 per person for half a day. All equipment is supplied and most charters offer optional meals and refreshments. Ontario Travel (416–965–4008) will supply all necessary charter information including amounts and types of fish that are safe for human consumption.

Even within Metro Toronto there are modest opportunities for anglers. The parks department stocks the trout pond at Hanlan's Point on the Toronto Islands. It's free. As well, some diehard fisherfolk can be observed trying their luck in the Humber River (behind Old Mill subway station) or in the suburban parks. Good luck to them.

Those thinking of chartering a boat on Lake Ontario should make reservations well in advance. And one can also enter the Toronto Star's annual Great Salmon Hunt. In 1983 the derby, held from mid-August to mid-September, attracted over 12,000 entrants from North America and Europe. The flotilla each year hunts for a tagged salmon—with $1 million going to the lucky sportsman who lands it.

For more information on fishing and licenses, see the *Fishing* section in *Facts at Your Fingertips* at the front of the book.

PARTICIPANT SPORTS. The four seasons of metropolitan Toronto provide such a range of activities for its sporting residents and visitors that you can almost exhaust yourself choosing. From the vast expanse of Lake Ontario to the south, to the rolling hills of the north, boaters and sail surfers, swimmers and skaters, joggers and cross-country skiers, tobogganists and golfers revel in accessible facilities and nature's bounty. Parks within the city and along the lakeshore, tennis courts and golf courses, skating rinks, and snow-covered hills are waiting for all who care to participate.

For information on public recreational facilities, call 392–7259 for the city of Toronto's pool and rink information, 626–4557 for Etobicoke Parks and Recreation, or 296–7411 if you're in Scarborough.

Golf. Though the season is shorter than most golfers would like (April to late October), there is ample opportunity to shave or inflate your handicap here. Toronto offers 47 courses within easy driving distance from downtown. Not all the courses are championship caliber, but for the low-handicapper and those who would like to test themselves on the site of the Canadian Open championship, a visit to *Glen Abbey* is a must. The course is open to the public when not being groomed for the Open. For starting times on this exquisite test, call 844–1800. Guests at the course, west of Toronto at the Doral Drive exit on the Queen Elizabeth Way, must rent an electric golf cart to deal with the rigors of the layout. Cart and green fees total about $50.

For the less adventurous, the *Don Valley Golf Course,* on Yonge Street just south of Highway 401 (225–6821), offers a twisting valley-floor course. The *Flemingdon Park Golf Club* at Don Mills Road and Eglinton Avenue (429–1740) is a comfortable nine-hole course. Highway 404, the extension of the Don Valley Parkway, will take you just north of the city to a cluster of fine courses. Take the Steeles Avenue East exit to get to the 36 holes of the *Parkview Golf Club;* 293–2833. Stouffville Rd. leads you to the *Firefighters Rolling Hills Golf Club* (888–1955) and 45 holes. For complete information on all the golfing adventures the Toronto area has to offer, call Ontario Travel at 965–4008 (English), 965–3448 (French).

Tennis. Throughout Toronto, the city provides courts free of charge, many of them floodlit. In the Western section, courts are available from 7:00 A.M. to 11:00 P.M. at *Stanley Park* (King Street W., three blocks west of Bathurst Street); *Wallace-Emerson Park,* which has four lit courts, on the west side of Dufferin Street, south of Dupont Street; *High Park,* which has three courts south of Bloor Street W. on the west side of Parkside Drive; and *Trinity-Bellwoods Park,* which has three courts on the north side of Queen Street W. between Crawford Street and Gorevale Avenue.

The central area of the city boasts eight parks with 28 courts. All are open from 7:00 A.M. to 11:00 P.M. with *Ramsden Park,* on the west side of Yonge Street four blocks north of Bloor Street W., having eight floodlit courts. *Otter Creek Park,* between Chatsworth Drive and Rosewell Avenue, one block south of Lawrence Avenue W., has four floodlit courts. So does *Eglinton Park,* on the north side of Eglinton, one block east of Avenue Road.

In the eastern area of the city, almost 40 courts are available at 11 different parks. The *Riverdale Park,* west of Broadview Avenue and east of the Don Valley Parkway, has seven; *Norwood Park,* on the west side of Norwood Road just south of Gerrard Street E., has five; *Fairmont Park,* on the south side of Gerrard Street E., two blocks east of Coxwell Avenue, has five; and the *Kew Gardens,* south of Queen Street E., just west of Lee Avenue, has 10 floodlit courts. Visitors may use the Kew Beach courts from 7:00 A.M. to 5:00 P.M., Monday through Friday; 7:00 A.M. to 10:00 A.M. on Saturday and Sunday; and 6:00 P.M. to 11:00 P.M. on Sunday.

Jogging. While it is difficult to find any Toronto byway without at least one jogger, the city has lovely parks and waterfront areas that are especially good for devotees. The Beaches area in the east end (Woodbine Avenue and Queen Street E.) offers miles of shoreline boardwalks for joggers and serious runners. And like the Beaches, High Park (Parkside Drive south of Bloor Street W. in the west end) and Eglinton Park (Avenue Road and Eglinton Avenue in the north-center area) provide jogging paths and "Vita Parcours" exercise stations.

Sail surfing. Windsurfing fans can sail to their hearts' content off Scarborough Bluffs and the boardwalk of the Beaches area, both in the east end of Toronto. Just behind the landmark Donald Summerville pool, you can rent sail surfers by the hour, afternoon, morning, or day. Bloor Street west of the High Park subway station is also beginning to sprout windsurfer rental shops. Real enthusiasts, aided by wet suits, are extending the season from May until late October. In the Bay, or out on Lake Ontario, the wind is always up for wind surfing.

Swimming. Public swimming is available in 16 Board of Education indoor pools, 12 outdoor pools, and 15 community recreation centers. The City of Toronto Department of Parks and Recreation (392-7259) will provide hours and seasons for the pools located in all areas of the city. As well, bathing stations with free change rooms are located at major Lake Ontario beaches on the Toronto mainland and Toronto Islands. But of late, the quality of Lake Ontario water at all but the island beaches remains dubious at best. Some people swim in the lake, others wouldn't if their lives depended on it—which they claim is the reason they won't. Still, the sunbathing is fine. If you're in doubt, ask the lifeguard or phone Metro Parks at 392-8186.

Cross-country skiing. Toronto's spacious parks, many ravines, and expanded waterfront offer splendid cross-country skiing in the heart of the metropolis. Skiers can make their own marks or follow trails through High Park (enter at the Keele and High Park subway stops or Parkside Drive south of Bloor Street W.) and glide past Grenadier Pond. Others choose to trace the ice-bound shore of the Lake along the Beaches (Queen Street east of Woodbine Avenue), and the reclaimed land of the Leslie Street spit (just east of the bottom of the Don Valley Parkway at the end of Leslie Street) takes skiers out into Lake Ontario, where they can pause and watch year-round residents—flocks of ducks and Canadian geese. There's a concentration of ski-rental shops on Bloor Street around the Runnymede subway station, and others are scattered throughout town. Check the Yellow Pages.

Horseback riding. The rolling hills north of the city are dotted with farms and many ranches and stables where horseback outings can be enjoyed. In Richmond Hill on Hwy. 11, the *Rocking Horse Ranch* (884–3292) offers scenic western trail rides year-round. There are four stables in nearby Stouffville, three in Markham, and four in Gormley. All are within an hour and a half of downtown. And *Central Don Riding Academy* is actually within city limits, located in Sunnybrook Park, the ravine that runs from Edwards Gardens south to Eglinton Avenue. The huge stable also runs classes and has a large convenient parking lot. Phone 444–4044 for details. For full information on stables, accommodations, and rates, call Ontario Travel at 965–4008.

Ice skating. Each New Year's Eve at City Hall on the *Nathan Phillips Square* rink (Bay Street and Queen Street W.) Toronto skates in the New Year.

At College Park (Yonge Street and College Street), in the west end at High Park (Parkside Drive and Bloor Street W.), and in the east end at Kew Gardens (Queen Street E. and Lee Avenue) all it takes in Toronto in winter is a pair of skates. Skating rinks dot the city. Just stop and listen and you will hear the cut of a blade over the ice or the slap of a stick on a puck. Almost all rinks have times designated for pleasure skating (often to waltz music)—usually that means 9:00 A.M. to 6:00 P.M.—as well as time set aside for the neighborhood kids with one puck (usually lunch hours and just after school). If you want to skate uptown, downtown, or all over town, stop and listen, or call 392–7259.

Weightlifting/Gym. Most major downtown hotels have workout gyms, but if yours doesn't, work out at the central YMCA at 20 Grosvenor (922–7765) (both men and women), or the *University of Toronto's* massive new complex at Spadina Avenue north of College Street (978–3437). Or check the yellow pages for the fitness clubs that dot the city.

SPECTATOR SPORTS. Every day of each season Torontonians can be seen rallying to the federal government's cry for "Participaction!"—jogging and in other ways supporting the sporting-goods industry. But it is only fitting that in a metropolis of Toronto's size there is ample outlet, too, for those who choose to read about exercise and pay to watch others play.

Hockey. The National Hockey League's Maple Leafs play 40 games (mostly Wednesday and Saturday nights) at the shrine of Canada's national game, Maple Leaf Gardens, through the seemingly endless October-to-April season. Despite the myths, tickets are available for every game. Call 977–1641. The Toronto Marlboros play top-notch Junior A hockey at the Gardens. Call 977–1641 for tickets.

Baseball. The Blue Jays of the American League East, with young stars and fine pitching, have become one of the toughest tickets in town. Their Exhibition Stadium home on Lake Ontario's shore is the worst baseball park in the major leagues, but the exciting team and, since, 1982, the cold beer, help make up for it. For ticket information call 595–0077.

Football. The Toronto Argonauts won the Canadian Football League championship Grey Cup for the first time in 31 years in 1983. The city fathers are promising a domed stadium, but until then, the Argos' eight home games will be played in the park they share with the Blue Jays, Exhibition Stadium. Call 595–1131 for tickets.

Thoroughbred racing. The sport of kings enjoys four annual meetings. At the Woodbine Race Track, a half-hour northeast of Downtown at Highway 27 and Rexdale Boulevard, the thoroughbreds run from late April to the first week in August; and from the first week in September to the end of October. The Queen's Plate, North America's oldest race for three-year-olds comes to Woodbine each July. The prestigious Rothman's International $100,000 purse for three-year-olds-and-up is run in the fall. Dates for both races fluctuate but can be obtained from the Jockey Club at 675–6110.

When not at Woodbine, the thoroughbreds run at the Greenwood Race Track in the city's east end at Queen Street E. and Woodbine Avenue along the lakeshore. The winter meeting runs from the end of October to the first week in December; the spring meeting from mid-March to the end of April.

Harness racing. The finest trotters and pacers prance at the beautiful Greenwood track at three annual meetings. The spring gathering runs from the New Year to mid-March; the summer meeting from the end of May to the first of September; and the brief winter meeting from the second week in December to the end of the year. The Jockey Club (675–6110) will provide details of feature races.

Tennis. The best in the world gather at the York University tennis complex in North Toronto each summer for the Player's International Canadian Open. The tournament is well attended by tennis fanatics, so be sure to make reservations well in advance. For tickets, call Tennis Canada 665–9784 or Bass ticket outlets at 872–2277.

Golf. Glen Abbey is the permanent site of the du Maurier Canadian Open golf championship. This Jack Nicklaus-designed course, a 40-minute drive west of downtown on the Queen Elizabeth Way, is a demanding one for the world's top pros and a pleasure for spectators. Nicklaus sculpted the championship layout to take advantage of natural amphitheaters. Fans can only blame themselves for missing a spectacular shot. The tournament, one of golf's big five, is played the last week in June. For weekly and daily pass information call 844–1800. The Ladies Professional Golf Association tour comes to Toronto's St. George's Golf and Country Club, 1668 Islington Ave. in Toronto's west end, for the du Maurier classic the last week in July. Call Bass (872–2277) and Ticketron outlets (872–1212) for daily and weekly passes.

Auto racing. The Can-Am racing circuit pit stops at Mosport Park, an hour's drive north of the city. For schedules of Formula and stock racing call 665–6665.

LOTTERIES. Even when the race tracks are dark, the bookies aren't answering their phones, and the church bingo halls are closed, Toronto's punters can flip a coin and choose between six different lotteries on sale at kiosks, tobacconists, and hotel-lobby gift shops throughout the city. Players can spend $1, $5, or $10 on a swing at the brass ring. The federal and provincial governments are the real winners, pocketing 30 percent or more of the take.

The most popular of the six is Lotto 6/49. It made headlines around the world in 1984 when its jackpot climbed to $13,890,588.80 and a working-class couple won the largest tax-free lottery prize in North American history. For $1 a chance, over 11 million players tried to predict which six of 49 numbers would tumble from an automatic scrambler. One winning ticket was sold, and ten second-place tickets earned those who had correctly predicted five numbers $443,481.60 each. The normal weekly draw has a jackpot of $500,000 with 14,000,000-to-1 odds against winning it all. If you honestly believe you've done it, call 870–9134 to check your ticket before beginning to spend all that money.

Two other lotteries, Super Lotto and the Provincial, originate outside the province of Ontario. Their tickets are available in Toronto convenience and smoke stores. Super Lotto has a monthly prize of $1 million and odds against winning are 500,000 to 1 for a $10 ticket. For winning numbers call 870–9135. The Provincial offers a weekly jackpot of $500,000 and a 1-in-1,200,000 chance, but the $5 ticket is good for five draws. Check your winnings at 870–9161.

Ontario's own lotteries are the Wintario and Lottario. Both cost $1, and draws are held each week. The Wintario top prize is $100,000; they'll tell you if you've won at 870–9170. There is a 1-in-1,000,000 chance of taking that home, but the lottery also has second prizes of $10,000 and mystery bonus numbers that can earn winners a luxury automobile one week, a vacation for two in Rio the next. Lottario usually has a jackpot of $500,000 and odds of 3,300,000 to 1 against grabbing it all. At 870–9122 someone will tell you if you're traveling or spending.

 BABYSITTING SERVICES. The major hotels can make arrangements to babysit for you. People at the front desk should be able to recommend registered, bonded babysitters who will let you enjoy some hours alone.

If your hotel can't help with arrangements, consider *Anderton Home Services,* 2911 Bayview Ave.; 222–5001. This bonded agency draws on mature, reliable sitters who will care even for newborns. There is a four-hour minimum in the evening, and a five-hour minimum during the day. Rates are $5 an hour, and you'll have to pay transit costs, or $3.50 if the sitter drives.

CHILDREN'S ACTIVITIES. Toronto is a good city to visit with children because it's clean, safe, and uncrowded, and there are scores of fascinating sights and activities that children will love.

No child should miss the *Ontario Science Centre,* a multi-million-dollar collection of hands-on exhibits that show, not tell, how science works. Plan to spend the day learning to make a computer talk, investigating lasers, videotaping, feeling static electricity, and generally being overwhelmed. It's open daily from 10:00 A.M. to 6:00 P.M., at 770 Don Mills Rd; 429–4100. Admission: $7 family, $3 adults, $2 youths 13–17, $1 children 12 and younger. Seniors are free. Parking will cost $1, but you can get there by TTC bus.

The *Royal Ontario Museum* (ROM) on University Avenue south of Bloor Street has been newly renovated to house its growing and priceless collections. The terrifying dinosaurs, West Coast Indian totem poles, and Egyptian mummies will impress even the most sophisticated children. The Discovery Room offers them a chance to touch flints and fossils, and to learn by doing. Hours are 10:00 A.M. to 6:00 P.M. daily; open Thursday and Friday until 8:00 P.M. Admission is $2.50 adults, $1.25 children, with occasional films added for free. For information, call 586–5549.

The *Metro Zoo* has been included elsewhere, but it is of special interest to children, who adore the infant gorillas. (They have a jungle gym right opposite one designed for human children. The two species watch each other.) The family of orangutans, chattering baboons, elephants, and fun-loving seals also delight children. Over 700 acres have been devoted to carefully engineered habitats for over 800 species from six geographic regions of the world. *The New York Times'* rating of the Metro as one of the ten best zoos in the world won't impress your child, but seeing exotic animals happily roaming in their own environments will. Drive east on Highway 401 to Meadowvale Road any day. Parking will cost $2 in summer, and admission is $5 adults, $2.50 seniors and youths 12–17, $1 children 5–11, while younger ones are free. Call 284–8181 to find out more.

All children will want to ride to the top of the *CN Tower,* 301 Front Street W. The tallest free-standing structure on earth, it has a revolving restaurant, large observation deck, an even higher Space Deck (admission costs $1 more), and a games room at the base. The glassed-in elevator ride to the top may be the most thrilling part. Hours are 10:00 A.M. to 10:00 P.M. Sunday through Thursday, 10:00 A.M. to 11:00 P.M. Friday and Saturday. Admission is $5 adults, $4 students, $3.50 children, $3.75 seniors. The information number is 360–8500.

Baseball fans will find plenty of special days with the Toronto *Blue Jays,* who play in Exhibition Stadium. Throughout the season children 14 and under can pick up freebies on Cap Day, Ragball Day, Bat Day, and Sportsbag Day. And everyone can get on the field for Autograph Day. Every Saturday there are half-price seats available for children under 14. Call 595–0077 for details on the dates and times.

The other professional sports clubs that may interest children are the Toronto Argonauts at 595–1131 (Grey Cup champions in 1983 after a 31-year wait), and the Maple Leafs of the National Hockey League (977–1641).

Young People's Theatre, at 165 Front St. E., is devoted to family entertainment. The productions range from Shakespeare to contemporary children's own writings, and the quality is first-rate. Call 864–9732 to find out what's going on. Drop by Five Star Tickets at Yonge and Dundas to see if other theaters are offering suitable productions, especially around Christmas. *The Nutcracker* is a standard with the National Ballet. The Toronto Symphony offers children's programs throughout the year.

There's always something for children happening at *Harbourfront,* 235 Queen's Quay W.; 364–5665. Parents and children can enjoy activities together, watch films or puppet shows, or children can make supervised messes in a crafts room equipped with paint and papier mâché. The program changes frequently and most events are free. Call for details.

If your children love books, drop by *The Children's Book Store,* 604 Markham St.; 535–7011. It claims to be the biggest children's book store in the world. *Boys and Girls House* at 40 St. George St. (on the U. of T. campus) is an excellent public library. The second floor is given over to The Spaced-Out Library, which is sure to pique any child's curiosity. Call 593–5351 for hours.

In case the children are famished by now, you should know about some restaurants they'll enjoy. *Fran's Family Restaurant* at three downtown locations (20 College, 21 St. Clair Ave., 2275 Yonge at Eglinton) is a sure thing. The children's menu features banana face pancake, jr. hamburg steak, chicken dippers (and more) in kid-size portions, but dinner-size sundaes!

The *Old Spaghetti Factory* and its neighbor, *The Organ Grinder* (54 and 58 The Esplanade), offer spaghetti and pizza in a wild, wacky setting. *Ginsberg and Wong,* at 71 McCaul St., offers giant-sized portions of burgers, fries, and milkshakes. Mom can get a full meal out of leftovers.

There's more for children to do, described in the sections on *Zoos, Free Events, Theme Parks* and *Tours;* inquire also at the Visitors Association at 979–3143.

HISTORIC SITES AND HOUSES. During the building boom in the 1950s and early 1960s, many of Toronto's oldest buildings were demolished to make way for the modern structures that now dominate the downtown core. Happily times have changed. Thanks to an active conservation grass-roots movement, politicians and citizens alike are more aware of their city's heritage, and old and important buildings are being restored and renovated for people to enjoy. Principal sites are listed below, but for more detailed information, contact the Toronto Historical Board at 595–1567.

Fort Rouillé. In the midst of the fairground paraphernalia at the Canadian Exhibition Grounds stands a granite obelisk, a monument marking the location of Fort Rouillé, a fur trade outpost built by the French in 1750 to intercept Indians trading with the English across the lake. To prevent the fort from falling into British hands, it was destroyed and abandoned by the French. Until the arrival of John Graves Simcoe, who came to found a new colonial capital four decades later, Toronto remained a wilderness.

Scadding Cabin. Also in the CNE Grounds (just west of the bandshell) is the oldest house in Toronto, a simple log cabin built by pioneer John Scadding in 1794. Scadding managed the estate of John Graves Simcoe, first lieutenant-governor of Upper Canada.

Old Fort York. Fleet Street West and Garrison; 595–1567. Tucked away under the maze of freeways that traverse the waterfront, Old Fort York narrowly missed being destroyed to accommodate the Gardiner Expressway. Since it was the first British military post established in the then-town of York, it is one of the city's most important links with the past.

The fort saw action during the 1812 war, when, on April 27, 1813, 1,700 American soldiers stormed into town, easily defeating the 700 or so militia who were defending it. The retreating Brits blew up their garrison with gunpowder and flattened the fort, killing or wounding 260 of the enemy in the process. One of them happened to be the leader of the expedition, General Zebulon Montgomery Pike (after whom Pikes Peak is named), who was killed by falling timber.

The fort was subsequently rebuilt; the eight log and stone buildings that remain date from that time. It was never used again in war, but each summer uniformed student-soldiers convincingly reenact the blood and thunder of that lively battle, firing off rifles and cannon and enveloping visitors in the sounds and smells of nineteenth-century warfare.

It's difficult to get to. Enter on Garrison Road (left off Fleet Street, between Bathurst Street and Strachan Avenue), which is north of Princes' Gate, the main entrance to the Canadian National Exhibition Grounds. Or take a subway or streetcar west from Yonge Street, then south to Bathurst.

Open Monday through Saturday, 9:30 A.M. to 5:00 P.M.; Sunday, noon to 5:00 P.M. Entrance fee: adults, $3, children and seniors, $1.50.

Mackenzie House. 82 Bond St.; 595–1567. Toronto's first mayor, William Lyon Mackenzie, was an outspoken, redheaded journalist whose checkered career reads like a Boys' Annual adventure story. After leading an unsuccessful rebellion against the colonial government of Upper Canada in 1837, he fled to the United States with a price of £1,000 on his head. Twelve years later he was allowed to return to Canada, where he joined the Legislative Assembly.

By the time he retired, in 1858, Mackenzie was broke and in ill health, and concerned friends banded together and bought this Victorian townhouse. It has been restored and refurnished by the Toronto Historical Board. Legend has it that the place is haunted. Both Mackenzie and a young woman clad in nineteenth-century dress are said to wander the rooms at night. Open Monday through Saturday, 9:30 A.M. to 5:00 P.M.; Sunday, noon to 5:00 P.M. Costumed guides show visitors around. Entrance fee: $1.50 for adults; $1 for seniors and children under 12; 595–1567.

Gibson House. 5172 Yonge St.; 225–0146. North York. Located behind Willowdale Post Office, this restored Georgian house was the onetime home of David Gibson, a Scottish-born surveyor who served as a lieutenant in Mackenzie's army during the 1837 rebellion. He, too, had to flee to the United States (where he helped to build the Erie Canal). On his return he built this handsome brick house.

Open Monday through Friday, 9:30 A.M. to 5:00 P.M.; Saturday, Sunday, and holidays, noon to 5:00 P.M. Admission: $1.50 adults, $1.25 students, $.75 children and seniors, $3.50 family.

Church of the Holy Trinity. 10 Trinity Sq.; 598–4521. Lost amidst the concrete and glass of the Eaton Centre is a nineteenth-century church whose twin towers were once so distinctive that they could be used by sailors to navigate across Lake Ontario—hard to imagine now, since the waterfront today is a mass of office towers. The Eaton Centre was planned around the church, which was built in 1847. Today the church is still used for services and as well is a lively place for drop-in lunches and community meetings.

Old City Hall. 60 Queen St. W.; groups of 10 or more should call 965–7518 for a talk before walking through. Individuals explore on their own. The solid and stately Old City Hall was upstaged by the opening of Toronto's innovative new City Hall in 1965, but at the turn of the century it was still considered to be one of the finest municipal buildings in North America. Designed by architect Edward James Lennox, who did much to change the face of the city (he was also responsible for Massey Hall, Casa Loma, and the King Edward Hotel), it remains one of Toronto's most memorable landmarks.

Casa Loma, 1 Austin Terrace, near Spadina and Davenport Rds., is an immense, 98-room castle-mansion built by financier Sir Henry Pellatt around 1913. One-and-one-half-hour self-guided tours. Open daily except Christmas and New Year's, 10:00 A.M. to 4:00 P.M. Adults $4, children 5–18 $2, seniors $1.00. 923–1171.

St. Lawrence Hall. 157 King St. E.; call 392–7986 for information about special events. The revamped St. Lawrence area (around King, Jarvis, Front, and Church streets) is fast becoming one of the most architecturally interesting areas of the city, and the St. Lawrence Hall, a dazzling example of Renaissance Revival style, is its crowning glory.

In its mid-nineteenth-century heyday, it was the city's cultural and social center. Operas, banquets, and balls were staged here, and such luminaries as Jenny Lind, the legendary "Swedish Nightingale," played here to packed houses. Sir John A. Macdonald, Canada's first prime minister, campaigned in the Great Hall—a magnificent room with ornate plaster friezes and a gas-lit chandelier—which has been faithfully restored to its former splendor. It is now used as a forum for public meetings and as a rehearsal studio for the National Ballet of Canada.

The Grange. 317 Dundas St. W.; 977–0414. This gracious Georgian mansion, which today is part of the Art Gallery of Ontario, was built in 1818 and was one of Toronto's first brick houses. Here the Boulton family—wealthy socialites and leading lights in law and politics—entertained the rich and the famous. Distinguished guests included Lord and Lady Elgin, Governor Simcoe and his wife, and Matthew Arnold, the English poet and writer. A well-illustrated paperback published by the Art Gallery of Ontario, *The Privileged Few,* provides a faithful and interesting guide to the Grange. Author John Lownsbrough chronicles the Boultons' reactionary role in times of rebellion; their small scandals (D'Arcy Boulton Jr. was twice charged with assault), and their subsequent fall. The last owner of the Grange was an American professor, Goldwin Smith, a moving figure behind New York's Cornell University. His library is here. The Grange is open Tuesday through Sunday, noon to 4:00 P.M.; Wednesday, noon to 4:00 P.M. and 6:00 P.M. to 9:00 P.M. Closed Monday. Adults $3.50, children $1.50; entrance fee includes admission to the Art Gallery.

CN Tower. 301 Front St. W., Harbourfront; 360–8500; cocktail and dinner reservations 362–5411. Not a historical site, but a great visitor attraction nonetheless, this, the tallest free-standing structure in the world, has an observation platform near the top, as well as, on another level, a bar-restaurant-nightclub. Platform open 10:00 A.M. to 10:00 P.M. Mon.–Fri., 9:30 A.M. to 11:00 P.M. Sat. and Sun.; adults $6; 13-17 year old $4.50; children and seniors $4.

LIBRARIES. Toronto's numerous industrial, educational, scientific, and medical institutions all have their own book and catalog collections, and there are over 300 libraries in Toronto alone. Some are highly specialized and of limited interest to the general public, but those worthy of note include the following:

Metropolitan Toronto Library, 789 Yonge St.; 393–7000. Opened in 1977, this is a dazzling, multi-storied building, with orange-and-white décor, glassed-in elevators, ornamental ponds, and hanging plants. It is the brainchild of Raymond Moriyama, the adventurous architect who also designed the Ontario Science Centre. Of special interest is the Arthur Conan Doyle collection.

Busy on Saturdays. Open Mon.–Thurs. 10:00 A.M. to 9:00 P.M.; Fri. and Sat. 10:00 A.M. to 6:00 P.M.; Sun. 1:30 P.M. to 5:00 P.M.

Thomas Fisher Rare Book Library, 120 George St.; 978–5285. Part of the University of Toronto and next door to the John P. Robarts Research Library, the largest in Canada. Thanks to budget restrictions, the Rare Book Library now closes on Saturdays, but during the week it's open from 9:00 A.M. to 5:00 P.M.

Osborne Collection of Early Children's Books, Toronto Public Library, 40 St. George St.; 593–5350. Fifty years ago Edgar Osborne, a librarian from Derbyshire, visited Toronto and was so impressed by the high standard of students' reading material that he donated his entire collection of children's books to this library. Since then the collection has grown from 3,500 books to over 17,000, and it includes a rare and valuable manuscript of Aesop's Fables that dates back to the fourteenth century. Hours are 10:00 A.M. to 6:00 P.M. weekdays, 9:00 A.M. to 5:00 P.M. weekends.

North York Public Library, Fairview Area Branch, 35 Fairview Mall Dr., North York; 494–6838. The Canadiana Department on the second floor is a must for history buffs. The more than 45,000 books and periodicals go back to the days of the earliest settlers and include several rare volumes.

Weekdays are less crowded than evenings or weekends. Open Monday, 12:30 P.M. to 8:30 P.M., Tuesday through Friday, 9:00 A.M. to 8:30 P.M., and Saturday 9:00 A.M. to 5:00 P.M.

MUSEUMS. Perhaps because it's the provincial capital, Toronto has more than its fair share of museums—large and small, esoteric and run of the mill.

The majestic **Royal Ontario Museum** (The ROM, as locals call it), on the corner of Bloor Street and University, is particularly renowned for its collection of Chinese antiquities. $55 million has recently been spent on renovating and enlarging the building. The ROM is unusual in that exhibits covering art, science, and technology are all shown under one roof.

Some exhibits have yet to be taken out of storage (the work of cleaning and restoring the prodigious collections is expected to go on for at least another five years) but there's still plenty to see: miniature Roman villas and Egyptian mummies; rare and exotic birds (including some which, such as the Labrador Duck, are now extinct); rocks, gems and minerals; shrunken heads, totem poles, and native Canadian beadwork—and the famed seventeenth-century sculptures found at the Ming Tombs.

Galleries with a common theme are linked together in "clusters" (for example, in the Mediterranean World Cluster, 4,000-year-old relics from ancient Egypt are grouped with Roman remains). Each cluster has an introductory area that explains the theme to visitors. Not to be missed is the Reptile Gallery, full of turtles, lizards, and snakes. The rattlesnake rattles—mechanically, as visitors activate a switch—and there is a horrific four-meter- (13-feet) long Nile crocodile. Don't pass up the Vertebrate Fossils Gallery with its giant dinosaurs: the Albertosauras (thus named because it was found in the western Canadian province of Alberta) and the rare Parasaurolophus, of which only three have ever been discovered.

Doors open at 10:00 A.M. and close at 6:00 P.M., except Tuesdays and Thursdays, when the museum stays open until 8:00 P.M. Family tickets cost $7. Individual entrance fees are $3.50 for adults, $2 for seniors, students and children. There are recorded tours for special exhibitions. For information, call 586–5549.

Next door to the ROM is the **McLaughlin Planetarium.** Here the cycles of the universe are simulated by dozens of projectors that flash stars, planets, the sun, and moon onto the building's domed ceiling. Special cosmic shows are staged to coincide with extraterrestrial happenings (comets, meteors, space launches, eclipses, and the like), and show times change according to the seasons and rotation of the earth. Older kids think this Star Wars stuff is just great. Under six not admitted. Once the presentation starts, museum officials won't admit latecomers. Admission: $5 adults, $2.50 seniors and students; 586–5736.

Also within walking distance of the ROM is the **Sigmund Samuel Canadiana Collection** (14 Queen's Park Crescent W.), an interesting little museum that owes much of its collection to Sigmund Samuel, a wealthy steel magnate whose hobby was picking up eighteenth- and nineteenth-century oils, watercolors, drawings, and prints. He also liked antique maps, and the ones on display here trace the mapping of Canada from 1513 to 1850. An upstairs room has been decorated in the style of nineteenth-century Quebec and the ROM has added bits and pieces from its bottomless treasure chest: silver, glassware, coins, medals, carvings, ceramics, etc. Open Monday through Saturday, 10:00 A.M. to 5:00 P.M.; Sunday from 1:00 P.M. to 5:00 P.M. No admission charge; telephone 586–5549.

Across from the ROM is the **George R. Gardiner Museum of Ceramic Art,** 111 Queen's Park; 593–9300. Opened in 1984, it was a $26-million gift to the city from the man who owned most of the country's Kentucky Fried Chicken franchises. That background notwithstanding, the museum is a tasteful oasis of calm, showcasing a world-class collection of pre-Colombian pottery, Italian Majolica, English Delftware. Hours are 10:00 A.M. to 5:00 P.M. daily, Tuesday through Sunday. Admission: $3 adults, $1.50 seniors, students, and children.

The Museum of the History of Medicine is a tiny, four-room museum attached to the University of Toronto's Academy of Medicine at 288 Bloor St. W.; 922–0564. It's fascinating. Inside are 300-year-old nursing bottles with chamois nipples; an Egyptian mummy and record of the autopsy recently performed on him; and prints by English satirical artists, including Hogarth and Rowlandson. Open 9:30 A.M. to 4:00 P.M., Monday through Friday. Admission by donation.

The Art Gallery of Ontario, 317 Dundas St. W.; 977–0414. The gallery dominates a city block right in the middle of Chinatown. At its northeast corner you will see a large Henry Moore bronze, and inside are more Moores—in fact, the world's largest collection of this noted modern English sculptor. The gallery also features Dutch and Italian masters, early Picassos, and pop artist Claus Oldenburg's giant hamburger. Open daily all year except Mondays, 11:00 A.M. to 5:30 P.M., 9:00 P.M. Wednesdays. Admission: $3.50 adults, $1.50 students.

The McMichael Canadian Collection, off Major MacKenzie Drive, via Highway 400; 893–1121. Just a short drive northwest of Toronto is this lovely rustic timbered gallery overlooking acres of wooded ravine. Inside are more than 2,000 works by Canadian artists. Open daily all year 11:00 A.M. to 5:00 P.M.; Admission: $2.50 adults, $1.50 seniors, $1 students, $6 family.

To children (especially adult children) the *Ontario Science Centre* (770 Don Mills Rd.; 429–4423) is a lot more fun than either the ROM or the McLaughlin Planetarium. Yet another of Raymond Moriyama's architectural masterpieces, this zany place could best be described as a cross between a mechanical kindergarten and Disney World, because it is a museum where people participate in, rather than just look at, the exhibits. There are buttons to press, pedals to push, and levers to pull, and you could easily spend days in this amazing building lost in the magic world of science and technology.

Exhibits are laid out in different sections: Environment Earth, Communication, Transportation, Energy, Life, and so on. In one section you might find a frustrated musician pounding up and down on an organ keyboard in a (thankfully) soundproofed room. In another, you'll see newborn chicks, scratching and wobbling their way out of broken shells. Ever wanted to fly to the moon? You can here, by simulating a moon landing or, less ambitiously, by launching an air balloon. Electronic gizmos show you how to walk away from your shadow or play tic-tac-toe with a computer. Then there's the Ontario Hydro exhibit—a literally hair-raising experience for those who participate in the demos illustrating static electricty.

When you've had enough, take time off to browse at the Science City shop, which stocks some very interesting educational books and gadgets. Better still, recharge your batteries at the licensed restaurant or one of the Centre's two cafeterias.

The Centre is a fair hike—11 kilometers (7 miles)—from downtown, but it's easy to get there by public transit. Take the Eglinton East bus from Yonge Street subway station and get off at Don Mills Road, or, if you're driving, head north up the Don Valley Parkway and turn off at the Don Mills Road (north) cutoff. The Science Centre is open seven days a week, from 10:00 A.M. to 6:00 P.M. Admission: $3 adults, youths $2, $1 children, and seniors free.

The following three museums can easily be covered in the course of a day because they're fairly small and all are in, or around, the grounds of the Canadian Exhibition and Ontario Place, which face each other across Lakeshore Boulevard. The amusement areas are busy during the summer months, especially when the CNE is running (late August to early September). So your best bet is to park the car (there are numerous lots) or take public transit (street car No. 511) and walk from one to the other, rather than try to drive.

Marine Museum of Upper Canada, Exhibition Place. For some inexplicable reason, a steam locomotive sits outside this marine museum, but there's also an 80-foot (24-meter) tug called the Ned Hanlan (after a famous oarsman), and the inside of the building, a former 1841 army barracks, is certainly dedicated to things nautical.

Exhibits concentrate on the exploration of Central Canada and the growth of shipping on the Great Lakes—old navigation instruments, diving helmets, hooters, and relics salvaged from shipwrecks. There's a licensed restaurant, the

Ship's Inn, in the basement. Opening hours are Monday through Saturday, 9:30 A.M. to 5:00 P.M.; Sunday, noon to 5:00 P.M. Admission: $1.50, adults; $1 children; 595-1567.

Five minutes' walk away is the building that houses the **Hockey Hall of Fame** and **Canada's Sports Hall of Fame** (595-1046), where sports fans can reminisce about past games and glorious victories. The Hockey Hall of Fame is more of a shrine than a museum. The mish-mash of reverential memorabilia includes trophies, masks, skates, and hockey sticks, amongst which is one used by ace player Bobby Hull. The Sports Hall of Fame highlights every other kind of sport—from running to rowing. Open Tues. to Sun. 10:00 A.M. to 4:30 P.M.; longer hours in summer. Admission: $2 adults; $1 children and students.

Across the way is the **H.M.C.S. Haida** (955 Lakeshore Blvd. W.; 965-6331), a floating museum docked near the East Island at Ontario Place. The ship, a former Canadian destroyer which saw service in both World War II and Korea, gets its name from the Haida Indians of British Columbia. It's a great place to take the kids because they can crawl all over the decks and gun emplacements. There are no organized tours, but uniformed sea cadets happily act as hosts, answering visitors' questions and pointing out things of interest. The *Haida* is open during the summer months only, from 10:00 A.M. until 7:00 P.M. Admission is $1 adults, $.75 children.

A 30-minute drive from downtown is the **Black Creek Pioneer Village** in Downsview (Steeles Avenue and Jane Street), where Daniel Stong, a pioneer from Pennsylvania, ran a prosperous farm back in the 1800s. Today his farm forms the nucleus of this "living history" museum that recreates the lifestyle of the settlers.

The Metro Region Conservation Authority has added another 25 buildings to Stong's original five (amongst which are his home, a piggery, and a grain barn), and has meticulously restored them to their original condition. The costumed guides who demonstrate the arts and crafts of the pioneers—weaving rugs, shoeing horses, grinding flour, etc.—make the whole thing come alive. The effect is remarkably authentic; so authentic, in fact, that the village is frequently used by film and television companies.

Buildings include a print shop, town hall, schoolhouse, harness shop, and a general store. An emporium sells homemade candy. Roblin's Mill, a solid structure with thick stone walls, houses a panoply of mechanical marvels, wheels and cogs and reels that clang and clank as they turn to grind the meal. Mouth-watering homemade bread, baked from the flour, can be sampled at the Half-Way House, a former coaching inn.

Opening hours vary according to the time of year, but in peak season (July and August) the village stays open from 10:00 A.M. to 6:00 P.M. From March to June and September and October, it's open from 9:30 A.M. to 5:00 P.M., to 6:00 P.M. weekends. Hours are limited during November and December; telephone 661-6600.

Throughout the year, pioneer-related activities such as sheep-shearing competitions, corn fests, and pumpkin parties are staged for visitors. Although the buildings are closed from January to March, winter activities such as skating, cross-country skiing, sleigh rides, and tobogganing can be enjoyed on the grounds on weekends.

 ART GALLERIES. Because the Toronto art scene is arguably the most dynamic in the country, it's not easy to compile a complete or even up-to-date guide of what's happening in the commercial galleries. Visitors will have to do what Torontonians do: consult The *Globe and Mail* for its regular "At the Galleries" advertisement feature and the *Saturday Globe's* listings and reviews. Or simply target one of Toronto's several gallery districts and start walking. (But please bear in mind that most commercial galleries are closed on Sundays and Mondays and don't open on Tuesdays until the civilized hour of 10:00 A.M.)

The three biggest concentrations of galleries lie along Queen Street west of University (Osgoode subway stop), in the uptown Yorkville shopping area, and in a complex at 80 Spadina Ave.

Yorkville sprawls between Bedford and Yonge streets, just north of Bloor. Its hub is Yorkville Avenue and Avenue Road, once a folky strip of coffeehouses that is now dominated by the huge Four Seasons Hotel and Hazelton Lanes.

In the shadow of the chic Hazelton Lanes complex, along poplar-lined Hazelton Avenue, lie some of the best-established commercial art galleries. The *Mira Godard Gallery,* 22 Hazelton, specializes in contemporary works by Canadians such as Christopher Pratt and Alex Colville, and such important international artists as Barbara Hepworth. The *Gallery Dresdnere,* 12 Hazelton, founded 20 years ago, has a stable of fairly well-known artists, such as Louis de Niverville. It handles wall hangings, graphics, and other works by major Canadian artists. The *Yaneff Gallery,* 119 Isabella St., also has an interest in Canadian painters and in nineteenth-century European prints. The Yaneff has also carried native and African works. The *Sable-Castelli Gallery,* 33 Hazelton, presents contemporary American artists, such as Warhol, Rosenquist, and Rauschenberg. (The gallery is associated with New York's Leo Castelli Gallery.) Canadian artists such as David Craven have also been featured. Also on Hazelton Avenue is *Nancy Poole's Studio,* 16 Hazelton, which carries works from the important school of London, Ontario, artists as well as folk art such as that of Canadian Indian woodcarver Joe Jacobs.

Near the corner of Avenue Road and Yorkville Avenue, the *Gallery Moos,* 136 Yorkville, belongs to Walter Moos, a knowledgeable pioneer of the Toronto gallery scene. Founded in 1959, Moos carries contemporary Canadian artists such as the popular magic realist Ken Danby, with a yearly Masters' Exhibition. Moos' second-floor gallery has stocked Dufys, Picassos, and Miros. On Scollard Avenue, the *Hollander York Gallery,* 120 Scollard, devotes itself to the works of contemporary artists. For those with an interest in architecture, *Ballenford Architectural Books,* 98 Scollard, features regular exhibitions of drawings and models.

Eastward on Yonge Street, Toronto's main drag, the *Carmen Lamanna*

Gallery, 840 Yonge, offers provocative shows of minimalist and conceptual artists, 3-D installations, films, paintings, and Polaroid art. Its next-door neighbor, the *Isaacs Gallery,* 832 Yonge, is another venerable leader in contemporary Canadian art. Look for the bannerlike paintings of Jack Meredith, the wit of Dennis Burton, and also North American Indian art and primitive art. Further north on Yonge Street, the *Alliance Française,* 895 Yonge, generally displays works by French-speaking artists.

In the mid 1970s, another, more adventurous gallery scene began springing up along the seedy Queen Street strip, west of University and east of Bathurst Street. Here, amid fabric jobbers, used furniture stores, and hip diners, there is a new community, full of funky vitality and creative energy. Out of the area's original second-hand bookshops (some still in business) has emerged a genuinely European book row. One of those bookstores, the *Edwards Books and Art,* 356 Queen St. W., stages small art exhibitions at the back of its store when certain artbook sales, in which it specializes, are held. Just across the street is *Gallery Eklektik,* 359 Queen St. W. Nearby there's a good print shop, *The Allery,* 322½ Queen St. W., and *Ydessa Gallery,* 334 Queen St. W.

In the same general neighborhood you might find Walker Evans' photographs or Jasper Johns' works at the *Yarlow/Salzman Gallery,* 50 Macpherson Ave. Across from the Art Gallery of Ontario is *Bau-Xi Gallery* at 340 Dundas W. Bau-Xi handles young surrealists such as Ian McKay and landscape painters such as Max Maynard.

The excellent *Jane Corkin Gallery,* 179 John St. (3rd floor), has a great interest in creative photography and has featured some of the world's greatest photographers—such as Avedon and André Kertesz—as well as local Polaroid art.

Canadian artists are displayed in many galleries. Lovers of Innuit (Eskimo) art visit mostly the *Innuit Gallery of Eskimo Art,* 9 Prince Arthur Ave.

Toronto also features one of the few holographic art (3-D) galleries in North America. Located in a small space, at 1179 King St. W., Suite 008, the intriguing *Interference Hologram Gallery* shows that three-dimensional techniques can translate into beauty.

Challenging works are often current fare at the art galleries of Toronto's Harbourfront, stretching along the shore of Lake Ontario west from the foot of Bay Street. Multi-media, prints, paintings, sculpture, lithos, and photographs are displayed on a year-round basis. Regular demonstrations of glass-blowing are featured daily, as well as many cultural events, including modern-dance concerts and exhibitions of kids' crafts. On occasion, exhibitions have also been held nearby at Queen's Quay Terminal, 207 Queen's Quay W. (5th floor).

 MUSIC. Birthplace of the late, world-ranked pianist Glenn Gould, Toronto is a major classical music center in North America. Music is everywhere. At certain subway stops you can hear surprisingly good soloists playing for your loose change. Just two big blocks west of the Bay subway, between the Royal Ontario Museum and the Royal Conservatory of Music, there's a leafy walkway, "Philosophers' Walk," where, when warm weather forces the musicians practicing in the Conservatory to open their windows, passersby stroll to the accompaniment of musical phrases and operatic fragments. To check the week's more formal performances consult the *Globe and Mail,* the *Toronto Star,* or *Toronto Life* magazine listings. Bass ticket outlets sell ballet, opera, and symphony tickets; 872–1111. Teletron is 766–3271. The Five Star Tickets booth outside the Eaton Centre (the southeast corner of Yonge and Dundas) sometimes has that day's performance tickets at half price; 596–8211.

The city's major concert hall is the Roy Thomson Hall (60 Simcoe), which opened in 1982. It is now home to the Toronto Symphony and the world-acclaimed Toronto Mendelssohn Choir. Located two blocks west of University Avenue on King, the new circular hall represents a triumph of architectural design and of acoustical expertise. The double-shelled structure is a honeycomb of glass that transforms itself into a transparent surface at night. The hall's main auditorium seats more than 2,800 people; it has been specially designed to allow maximum visibility and luminous sound reverberation. Acoustician Theodore J. Shultz has provided for thirty movable discs to reflect sounds from their overhanging position above stage. Roy Thomson Hall is considered to be one of the great concert halls of the world. A 45,000-pipe organ, equipped with digital electronics and designed by Canadian Gabriel Kney, could by itself justify this reputation.

Roy Thomson Hall has facilities for the disabled. Group tours can be arranged. It is easily accessible by subway (exit at St. Andrew Station, walk west). Parking is available. Phone 593–4822 for information.

Toronto's very first concert hall was Massey Hall (178 Victoria), built in 1894 just off Yonge Street on Shuter. As a gift from Hart Massey, a man said to be "rather averse to the theater," Massey Hall was intended to be a general-purpose establishment. Paderewski, Caruso, Pavlova, and the young Yehudi Menuhin performed on its stage, as have countless other celebrated artists. Jack Dempsey fought at Massey Hall. In 1939 Hitler's nephew made a speech there in which he predicted Nazism would never survive. Many early radio broadcasts originated from the hall.

While it attracted many rock groups in the '60s, Massey Hall has continued its classical vocation, although it has lost artists to the Roy Thomson Hall. Massey Hall has few facilities for the handicapped. Open seven days a week (with a variable break during the summer months), it is accessible by subway (exit at Queen station, walk north on Yonge and turn right at Shuter). For information, phone 593–4828.

Symphony, chamber music, solo concerts, and other musical events are also featured at the Edward Johnson Building of the University of Toronto (80 Queen's Park Crescent, near the Parliament Buildings). The box office number is 978–3744. The EJB also hosts many of the city's avant-garde music concerts.

During the summer months outdoor concerts are held at Ontario Place under the canopy of the Forum. For program information call 965–7917. In recent years the Toronto Symphony and the Hamilton Philharmonic have appeared, along with many other guest artists. The City Parks Department has also organized annual Summer Music Festivals. Summer concerts have also been held at the TD Centre Plaza at King and Bay. For information phone 392–7291.

The *Toronto Symphony* has acquired an enviable reputation in its six-decades-plus history. The *Financial Times* of London has called the symphony a "first-rate virtuoso orchestra." Some of its conductors have included Seiji Ozawa, Sir Ernest MacMillan, Sir Thomas Beecham, Sir Malcolm Sargeant, and even Igor Stravinsky. Its present conductor is Andrew Davis.

The Toronto Symphony has thrice-weekly subscription concerts from September to May. Its offices are located at Roy Thomson Hall. Tickets usually cost from $12 to $33. For ticket information call Teletron, 766–3271; Roy Thomson Hall, 593–4828; or Bass ticket outlets, 698–2277.

A frequent guest of the Toronto Symphony is the internationally acclaimed Toronto Mendelssohn Choir. Its festival character has contributed to the great popularity of this 180-singer group. The choir's rendering of Handel's "Messiah" at Christmastime has become a local institution. Its first concert was held on January 15, 1894. For program information phone 598–0422. For tickets call Bass, 698–2277, or Roy Thomson Hall, 593–4828. The choir has also provided encouragement to young singers through the Toronto Mendelssohn Youth Choir. Another Toronto choir, the Elmer Iseler Singers, 20 members strong, has performed around the world, notably in the Library of Congress in Washington, D.C. For program information, phone 482–1664.

Based in Toronto, The *Orford String Quartet* is in residence at the University of Toronto's Edward Johnson Building. Founded in 1965, it is held in high esteem in Canada and abroad. Its broad repertoire includes chamber music of Ravel, Beethoven, Mozart, Debussy, and Bartok, and it has commissioned works from noted Canadian composers Irving Glick and R. Murray Schafer.

In the past decade the churches of "Toronto the Good" have ceased to reverberate only with godly Methodist hymns; today, many of the grand old downtown churches feature chamber music and organ and choral concerts. Consult the newspapers for notices of performances by *Tafelmusik* (literally, "table music"), an orchestra devoted to playing Baroque music with original instruments. It plays at the St. Paul Centre at Trinity Church, 427 Bloor St. W. (Spadina subway). Tafelmusik's box-office number is 964–6337.

There are a score of semi-professional musical groups and symphonies in Toronto and its suburbs. Consult the newspapers for up-to-date listings of their inexpensive concerts. As well, check with the Canadian Broadcasting Corporation, 925–3311, extension 4835 (the CBC's ticket office), for information about its concerts.

And watch for concerts by the *Canadian Brass*, which combines chamber music, ragtime, jazz, opera, other musical forms, and humor.

OPERA

In recent years, the *Canadian Opera Company* has received wide acclaim for its productions of Handel's operas, which it recently introduced to New York. Also acclaimed are its "Joan of Arc" by Tchaikovsky, "Norma" by Bellini,

"Death in Venice" by Benjamin Britten, and "Louis Riel" by Canadian compos-er Harry Somers. The company was founded in 1950 and is now one of the largest in North America. It has a year-round resident-artists corps and allows students to attend some of its dress rehearsals. The Canadian Opera Company has also pioneered the use of "surtitles," which allow audiences to follow the libretto in an abridged version in translation. The company holds an annual summer festival at Harbourfront's York Quay Centre, where, along the shores of Lake Ontario, shorter versions of operatic works are presented in a big tent—sometimes with operatic singalongs. In winter the C.O.C. performs at the O'Keefe Centre at the corner of Yonge and Front. The O'Keefe's box-office number is 365-9744.

POP MUSIC

Toronto is the pop music capital of Canada. All of the major multi-nationals and most of the Canadian independent recording companies have offices here; thus a regular parade of new or established talent performs for huge crowds or trys out in front of wary recording executives in satin jackets. International talent, whether young and eager with a first album under its belt or seasoned and successful, almost always stops in Toronto on any jaunt to North America. When the record business is thriving, Toronto is always hot with music.

The big venues book talent on long-term notice; therefore performances are advertised well in advance. Check the *Globe and Mail,* the *Toronto Star,* and underground newspapers such as *Now* for concert information. For the big places, tickets can often be purchased in advance and charged at the Bass outlet (872–2277).

The biggest pop and rock stars can easily fill *Maple Leaf Gardens,* at 60 Carlton St.; 977–1641. The Who chose it as site of their final concert. For sports fans this 14,000-seat arena is the home of the Toronto Maple Leaf Hockey Club. But for music fans it's the Toronto home of rock spectacle. Every act of long-standing significance to the music industry, from The Beatles to Barry Manilow, has played here. Concert Productions International, the largest national rock promoter, has an exclusive hold on the Gardens, and the company goes for big names with broad appeal. The daily newspapers will carry ads for the big shows, unless they're sold out, in which case they won't spend the money. Look in the listings sections rather than the display ads, and keep your ears tuned to pop radio stations such as CHUM, CHUM FM, Q107, and CFNY for news of current concerts. Or watch MuchMusic (CITY-TV) or Toronto Rocks (CBC-TV).

Big names such as Harry Belafonte also play the *O'Keefe Centre* (at Yonge and Front streets). Call Bass, 872–1111 or 872–2277, when you see such a concert in the listings. In late summer the place to catch pop's biggest stars is *Exhibition Stadium,* in the Canadian National Exhibition grounds. In the sum-mer the stadium is used for large outdoor concerts, with big-name acts like The Police. There is also a nightly lineup of pop talent coinciding with the Canadian National Exhibition in late August. The concerts are well-publicized. To get to

DANCE

the CNE, take the Bathurst Street streetcar from Bathurst station. Exhibition information is available by calling 393–6000.

The Concert Hall, 888 Yonge St., was once the central Masonic Temple for Toronto; it is now a medium-sized hall, used generally by newer acts on their way to the Gardens. But B B King has appeared here as well. In the summer it can be unbearably hot, smoky and crowded—in short, a place with the essence of rock and roll. For information call 922–6310.

Convocation Hall. On the University of Toronto campus north of College Street between University Avenue and St. George. No phone. Theater-in-the-almost-round, a forum for blues, folk, light pop, and ethnic music. Rock is rarely heard here, and the no-smoking rules are strictly enforced in this classic old academics' hall.

Kingswood Music Theatre, 9560 Jane Ave., Near Highway 400 and Major Mackenzie Dr., northwest of Toronto. There's a summer lineup of rock and pop entertainment here, in a large, open-air venue. Call 832–8131 for information.

The Palais Royale Ballroom, at 1601 Lakeshore Blvd. W., is another summer spot, usually for bands that inspire dancing. A peaceful place on Lake Ontario, with an outside terrace. Call 532–6210.

The local blues scene is quite a vibrant one, perhaps because of Toronto's proximity to Detroit and Chicago. Motown and R & B live at the *Club Blue Note,* 128 Pears Ave.; 921–1109, and at *Albert's Hall* in the Brunswick House, 481 Bloor St. W., 964–2242. Punk and new-wave bands gravitate to the *Bam-Boo Club* at 312 Queen St. W. (593–5771), the nearby *Rivoli,* at 334 Queen St. W. (596–1908), and for Reggae try *Tiger's Coconut Grove,* 12 Kensington Ave. (593–8872). Unlicensed, but the music is good. The premier rock club is the *El Mocambo,* 464 Spadina Ave. (961–2558), the only small club where the Rolling Stones have played since 1968.

 DANCE. As the dance capital of Canada, Toronto is one of the continent's leaders in this area. Home to the National Ballet School, it is also on the touring circuit for everything from the Wu Shu martial arts dancers from mainland China to the Bolshoi Ballet. It was in Toronto that the artistic director of the New York City Ballet, Mikhail Baryshnikov, defected to the West; he's a popular visitor and guest artist, as are his compatriots Rudolf Nureyev and Natalia Makarova. Meanwhile Toronto's native experimental dance scene, which until recently was dominated by derivative companies led by American expatriates, is developing several distinctive individual approaches of its own.

Consult the *Toronto Star,* the *Globe and Mail,* and *Toronto Life* magazine for major concerts, and underground papers such as *The Toronto Clarion* and *Now* for modern and avant-garde performances. And in the summer, from Yonge Street's downtown strip to the suburban subway stops, look out for street mime and breakdancing . . . free, of course.

The *National Ballet of Canada* held its first performance in 1951. Since then, it has moved on to international recognition and an impressive home at the O'Keefe Centre, located at Front and Yonge. In recent years, the company had attempted to change its somewhat British image through the efforts of Eric Bruhn, its artistic director. Bruhn, who died in 1986, is considered one of the century's greatest male dancers. Principal dancers Karen Kain and Frank Augustyn, who won prizes at Moscow in 1973, have gone on to international stardom. The company now has 65 dancers and is in a period of great creative vitality, commissioning new works from modern-dance choreographers.

The year 1972 marked the troupe's European debut and was also the first time Rudolf Nureyev danced with the National Ballet. Since then, it has performed at Covent Garden and toured extensively. While tickets are usually available for most performances (the National averages 70-percent capacity audiences), you'll be hard-pressed to get tickets for "The Nutcracker Suite," performed each Christmas season. For information about the National's fall and early spring seasons and tickets, phone 362–1041, or Bass at 872–1111 or 872–2277. Tickets run from $8 to $35.

The O'Keefe Centre, which is home to the National Ballet, is located at 1 Front St. E. and is easily accessible through the subway (exit at Union Station, with a short walk east to the hall). The O'Keefe's box office number is 365–9744.

Celebrating its sixteenth anniversary is the *Toronto Dance Theatre* (80 Winchester) about whom the *Toronto Star* has said: "For intensity, energy, physical discipline and grace, the Toronto Dance Theatre is the most stunning in Canada." Its strictly modern repertoire ranges from pieces based on Debussy to original commissioned works. It developed out of Martha Graham but today has evolved a less melodramatic but still strongly emotional style. One of its choreographers, David Earle, is now doing original works for the National Ballet. It usually performs at the Premiere Dance Theatre (235 Queen's Quay W.), a 450-seat theater designed especially for modern dance and located in an impressively renovated high-tech former warehouse overlooking Lake Ontario at Harbourfront. For information phone 869–8444.

As the lines between visual art, dance, and performance grow more blurred, Toronto's commercial galleries are entering into the modern-dance scene with occasional avant-garde performances. Check the student and underground press (*The Clarion, Now,* the University of Toronto's *The Varsity* and *The Ryersonian*) for dance listings at galleries such as Gallery YYZ, 116 Spadina (367–7601) and A Space, 204 Spadina Ave. (364–3227 or 364–3228).

Other dance performance theaters include: *Hart House,* on Hart House Circle in the University of Toronto campus (just south of the Queen's Park subway stop); call 978–8668 for information. Ryerson Theatre, 43 Gerrard St. E., call 977–1055. And Solar Stage, 1st Canadian Place; 368–5135.

Solar Stage and the Premier Dance Theatre have both staged performances of another major Toronto modern-dance company, *Dancemakers.* This company, composed chiefly of graduates of York University's school of dance, reflects its eclectic background, drawing on Martha Graham, José Limon, and Merce Cunningham influences. Call 535–8880 for program information.

Another troupe is the popular *Danny Grossman Dance Company,* which performs original works choreographed by the company's American-born founder, Danny Grossman. Grossman, who also choreographs original material for the National Ballet, has an original and critically acclaimed style of abrupt contorted movement and politically charged themes. Call 531–8350 for information.

Founded in 1978, the *Toronto Independent Dance Enterprise,* also known as T.I.D.E., has its headquarters at 81 Portland. It has five dancers who perform at Harbourfront or the Winchester Street Theatre and tour nationally. The company features post-modern, contact, and improvisational dance. Phone 596–8384 for information.

The *Paula Moreno Spanish Dance Company* (59 Pears Ave.), which was founded in 1969, is a colorful local company that performs classical Spanish folk and flamenco dances. There are five dancers and a guitarist in this troupe, which also operates a studio and a school. Call 924–6991 for information.

The first *Toronto International Festival* in 1984 brought an impressive mix of modern, classical, and traditional dance troupes to the city in mid-June: Kathakali of India, The Pina Bausch avant-garde German company, the Hamburg Ballet, and the Harlem Dance Theatre. The Festival organizers promise more of the same spirit and quality in the future.

You can do it yourself, too. The public can do ballroom dancing and swing at Harbourfront during the summer. Toronto's City Parks Department has also organized special evenings for square dancing, notably at Eglinton Park. Call the Metro Parks department at 392–8186 for information.

THEATER. Toronto is the heart of a renaissance in English-language Canadian theater that started in the early 1970s and continues today. Fired by a renewed nationalist spirit, after Canada's centennial in 1967, playwrights focused on Canadian themes that have drawn a powerful response from audiences. The best of these works, such as *Balconville,* supported by casts trained in an indigenous theatrical style, toured Canada and North America.

To encourage the growth of Canadian culture, government agencies at the federal, provincial, and municipal levels still partially subsidize the operations of many Canadian theaters. Top-ticket prices are therefore very reasonable compared to other countries'.

Many smaller Toronto theaters offer "pay what you can" Sunday matinees. Call individual theaters for more information. There is also a half-price ticket booth, Five Star Tickets, outside the Eaton Centre at Yonge and Dundas, where tickets are available at half price on the day of performance. For the Stratford and Shaw Summer Festivals outside the city the booth also offers half-price tickets on sale the *day before* each performance; call 596–8211. For further information and tickets for Stratford, call 363–4471; for Shaw, call 690–7301.

With more than 50 performing spaces, Toronto, along with New York and Chicago, is among the three biggest North American cities for theater. New York and Chicago. The largest theater in the city is the *O'Keefe Centre* at 1 Front St. E. A theater this massive does not take many risks. Look for only the most popular sellers here, such as productions of Broadway musicals. Call 872–2262 for information. The *Royal Alexandra Theatre* at 260 King W. is the grande dame of Canadian theaters, a 100-year-old, gilt-painted historic monument that leans to a conservative repertoire of touring Broadway musicals such as *A Chorus Line* and Neil Simon comedies. Call 593–4211 for details about what's on at the Royal Alex. Since March 1985, the Andrew Lloyd Webber musical *Cats* has been playing to capacity audiences at the *Elgin Theatre,* 189 Yonge St. (872–2287).

The St. Lawrence Centre, 27 Front St. E., is the city's largest not-for-profit performing space, housing two theaters. The main stage and lobby were recently remodeled at a cost of $3.5 million to create a luxuriously appointed theater for the resident CentreStage company. The winter season at CentreStage offers a mix of classical, Canadian, and contemporary plays. The other theater is occupied by Theatre Plus, the city's only subscription summer theater focusing on international contemporary drama. Call 366–7723 for information.

Farther east along Front Street—which was the pre-landfill waterfront edge of the original Village of York (Toronto) downtown area—lies the *Young People's Theatre.* Located at 165 Front E., YPT houses two theaters in a renovated warehouse. The theater mounts imaginative productions aimed at young people from four-year-olds to teenagers. For example, it has done an abbreviated punk version of Shakespeare's *Twelfth Night* and has produced *The Diary of Anne Frank,* starring Eli Wallach. The YPT tours many of its plays throughout the province's schools and theaters. Call 684–9732 for information. Also of special interest is the *Théâtre du P'tit Bonheur* at 57 Adelaide E., one of the most popular French theatres in English Canada, with a repertory of classical, contemporary, French, and French-Canadian theater. The company is resident in the Adelaide Court Theatre, a sedately beautiful, renovated former courthouse, where one can also catch productions by independent producers. Call 392–5193 for program information.

Many of the internationally acclaimed Canadian plays of the past two decades, such as *Billy Bishop Goes to War,* first attracted public attention in one of the four Toronto "alternate" theaters. *Tarragon Theatre,* at 30 Bridgman, is the country's showcase for new English Canadian playwrights and new work by established dramatists. It also introduced the works of the renowned Quebec playwright Michel Tremblay to English Canada. Call 531–1827 for information.

Theatre Passe Muraille at 16 Ryerson, Bathurst and Queen district, is famous for Canadian plays, including the controversial hit *Maggie and Pierre,* starring Linda Griffiths, which went on to New York. The essentially journalistic approach of Passe Muraille to theater has been imitated by companies across Canada. Call 363–2416 for information.

Toronto Free Theatre, at 26 Berkeley, mixes innovative foreign works with new Canadian plays. Artistic director Guy Sprung, a conscientious nationalist, has won many awards for direction. The company also mounts free productions of Shakespeare-in-the-park in High Park at Bloor and Keele during the summer; call 368–2856. All of the above alternate theaters also have smaller performing spaces for new plays in progress and experimental work.

The oldest established alternate theater is *Toronto Workshop Productions,* founded in 1959 by its present artistic director, George Luscombe. The theater, at 12 Alexander, focuses on social and political issues; its collective creation, *Ten Lost Years,* a memoir of the Great Depression, toured widely in Europe and North America. Call 925–8640 for information.

A recent arrival on the Toronto alternate scene is the *Canadian Rep Theatre,* 121 Ave. Rd., which divides its all-Canadian content between new works and significant plays from the past two decades. Call 925–0025 for information.

Hit productions from the subscription theaters are often transferred to producer Peter Peroff's *Bayview Playhouse* at 1605 Bayview (call 481–6191) or his *Bathurst Street Theatre,* 736 Bathurst (call 533–1161). Both theaters present independent productions, too. Peroff also runs *Toronto Truck Theatre* at 94 Belmont, where Agatha Christie's *The Mousetrap* is in its tenth year. Call 922–0084 for information.

Two theaters in the suburb of North York offer unique programming. The *Leah Posluns Theatre* at 4588 Bathurst presents international contemporary works, especially by Jewish playwrights. Call 630–6752 for information. *Skylight Theatre* operates a free, open-air summer theater in Earl Bales Park at 4169 Bathurst. Call 630–4868.

Toronto is rich with companies and theaters exclusively devoted to innovative work. *Factory Theatre,* 125 Bathurst at Adelaide W., specializes in presenting new works in progress. Call 864–9971 for information. The company at *Actor's Lab,* 155A George St., creates its own works and exchanges actors and ideas with innovative theaters throughout Europe. Call 363–2853. *Mercury Theatre,* at the Bathurst St. Theatre, presents contemporary international playwrights, from Edward Albee to Brian Friel; call 533–1161. The *Theatre Centre* at 296 Brunswick is a performing space jointly operated by three experimental companies (call 927–8998). *AKA Performance Interfaces* focuses on multimedia works; *Buddies in Bad Times* features poetic and musical dramas; and *Nightwood Theatre* is a feminist collective. Call 862–0659 for information. Unusual theater, everything from local mime troupes to Italian *commedia dell' arte,* can also be found at *Harbourfront,* a performing and visual arts complex in a picturesque lakeshore setting at 235 Queen's Quay W. Call 869–8412.

Environmental theater performed in different locations around the city is the speciality of *Autumn Leaf,* at the Adelaide Court Theatre. Call 363–6401 for information. *Comus Music Theatre* is also a roving company whose works combine dramatic, musical, and operatic elements. For example, it recently presented an 11-hour musical, gastronomic, and theatrical extravaganza based on the *Egyptian Book of the Dead,* featuring opera star Maureen Forrester. Call 363–5868 for information.

Local productions of Broadway musicals and comedies are often found at Toronto's many dinner theaters. Among them are *Harper's East,* at 38 Lombard (call 863–6223); *Limelight,* at 2026 Yonge (call 482–5200); *The Strand,* inside the 1st Canadian Place building at 77 Adelaide W. (call 368–2761); the *Teller's Cage,* inside the Commerce Court building at King and Bay (call 862–1434); and the *Variety,* at 2335 Yonge (call 489–7777). The most famous is *Second City* at 110 Lombard, which specializes in topical satire and is the original home of the popular television series, *SCTV.* Call 863–1111 for information. *Yuk-Yuk's Komedy Kabaret* at 1280 Bay showcases stand-up comics; call 967–6425.

Cabaret and satirical revues are frequent fare at Toronto's nightclubs. Established venues include the *Basin Street Cabaret* at 180 Queen W. (call 598–3013); *Club 21 Cabaret* at 21 Yorkville (923–3263); *Garbo's* at 429 Queen W. (593–9870); *Old Angelo's* at 45 Elm (597–0155); and the *Theatre In The Dell* at 300 Simcoe (598–4802).

 SHOPPING. Although some of the fashions lag a little behind Milan or New York City, shopping in Toronto can provide for the most sophisticated appetites. Not that everything is wildly expensive; there are bargain outlets to excite the most rigid budget keepers. Be prepared to pay 7% provincial sales tax. Most stores accept major credit cards (Visa, MasterCard, American Express) and some will honor personal checks.

Overlooking Lake Ontario, **Queen's Quay Terminal** is a dramatically renovated warehouse. This chrome-and-glass building at the foot of York Street is filled with clothing boutiques, kite shops, a quality tobacconist, patisseries, and, upstairs, crafts stalls.

A little north, at Front and Bay, is the Merchant's Mall of the Royal Bank Plaza, the beginning of a massive system of **underground shopping concourses.** This connects the Toronto Dominion Centre, Commerce Court Mall, First Canadian Place, the Richmond-Adelaide Centre, and the Four Seasons Sheraton Centre. The stores here include the city's successful, medium-priced dress and shoe chains.

A little east, at Yonge and Queen, is *Simpson's,* one of the three biggest department stores. (The other two are Eaton's and The Bay.) The main downtown store connects by a glass walkway to the **Eaton Centre,** an enormous structure with several levels of shops, fountains, and restaurants. The cheaper stores are in the lowest levels of the mall. On the upper floors are expensive shoe stores such as *Pino Carina* and good jewelers such as *Birks.* The six floors of *Eaton's* fill the north end of the Centre, going right to Yonge and Dundas. The designer fashions are at the north end of the second floor. Everybody's favorite meeting place is at "Timothy's Toes," the foot of the bronze statue of Timothy Eaton, at the store's main entrance. Notice the shiny left boot; for years it's been rubbed for luck.

Outside, just steps north of Yonge and Dundas, are *Sam's* and *A&A,* two enormous record shops carrying everything from the latest rock to the finest quality classical recordings. Sam Sniderman (of Sam's) helped his wife start a Canadian classical recording company, Aquitaine records—her name is Eleanor. On Edward Street just west of Yonge is *The World's Biggest Bookstore.* The size of a supermarket, with discount bins and glaring lights, it's not a cozy corner bookshop. Despite its size, it doesn't carry everything, and locating a particular book can be difficult: but it's a browser's heaven.

One subway stop farther north is *College Park,* a marble and art-deco renovation of an old Eaton's store. Its malls concentrate on furnishings and women's clothes. North, at Yonge and Bloor, The **Hudson's Bay Centre** houses women's clothing stores, gift shops, and a disco beneath The Bay department store. From this center, walk underground to *Cumberland Terrace*, a three-level complex of bookstores, clothing stores, and shoe stores. Just north of The Bay is *Albert Britnell Book Shop* at 765 Yonge St.—one of the city's best.

The **ManuLife Centre** is at Bloor and Bay. Here, *Creed's* offers Cartier watches, Sonia Rykiel designer clothes, and Maud Frizon shoes. *Birk's*, carries quality silver, plate and jewelry, fine stationery, and gifts. At the Northwest corner of Bay and Bloor is *David's*, considered to be Toronto's best and most expensive shoe store. Beside it is a cheaper shoe store, *Capezio*, while 10 doors east of Bay on Bloor is *Bally*, also for shoes. Fine clothing is offered at *Holt Renfrew, Harridge's, Your Choice, Celine, Classica Uomo, Brogue,* and others. *Clotheslines Inc.* carries imaginative Canadian designer fashions. Other stores on the Bloor Street strip between Yonge and Avenue Road include *Eddie Bauer* for top-quality outdoor clothing and camping goods; *William Ashley* for Wedgwood, Royal Doulton, and Waterford; *European Jewellery*, with windows so laden with gold that a policeman is usually on duty outside; *The Irish Shop*, displaying lovely hand-woven woolens and playing recorded traditional music; and *Bob Miller Book Room*, just west of Avenue Road in a basement on the north side of Bloor, a favorite among academics.

Hazelton Lanes at Avenue Road and Yorkville is a gathering of exclusive, expensive shops for the most particular buyers. Women will find Canadian designer clothing at *Alfred Sung* and the best of imports at *Chez Catherine*. *Turnbull & Asser* is a quality British men's clothier, while best-dressed children can find fashions at *La Petite Gaminerie*. *Davidoff*, also in Hazelton Lanes, offers tobacco, Havana cigars, and smoking accessories—such as $100 cigar clippers. *Penhaglion's* blends its own perfumes and toiletries; *Fabrice* displays French costume jewellery. It's *Roots* for Canadian-designed, rather sporty shoes, boots, bags, leather, and clothing. Still in The Lanes, *Beaver Canoes* actually sells "designer" canoes and outdoor wear, and the *General Store* sells handmade paper from Nova Scotia, as well as marbled paper products from Il Papiro in Florence, Italy.

Suburban plazas include *Yorkdale* on the Spadina subway line, with branches of Eaton's, Simpson's, and Holt Renfrew; the *Don Mills Shopping Centre* at Don Mills and Lawrence, where you'll find another Eaton's; *Fairview Mall*, with The Bay and Simpson's, at Sheppard Avenue and Don Mills Road; and the huge *Scarborough Town Centre* in the northeast at McCowan Road and Highway 401, with Harridges, Lipton's Fashions, Harry Rosen Men's Wear, and many others.

SHOPS BY NEIGHBORHOOD

Some of Toronto's neighborhoods, villages, and areas have evolved into unique places to shop, meet, and linger. One of the best things to do on a Saturday morning or whenever you're planning a party is to go to the markets.

Once a week **St. Lawrence Market** at 92 Front St. E. brings together farmers, their freshest produce, and eager buyers. Buy a slab of fresh butter and have it wrapped in a sheet of paper, or choose a fruit pie and buy it from the baker.

Kensington Market is just off Spadina Avenue along Kensington and Baldwin. Sample the variety of cheeses at the Kensington Dairy, and wander past produce spilling onto the sidewalks while listening to reggae music from West Indian record stores. The area is colorful, pungent, crowded, and not to be missed.

While you're in the area, prowl down **Spadina Avenue** south of College. Both sides of the widest street in Toronto are crammed with fascinating fabric, clothing, and hardware stores, as well as jobbers. This is the biggest bargain district; while overhead and prices are low, quality is high. South of College is Fortune Hardware & Importing, with more than you'll ever need for your kitchen. Gwartzman's Art Supplies is a little old shop crammed with goodies like quality paints, papers, pens, and blank journals. Farther down, near Queen Street, are the bargain retail-fashion outlets. Good bets are Lady Manhattan Sportswear, Stitches Warehouse Outlet (claiming to "please the bargainese"), La Coquette for French and Italian imports, Gimpex for fur, leather and sheepskin, and Ritche for discounts on exclusive bridal designs. Two buildings to investigate are the Fashion Building at 130 Spadina and the Balfour Building down the street at 119. Bargain hunters will want to continue right down to Front Street, where the historic garment district ends.

Chinatown intersects Spadina Avenue on Dundas Street, and continues east to Bay. Restaurants and Korean and Vietnamese food-trading companies abound, as do gift shops like James Imports for wicker and china and Hong Kong Emporium for fine linens and wooden carvings; clothing from Kwok Sun Silk Importers and the Great East Trading Co.; and fascinating specialty shops like Great China Herbs Centre.

Along **Queen Street,** west of University and east of Spadina, is a strip of different, but equally fascinating, shops. This district is one of the most recent "discoveries." Galleries, fashionable cafés, and bars are scattered among new-wave clothing stores, used bookstores, and the original used office-furniture stores. It's a strange world of dusty, neglected stores next to popular nightclubs. The Allery displays original seventeenth to nineteenth-century etchings, engravings, and lithographs. Two shops on the south side, owned by Canadian designers, are Marilyn Brooks and Club Monaco. The latter is the affordable end of Alfred Sung's sportswear line. A chic espresso bar in the back offers shoppers refreshment. Also on the south side of Queen, west of Spadina, is Abelard Books (used and rare). On the north side, east of Spadina, is Bakka (sci-fi), and on the south side is the Can-Do Bookstore (devoted to how-to books). On the north side, Koochee carries colorful South American textiles and crafts. Zephyr has a unique selection of shells, rocks, toys, prisms, and fossils. Gold's Luggage Shop, Canada's largest, will repair any kind of luggage, even vinyl.

East along Queen Street from Coxwell to the Reltam's Filtration Plant is an area fondly called **The Beaches.** While the restaurants and latest merchandise in the specialty shops reveal a big-city influence, the atmosphere is that of a main street in a beach resort. The Beaches Book Shop is a good place for browsing. Nostagia Villa and Queens Comics and Memorabilia are two spots crammed with such collectibles as comic books, street signs, Coca Cola coolers, and even an old gasoline pump. Used clothing fills 20th Century Frox, From Here to Eternity, and the South Pacific Clothing Company. For gadgets, novelties, incense, mobiles, and lots of gift ideas, visit Miracles.

Bloor West Village along Bloor from Runnymede Subway stop to Jane Street is another area with a small-town feeling, but the Polish, German, and Ukrainian shops provide a European atmosphere. Watch your waistline, because the bakeries and sweet shops such as Cakemaster and the Sweet Gallery are tempting. There are several German, Polish, and Ukrainian gift shops, including the Ukrainian Ceramic Art Centre and West Arka, which offer amber, crystal, and embroidered gifts from the Ukraine. The carefully tended sidewalk flower boxes reveal the shopkeepers' pride in their "village."

Markham Village is one short block on Markham south of Bloor. Honest Ed's enormous bargain center, carrying clothing, housewares, drugstore goods, records, and tapes is on the northeast corner, with Ed's Ice Cream Parlour just opposite. Antique shops such as Upper Canada Antiques and Journey's End, and bookstores such as the stunningly beautiful David Mirvish Books on Art and the Children's Bookstore stretch down the street. Here you'll also find Memory Lane, with posters, comics, and all kinds of memorabilia, and Clayworks, with hand-crafted porcelain and stoneware.

Yorkville is located along Cumberland and Yorkville Avenue, stretching from Bay to Avenue Road just north of Bloor and just west of Yonge. The area has seen many changes over the years. In the late sixties it became Toronto's idea of Haight-Ashbury, and since then it gradually went from funky occult shops to designer fashions, antiques, and select jewelry. Norma on Cumberland Avenue is a shop for locally made, internationally famous, high-fashion sweaters. You'll find model clothes and samples up to size 15 at Miranda's on Yorkville Avenue; and next door Madelaine has fashion for children. Fidani carries Giorgio Armani for men. Swimsuits etc. has swimwear for everyone, even the hard to fit. For crafts, look into the Guild Shop on Cumberland at the corner of Old York Lane; for stationery, wrapping paper, and cards, it's The Papery. For the man or woman who has everything, browse through Yorkville Avenue's Lovecraft, Toronto's most upbeat sex shop. Never take your car into this narrow maze of one-way streets. Go on foot, poke into the tiny shops and, when you're tired, watch the parade from a sidewalk café. During the summer evenings it looks like a street carnival; single women will not be alone for long.

These are the most interesting areas. If there's something in particular that you want, the following suggestions can get you started. Here is a brief list of types of merchandise and the stores where you'll find it.

Art Supplies. *Curry's,* 756 Yonge St.; every possible kind of Letraset. *Gwartzman's,* 448 Spadina Ave. *Loomis & Toles,* 214 Adelaide St. W.; the professionals' choice.

Bargains. *Honest Ed's,* 581 Bloor W.; the king of bargain houses, with three floors of housewares, clothing, toys, grooming products. *Hercules,* 577 Yonge St.; Army surplus goods and camping gear.

Books. *Albert Britnell Book Shop,* 765 Yonge. *Longhouse Book Shop,* 630 Yonge St.; specializes in Canadiana. *This Ain't The Rosedale Library,* 110 Queen E.; rock, poetry, and the latest from small Canadian presses.

China. *William Ashley,* 50 Bloor St. W.; Wedgwood, Royal Doulton, Waterford. *The Bronze Dolphin,* 1365 Yonge St.; Lalique, Kosta Boda, Rosenthal. *Tabletop Gallery,* Hazelton Lanes: Baccarat, Fitz & Floyd.

Gourmet Foods. *Dinah's Cupboard,* 50 Cumberland; teas, seasonings, and food from around the world. *Carole's Cheesecake Company,* 2 Bloor W.; nothing but wicked cheesecakes. *Oliver's Fine Foods,* 2433 Yonge St.; homemade pâtés, pasta, and baking worth going out of your way for. *Paul's French Food Shop,* 425 Spadina Rd., *David Wood Food Shop,* 1110 Yonge St., and *Fenton's Food Shop,* 2 Gloucester St. are two of the finest.

Housewares. *Fortune Houseware & Importing,* 388 Spadina, 1235 Bay, *The Compleat Kitchen,* 87 Yorkville; all make you want to restock your entire kitchen.

Jewelry. *Secrett Jewel Salon,* 14 Avenue Rd. *European Jewellery,* 111 Bloor St. W.

Magazines. *Pages Book Store,* 256 Queen St. W. *Lichtman's News & Books,* 34 Adelaide W., 595 Bay, 1430 Yonge.

Tobacco. *Davidoff,* Hazelton Lanes. *Winston & Holmes,* 138 Cumberland St.

Toys. *The Toy Shop,* 62 Cumberland St. *The Toy Circus,* 2036 Queen St. E. *Topp's Toy Town,* 914 Eglinton W.

DINING OUT. There is no such thing as a "typical Toronto meal." If a visitor wanted to put one together—speaking hypothetically—he or she would have to do some traveling. The most typical Toronto meal would probably start with a bowl of Szechuan hot-and-sour soup on Spadina Avenue, followed by a cold plate of marinated fish, *ceviche,* at the Latin-American influenced Boulevard Café on Harbord Street, or possibly one of the fabulous Italo-Yugoslav fish-and-pasta specialties at Joso's on Davenport Road. For a really fancy dinner, the next course would have to be a *sorbet,* maybe a tangy scoop of lemon ice from the Sicilian Ice Cream Company on College Street, then back downtown to the city's most opulent French restaurant, Napoléon, for filet mignon with chopped mushrooms and truffles under a pastry carapace with the emperor's monogram "N" baked into the top. The salad course should be something tart and refreshing, maybe one of the Middle-Eastern salads served at The Jerusalem, on Eglinton Avenue. Any number of Swiss restaurants—Auberge Montreux, Mövenpick, Le Valais, Raclette—could lay on a proper cheese course after that. And for dessert? Well, what about the ultimate Austrian soufflé, a *Salzburger nockerl,* from either Barberian's on Elm Street or the Old Viennese on St. Joseph? No one could possibly eat such a meal, of course, nor would you want to pay for the taxis or the parking, but the menu makes a point.

In the twenty years between 1950 and 1970, Toronto's Anglo-Saxon population dropped significantly—from 70 percent of the total population to less than 50 percent. That trend has continued, with the overwhelming majority of the non-Anglo-Saxons being new immigrants. These people have had an immeasurable impact on the city, especially on its eating habits. Name a national cuisine you've never tried—Thai? Korean? Scottish? Cuban? Finnish? Russian? Moroccan?—and there's a restaurant serving it in Toronto. You can also find French scallops, flown in fresh, with the pink "coral" still attached, or a mixed platter of bear, bison, and wild-boar meat from a place that specializes in game, or the best bagels west of New York City.

These outside influences have been a good thing for Toronto, since the city itself never really had a cuisine of its own worth discussing. (Most nineteenth-century British cities didn't.) Even the best Canadian foods came—and still come—from elsewhere: seafoods from the Maritime provinces, grain and flour from the Prairies, beef from Alberta, maple sugar pie and pork pâté from Quebec.

The weather has always been a problem for Toronto cooks trying to work with local ingredients. In high summer the Niagara Peninsula explodes with grapes and tree fruits and the Holland Marsh north of town brings forth tomatoes, asparagus and the like. But for the rest of the year, all fruits and vegetables have to be imported, and along about March everybody gets pretty tired of broccoli and Brussels sprouts and Florida tomatoes with thick skins and no taste.

The shock for visitors dining out in the city will be our wine and liquor prices. Don't blame the restaurateurs. All restaurants, especially in North America, mark up wines and spirits by about 100 percent. It's just one of those restaurant-administration rules, to offset the costs of tying up capital in a wine cellar, as well as the cost of storage space and labor. But Toronto restaurants must, by law, purchase such beverages from a provincial government monopoly that has already marked its prices up by well over 100 percent, *after* shipping and federal excise taxes. And restaurateurs, instead of getting volume discounts, actually pay more for their wines than one-bottle-at-a-time consumers. Under the circumstances, it sometimes seems miraculous that Toronto's restaurants can be as good and varied as they are.

Formality is a sometime thing in Toronto. Very few eating places—and usually not very good ones at that—require gentlemen to wear jackets and ties. However, a good many of the pricier places might well seat you in their private Siberias if you show up in anything else. This is less true the farther you get from Anglo-Saxonism, with some of the best new Italian places (which are some of the best places of all) being very informal indeed.

Service is generally competent, and what many Americans mistake for unfriendliness is really only a certain reserve. Canadians have never gone for the "Hi-my-name-is-Bruce-and-I'll-be-your-waiter-tonight" style of false *bonhomie*. Waiters and waitresses here will be friendly enough if a customer strikes up the conversation; otherwise they tend to just get on with the work at hand. They expect tips of 10 to 15 percent, rarely more.

Reservations are almost mandatory at better restaurants on the weekends and at some of them every night, although few places are booked solid on weeknights before 2:00 P.M. on the same day. At businessmen's favorites, it's also a good idea to book tables for lunch.

Price classifications in the following, partial listings are based on the cost of an average three-course dinner for one person *for food alone;* beverages, tax, and tip would be extra. Prices have been calculated in Canadian dollars. The price categories are: *Deluxe,* $30 and up; *Expensive,* $20 to $30; *Moderate,* $14 to $20; and *Inexpensive,* less than $14.

Credit card abbreviations are: AE, American Express; CB, Carte Blanche; D, Diners Club; MC, MasterCard; V, Visa. Some restaurants also accept the Canadian credit card, En Route. Meals are abbreviated as: B, breakfast; L, lunch; D, dinner; it's best to phone ahead for the times of the first and last seatings.

INTERNATIONAL

Deluxe

Chateauneuf (Toronto Hilton Harbour Castle). 1 Harbour Sq., Waterfront; 869–1600. This sumptuous room, the main dining room of the Toronto Harbour Castle Hilton, is expense-account city. Many of the knowledgeable chef's ingredients are flown in from Europe, including his French scallops with coral. L,D, Monday–Friday; D, Saturday. AE, CB, D, En Route, MC, V.

Sanssouci (Sutton Place). 955 Bay St., at Wellesley; 924–9221. This room has recently been redecorated to look like an Italian villa: marble, lattice-work, and mirrors. The chef is inventive and audacious, known for his scallops in Campari-laced sauce. The bar makes the best martinis in town. The clientele includes Queen's Park (Ontario government) lobbyists. B,L,D, Monday–Saturday; B, brunch, D, Sunday. AE, En Route, MC, V.

Truffles (of Four Seasons Hotel–Yorkville). 21 Avenue Rd., Yorkville; 964–0411. Truffles is open for lunch on weekdays, but to "club members" only—and, of course, their guests. Membership costs $100 per year. Dinner is another matter—anyone can enjoy some of the city's most marvelous cooking. The Danish chef plays with classic French cuisine, for example, hiding a tiny mound of truffles under a pastry crust in one of his aromatic soups. Kind waiters, elegantly understated décor. D, Monday–Friday; L,D, Saturday; brunch, D, Sunday. AE, CB, D, En Route, MC, V.

Winston's. 104 Adelaide St. W., near Bay; 363–1627. This restaurant caters to the people who occupy the top floors of the office towers that surround it. Its rich, meaty menu is pushing its overwhelmingly male clientele to early cardiac arrest. Famous for pâté, beef Wellington, and a superb wine list. L, D, Monday–Friday; D, Saturday. AE, CB, MC, V.

Expensive

Beaujolais. 165 John St.; 598–4656. Founded by two West Coast chefs, this large, airy, pastel room is one of the city's most adventuresome restaurants. California-style cooking dominates—appetizers combine pizza with goat cheese, or tropical fruits with raw cured meats. The entrées are rare, exquisite, and small. Licensed. L,D, Tuesday–Saturday. V.

Courtyard Café. In the Windsor Arms Hotel, 22 St. Thomas Ave., Bloor and Bay; 979–2212. Also known as "Cafe Yoo-hoo," because it is a place to be seen as much as to be fed. The menu is *nouvelle* cuisine with quenelles, forcemeats, juliennes, and watercress in abundance. The Canadian film and TV-producer community lingers here over Perrier while starlets ogle the dark chocolate desserts. One of the best breakfast meeting spots, with some evening entertainment. B,L,D (open late), daily. AE, CB, D, MC, V.

Fenton's Front Room, Garden and **Downstairs.** 2 Gloucester St., Yonge and Wellesley; 961–8485. The Garden is the most popular of Fenton's three rooms. It is a chic area with indoor trees hung with lights. The food is beautifully presented but sometimes a little bland. The Front Room is lovely in mid-winter; there's a roaring fire and a bar equipped with international newspapers. The best place to eat is the least popular room, Fenton's Downstairs. Here the chef tries things out, and tries a little harder. L,D, daily; D only Downstairs; brunch, L, D. Sunday. AE, MC, V.

Palmerston. 488 College St.; 922–9277. One of the city's star chefs, Jamie Kennedy, formed his own restaurant to experiment with the flavor combinations that interested him most. Bitter salads and artichoke hearts with fresh sole are specialties. The food is always fresh, expensive, and unusual. Licensed. D, Tuesday–Saturday. V.

Scaramouche. 1 Benvenuto Pl., Avenue Road and St. Clair; 961–8011. Arguably the most exciting cuisine in Toronto. Hidden in the depths of an uptown apartment hotel, it overlooks a splendid view of the Toronto skyline. The decor is pink and purple paintings based on *Commedia Dell'Arte* characters, including, of course, Scaramouche the Rogue. The menu changes but food is fresh, delicately and deftly prepared, some recent examples being capon poached in raspberry vinegar, mussel bisque, hot seafood salads, and mocha rum cakes. D, Monday–Saturday. AE, MC, V.

Three Small Rooms. Windsor Arms Hotel, 22 St. Thomas Ave., Bay and Bloor; 979–2212. Each of these three low-key, tastefully under-decorated rooms falls into a different price category. The *Restaurant* room is expensive, the *Grill* and *Wine Cellar* progressively less so. *The Restaurant* is where you'll find Beluga caviar, authentic fresh Dover sole, salsify, and meltingly tender lamb worthy of accompanying the best wines on the list—which are pricey indeed. *The Wine Cellar* has a more limited menu, but the same superb pâté and wines. It is intimate, with small tables and soft banquettes. *The Grill's* menu, on a blackboard, changes every day, but its steaks, chops, and grilled seafood are always simple and splendid. Unfortunately, *The Grill* is the least comfortable of the three rooms. L,D, Monday–Friday; D, Saturday. AE, MC, V.

Moderate

Parrot. 325 Queen St. W., downtown; 593–0899. This pretty little restaurant is one of the city's best deals. Walls of exposed brick are hung with paintings and graphics by local artists. The music and the waiters are hip. The food is fresh, light, basically vegetarian or fish, and imaginatively prepared. Desserts are rich, and run to pecan pries, dark chocolate pastries, and trifles. Licensed. L,D, Tuesday–Friday; D, Saturday–Sunday; Brunch, Sunday. AE, V.

Peter Pan. 373 Queen St. W., downtown; 593–0917. This Depression-era street-corner coffee shop miraculously made it into the 1970s almost without alteration and has since been lovingly spruced up by young entrepreneurs. Simple menu items seem to work best: salads, soups, quiches, burgers. The clientele is typical of the art-school-and-alternative-fashion-boutiques neighborhood. L, D, Monday–Saturday; brunch, Sunday. AE, MC, V.

Rhodes. 1496 Yonge St., near St. Clair; 968–9315. The children of the Sixties graduated from old standard junk food to new affluence, and Rhodes caters to them with sophisticated burgers, cold barbecued chicken marinated in Hoi Sen sauce, and homemade ice cream. Busy bar. Local clientele are upwardly mobile singles. L,D, daily. AE, MC, V.

The Senator. 249 Victoria St.; 364–7517. A former greasy spoon, the Senator still features collapsing bankettes and formica tabletops. But the fresh cornbread filled with ricotta that greets dinner guests is always followed by wonderful food: spicy sausage, blackened chicken, couscous, purple rice and gumbo. Licensed. L, D, Tuesday–Saturday. V.

Stelle. 807 Queen St W.; 868–0054. An odd mixture of Indonesian, Italian, and experimental North American cooking, this modest, out-of-the-way restaurant has become hot. And it only seats 30, so reserve. Its most famous dishes include Thai chicken with chilis to make your hair stand on end (available with milder seasoning, too), a North African-style rack of lamb with apricots and couscous, and veal with a sauce of roasted garlic. Handicapped accessible, with a non-smoking section. Licensed. L, D, Tuesday–Saturday. V.

FRENCH

Expensive

Café des Copains. 48 Wellington St. E., downtown; 869–0898. Downstairs there's a bistro with entertainment; upstairs, an elegant, airy restaurant decorated with brass railings and Belle Epoque posters is the site of many business and magazine-publisher lunches. Cold duck salad, steak frites, *tarte aux poires* for dessert. L,D, Monday–Saturday. AE, CB, D, MC, V.

Le Trou Normand. 90 Yorkville Ave., Yorkville; 967–5956. In summer the Trou Normand spreads out onto a patio. In the winter it's a little more difficult to find, but well worth it. Northern (Normandy) French entrées, including rabbit, are supposed, by Norman custom, to be separated from adjacent courses by a gulp of Calvados, the Normandy apple brandy. L, D, Tuesday–Saturday; D, Sunday. AE, CB, D, En Route, MC, V.

Maison Basque. 15 Temperance St.; 368–6146. The décor is stolid, bourgeois Basque, with plates and scenes of the countryside of Southwest France. The menu is strong on grilled meats, beautifully prepared. Alas, the clientele tends to be male businessmen, which is perhaps why women diners can experience less-than-friendly service. L, D, Monday–Friday; D, Saturday. AE, MC, V.

Expensive–Moderate

Auberge Gavroche. 90 Avenue Rd, just north of Yorkville St.; 920–0956. The main thing here is the classical French cuisine at relatively modest prices. The two-story restaurant has a terrasse with bar in front for good-weather sitting, and the L'Entrecôte bistro upstairs, with a prix-fixe $7.95 dinner Monday–Saturday. The main part of the Auberge is open for L and D Monday–Friday; D only Saturday. Major credit cards.

Le Canard Enchaine. 12 Amelia St., just off Parliament St.; 924–9901. This small and homey place is one of the best-kept secrets in town, with excellent food, friendly service, and sometimes music. There is a terrasse in good weather. L, Monday–Friday; Saturday, Sunday. D only. Major credit cards.

Le Pigalle. 315 King St. W., downtown; 593–0698. The décor is Gay Nineties with Toulouse Lautrec posters, lace curtains, and dark wood. In summer the peach-colored back patio is a wonderful place to squander a long lunch. Beef, lamb, liver, *poulet chausseur*. Licensed. For some reason a lot of well-dressed lady lawyers seem to come here. L, D, Monday–Saturday. AE, MC, V.

Moderate

La Folie. 349 Queen St. W.; 593–8812. Thanks to the *prix-fixe* menu a visit to this art-deco eatery won't lose you your shirt. Steak frites is a good bet, as are tarragon sauce on fresh fish, veal, and *gateau* St. Honoré. L, D, Monday–Friday; D, Saturday. AE, D, MC, V.

Le Select Bistro. 328 Queen St. W.; 596–6405. This restaurant is not only one of the best medium-priced French restaurants in town, it also has terrific jazz and blues taste in its music. Perhaps that's because the crowd here usually includes a sprinkling of Francophone CBC Radio Canada personnel. Lamb, salmon, cornish hen, capon, and a huge *plat des crudites*—which is a meal in itself. L, D, Monday–Saturday; D, Sunday. AE, D, V.

Moderate–Inexpensive

A La Broche. 1505 Bayview Ave.; 485–1111. A neighborhood French restaurant with changing daily specials. Watch for their cassoulet (Occitaine's goose-sausage-and-bean stew). It's a friendly, warm, husband-and-wife managed eatery. L, D, Tuesday–Friday; D, Saturday–Sunday. MC, V.

Café du Marché. 45 Colborne St., King and Church; 368–0371. Bare brick walls and a cafeteria at the entrance, but it's still a pleasant place for a salad or croissant and coffee. Omelettes can be heavy. Entrées are chicken and beef bourguignon. Clients are young urbanites heading to the nearby St. Lawrence Market to shop. L, D, Monday–Saturday. No credit cards.

La Chaumiere. 77 Charles St. E., near Yonge; 922–0500. This by now ancient-seeming restaurant of three dark, varnished, French-travel-poster-hung rooms was Toronto's first Gallic eatery. Its older clientele is still thrilled by the trolley of appetizers (*amuse-geules* of chick peas, pâté, olives, herring salad, etc.) that precedes the entrées, which include such old classics as *coq au vin* and sweetbreads. L,D, Monday–Saturday; D, Sunday. AE, CB, D, MC, V.

Le Petit Gourmet. 1064 Yonge St., Midtown; 966–3811. The trouble is, it's too crowded. For microwaved food, it's quite good. Beef Bourguignon, veal stew, chicken *chausseur* are among the daily choices, as are cold salads, including avocado and shrimp. Local Rosedale matrons come here to buy croissants and the famous custard-hearted Basque cake. Not licensed. B,L,D, Monday–Saturday. No credit cards.

CAFÉS AND BISTROS

Moderate

Bersani & Carlevale. 138 Avenue Rd., midtown; 964–9639; 86 Bloor St. W., midtown; 968–9143; 595 Bay St., downtown; 595–0881; 406 Bloor St. E., midtown; 921–9349. The various B & Cs have less in common with each other than the links in most chains, though all offer greater or lesser choice from the same basic menu and the same stock of takeout specialties. The Avenue Road branch acts more like a classy Italian deli-cum-takeout, Bloor Street West is hardly more than an espresso bar. The Bay Street address (the Atrium building, where B & C actually faces Dundas Street and is nearer to Yonge than to Bay Street) tends toward fast meals for shoppers and office workers and is licensed to serve alcohol. Bloor Street East caters more to a neighborhood of primarily singles. Avenue Road: L, D, Monday–Friday; L (open till 6:00 P.M.), Saturday–Sunday. V. Bloor Street West: B, L, D, daily (open late). V. Bay Street: B, L, D, Monday–Saturday. V. Bloor Street East: L, D, Monday–Friday; D, Saturday. AE, MC, V.

Bregman's. 1560 Yonge St.; 967–2750. Bregman's is a fine bakery with a good noshery attached. Upstairs you'll find salads, soups, elaborate sandwiches, and a young, noisy, appreciative crowd of local Forest Hill and Rosedale families. Licensed. L, D, daily. AE, V.

Emilio's. 127 Queen St. E., downtown; 366–3354. Young staffers prepare and serve fine lunches and light dinners that have a whole-earth honesty about them, but they don't preach. For once, high-quality sandwich fillings are equaled by high-quality breads. The soups rarely disappoint; table service sometimes does. L, D, Tuesday–Saturday; L, Monday. AE, V.

Joe Allen. 86 John St., downtown; 593–9404. New York, London, and Paris have Joe Allens, too. Like this one, they're generally on low-rent back streets near a lively theater scene and are unannounced except for a small brass plate near the door. The food is best the closer it gets to American high school hangout favorites—chili, fried chicken, ice cream. Less a place to eat than to see and be seen. Has some of the best mixed drinks—especially martinis and Bloody Marys—in town. L, D, daily. AE, V.

Moderate–Inexpensive

The Boardwalk Café. 2 Wheeler Ave., Beaches; 694–4795. The Boardwalk, a splendid snack stop on a stroll through the Beaches, does, we know, serve soups, sandwiches, quiches, and cakes. But we've never been able to get past the homemade ice creams, especially the rich-but-not-sweet chocolate, and the very good espresso variations. L, light dinner, daily (open late except Monday). MC, V.

The Coffee Mill. 99 Yorkville Ave., midtown; 920–2108; 110 Bloor St. W., midtown; 928–3126. The best full meal—and a real bargain, especially in Yorkville—is the Saturday goulash soup special, with a couple of slices of rye bread on the side. But the best time is about 4:00 P.M. any day, when the Coffee Mill, particularly the Cumberland branch, becomes the closest thing Toronto's got to a proper Middle-European café, complete with aging boulevardiers and ladies in hats. L, D, daily. En Route, MC, V.

Dooney's Café. 511 Bloor St. W.; 536–3293. With its huge glass windows, brightly lit pastry cases, and airy little wooden chairs, Dooney's looks cold in midwinter. But it is a popular and elegant neighborhood sandwich and pastry place, with Dufflet's famous pastries as the big drawing card. Licensed (not all Toronto cafés are). L, D, daily. MC, V.

Inexpensive

Fabian's. 876 Markham Rd., east; 438–1561. Horst Fabian gave up a career as Toronto's foremost big-hotel pastry chef to open this modest German-style café in a more modest roadside strip of shops. The best place for a treat and a coffee after the Metro Zoo. Avoid the crêpes and pig out on Fabian's fabulous cheesecake, layer cakes, or chocolate truffles. L,D, daily. No credit cards.

Sicilian Ice Cream Parlour. 712 College St., west; 531–7716. You could almost think you've been beamed up out of WASPy Toronto to a streetcorner in one of the seedier quarters of Palermo. The Sicilian Ice Cream folks sell spumone and tartufi to half the Italian restaurants in the city, but it's more fun to eat their product at the source, after dinner, with a demitasse of Stygian espresso, the exhaust fumes from College Street wafting over the tables and always, somewhere nearby, a proper Italian argument going on in full, arm-flailing vehemence. No booze. Daily (open late). No credit cards.

The Sweet Gallery. Eaton Centre. 220 Yonge St., downtown; 979–3118; Queen's Quay Terminal, 207 Queen's Quay W., waterfront; 864–1589; 2312 Bloor St. W.; 766–0289; 350 Bering Ave.; 232–1539. The Sweet Gallery's pastries seem a little long on flour and short on eggs and butter these days. But they are gorgeous to look at, still very good to eat, and are served at the Bloor Street W. address in pseudo-Viennese elegance. For a first course try the sandwich cake—layers of unsweetened cake separated by deviled ham or egg salad, with a sour-cream icing. Soups are good, too. L, and early supper, Monday–Saturday. Various branches keep hours of adjacent shops (Eaton Centre later than others, Queen's Quay Terminal open Sunday afternoon). MC, V (Eaton Centre branch only).

SEAFOOD

Expensive

Joso's. 202 Davenport Rd., midtown; 925–1903. Joso is a Yugoslav, an ex-folk singer (his TV show used to fill the flexible time slot between the end of the hockey game and the beginning of the news), and a former proprietor of a Yorkville coffee house in that street's hippie days. He's also a part-time sculptor whose pneumatic female nudes dominate the restaurant's décor. Now he runs our nominee for Canada's best seafood place, and that includes those in Halifax and Vancouver. If you dare, try the garlicky spaghetti with cuttlefish in a black sauce of cuttlefish ink. L, D, Monday–Friday; D,Saturday. AE, V.

Mermaid Seafood House. 330 Dundas St. W., downtown; 597–0077. The name refers to Hans Christian Andersen's fictional creation, and there's a reproduction of her statue from the Copenhagen harbor. Take the hint. The best dishes are based on Scandinavian recipes. Freshwater fish fare less well. L, D, Monday–Saturday. AE, CB, D, En Route, MC, V.

Moderate

Lobster Trap. 1962 Avenue Rd., north; 787–3211. This informal seafood house—tongue-and-groove booths and gingham—specializes in lobster, and at about the most reasonable price in town. Lobsters, priced by weight, are available broiled or steamed, but only barbarians order the former. D, daily. AE, CB, D, En Route, MC, V.

Old Fish Market. 12 Market St., downtown; 363–0334. The room is very informal, and it's just across the street from the fishmongers' counters of the St. Lawrence Market. Because of the market's proximity and the management's fetish for freshness, the menu regularly features fish never seen on other fishhouse cards. Upstairs is a pleasant, funky oyster bar. L, D, daily. AE, CB, D, En Route, MC, V.

Phebe's. 641 Mount Pleasant Rd.; 484–6428. A New England atmosphere with raw oysters to start. L, D. Closed Sundays. AE, V, MC.

BRITISH

Moderate

Duke of York. 39 Prince Arthur Ave.; 964–2441.
Duke of Westminster. 1st Canadian Place; 368–1555.
Duke of Richmond. Eaton's Centre; 598–4454.
Duke of Marlborough. 680 Silver Creek, Cooksville; 275–9301.
Duke of Kent. 2351 Yonge St.; 485–9507.
The Dukes Gloucester. 649 Yonge St.; 961–9704.
All the Dukes—Toronto has a chain of them—are instant Brit pubs, their atmosphere created overnight with wallpaper, paneling, and Toby signs. But the expatriate Brits who flock here to talk rugby and feast on ploughman's lunch, steak and kidney pud, and shepherd's pie seem to feel right at home. L, D, Monday–Saturday. AE, D, En Route, MC, V.

Hop & Grape. 14 College St., Downtown; 923–2715. This place looks like a theater set for an Edwardian play, with paneling, wallpaper, and pseudo-gas lamps. Downstairs is a popular pub and chop house; upstairs in the wine bar and restaurant there are good lamb or fish dinners and before-theater snacks. The clientele is a mixture of Brit expatriates, CBC-TV and magazine journalists, and movie buffs on their way to Cineplex. L,D, Monday–Saturday. AE, CB, D, En Route, MC, V.

Parkes. 226 Carlton St., Cabbagetown; 925–8907. A small neighborhood restaurant in the heart of Cabbagetown's most renovated former funk. The owner shops for fresh ingredients and specializes in conservative but splendid British cooking. You might find kidneys as the daily special, but can always count on chicken or lamb. The bar has good bargains—ask about house wines and brandies. L,D, Monday–Friday; D, Saturday–Sunday. AE, MC, V.

Pimblett's. 249 Gerrard St. E., east; 929–9525. Pimblett's is British as in eccentric. The seemingly wacko proprietor breaks all the rules laid down in restaurant management courses but has built himself a small, devoted clientele. He has sometimes offered free meals to any table that gets two pieces of matching china, and a few years back he began "laying down" his English-style Christmas puddings like vintage wines. The kitchen experiments, to wildly mixed results. Not for everyone. L, D, daily. MC, V.

DELICATESSENS

Moderate

The Bagel. 285 College St., downtown; 923–0171. Early Formica décor, motherly waitresses who complain that "you eat like a bird, dear," and the best chicken soup in town. Located between the garment district and the university, and equally patronized by habituees of both. An institution. B, L, D, daily (except Jewish holidays). No credit cards.

Dunkelman's. 1427 Yonge St., near St. Clair; 923–8224. Yiddishkeit meets *nouvelle cuisine:* blintzes with graavlaks. The art on the walls is very good: the restaurant's owners, Yael and Ben Dunkelman, used to own Toronto's progressive Dunkelman Gallery. L,D, daily; brunch, Saturday–Sunday. AE, MC, V.

Inexpensive

Switzers. 322 Spadina Ave., Spadina and Dundas; 596–6900. The anarchist Emma Goldman died in a room above above this venerable Spadina Avenue garment-district deli. Expensive cigars and poppyseed cookies in the window are your first introduction to a brightly lit room with red leatherette banquettes. Great pastrami, kishkes, red peppers, chopped liver. Licensed. L,D, daily. V.

United Bakers. 338 Spadina Ave., downtown; 593–0697. A Kosher dairy restaurant that has served fake chopped liver, salted salmon and scrambled eggs, and famous blintzes to three generations of loyal clients. Not licensed. B,L,D, Monday–Friday, Sunday. No credit cards.

MIDDLE EASTERN

Moderate

Arax. 1190 Eglinton Ave W.; 782–0494. A small, formal, family-run restaurant. The Asparian family's array of particularly wonderful appetizers include crisp, deep-fried eggplant, homemade yogurt and cheese, and a chicken shish kebab with a strong garlic sauce. The baklava is also homemade and not as sticky as most. Licensed. Tuesday–Saturday. V.

Jerusalem. 955 Eglinton Ave. W., north; 783–6494. Better for families than for spooning couples, the Jerusalem can be noisy and bright, but the *hummous, taboulleh,* and other Middle Eastern favorites always please. The main courses of fresh lamb set local standards. L, D, daily. AE, MC, V.

The Sultan's Tent. 1280 Bay St., Midtown; 961–0601. The address is surely the ugliest new building to be erected in downtown Toronto in the past ten years, but once into the caravan-tent setting of the restaurant you can forget that. The many lamb-based main courses are standouts, as are the honeyed desserts. The belly dancer isn't bad, but her prerecorded accompaniment gives new meaning to the words wow and flutter. D, Monday–Saturday. AE, CB, D, En Route, MC, V.

Inexpensive

Aida's Falafel & Shish-Kabab. 597 Yonge St., midtown; 925–6444. This deep, narrow, almost windowless and utterly unprepossessing establishment attracts a mixed clientele, including some of the riff-raff from this inexpensive stretch of the Yonge Street Strip. It also happens to make the best *falafel* sandwiches (deep-fried vegetarian "meatballs" served in pita bread pockets with tahini sauce and Middle Eastern salad) in town. L, D, daily. No credit cards.

LATIN

Moderate

The Boulevard Café. 161 Harbord St., midtown; 961–7676. In the heart of the university district, with a clientele to match, the Boulevard specializes in Latin-American fare prepared and served by Latin Americans immigrated recently enough not to have lost any of the touch. The *ceviche* starter—cold, marinated fish—is particularly good. L, D, daily. AE, MC, V.

Don Quijote. 300 College St.; 922–7636. Some corny iron sculptures of the Don himself adorn the white plaster walls of this restaurant, and diners are occasionally irritated by stomping from the flamenco dancers upstairs. But the service is friendly and the garlic shrimp, *paella, calamares* (squid), and chicken dishes are satisfying. L, D, Monday–Friday; D, Saturday–Sunday. AE, MC, V.

Costa Basque. 124 Ave. Rd.; 968–0908. Terra-cotta walls and ceramic floors lend a folkloric feel to the place. The menu features a fine fish soup, quails, and a perfect salt cod dish that demands a reevaluation of that fish. L, D, V.

Inexpensive

Chile's Mexican Flavours. 936 Gerrard St. E., 465–1247. This is basically a takeout place, with very few counter seats, but it continues to purvey the best Mexican food in Toronto by far. Daily menu specials regularly introduce dishes rarely found north of Mexicali. D, daily. V.

INDIAN

Moderate

Bombay Palace. 71 Jarvis St., downtown; 368–8048. Toronto probably has North America's largest population of born-and-raised Londoners—who care about their curries—not to mention a substantial group of born Indians. Competition among the top Indian restaurants is fierce, but this one was an instant hit the minute it opened its doors in an unlikely location near the St. Lawrence Market. L,D, daily. AE, CB, D, MC, V.

Moghal Restaurant & Tavern. 33 Elm St., downtown; 597–0522. 555 Bloor St. W., midtown west; 535–3315. A curry house with red flocked wallpaper and elaborately carved wooden panels, it serves a bargain lunch for around $6 with chutneys, *popadums,* and *gulab jamon* (Indian milk-based sweets in syrup) for dessert. The downtown Moghal is smaller and prettier than the Bloor and Bathurst Street Moghal; both are equally good. L,D, daily. AE, CB, D, MC, V.

Inexpensive

Sher-E-Punjab. 351 Danforth Ave., East Toronto; 465–2125. A recently moved and modestly renovated restaurant with *pukkah* (authentic) curries and *pukkah* tea—Indian tea boiled with milk and spices. When Torontonians first discovered this restaurant, they begged restaurant reviewers not to mention it. But word got out, as occasional lineups attest. D, daily. MC, V.

ITALIAN

Deluxe

Il Posto. 148 Yorkville Ave., midtown; 968–0469. The location, a hidden corner of the York Square courtyard at Yorkville Avenue and Avenue Road, has killed more than one good restaurant with its obscurity. At this writing, Il Posto appears to have beaten the curse with very elegant service and food, flattering lighting, framed etchings of Italian ruins, and every record Gheorghe Zamfir ever made. L, D, Monday–Saturday. AE, MC, V.

Expensive

Noodles. 60 Bloor St. West; 921–3171. Years after this place opened it was featured in *Progressive Architecture* and *Fortune* magazines; its glossy pink-neon, orange-tile, and leather-banquette interior is comfortable, service is friendly, and the food, loosely inspired by Italian cuisine, can be very good. Italian chefs do week-long guest spots here. At other times, look for *polenta* with *Osso Buco,* fresh asparagus with asiago, figs in Italian liqueurs. A friendly if cliquish wine bar is adjacent. L,D, Monday–Saturday; D, Sunday. AE, MC, V.

Pronto. 692 Mt. Pleasant Ave., 486–1111. Many hold this to have the best Italian food in the city—or maybe the continent. The service is first rate, the menu very inventive. Owner Franco Prevendello has his own vineyard in northern Italy. D Monday–Saturday. Major credit cards. (The restaurant across the street, **Biffi's,** is neither as special or as expensive.)

Expensive–Moderate

Vittorio's Osteria. 2637 Yonge St.; 483–3694. Graffiti in the dining room, a zesty staff, homemade pasta, and a blackboard menu that changes frequently help account for the lines at the door. D, V, MC.

Cibo. 1055 Yonge St., midtown; 921–2166. The pasta is scrumptiously fresh and available "to go." The menu breathes originality into many classics—for instance, poached trout topped with a thick sauce of pureed watercress and lime juice. The "neighborhood place" for the city's most luxurious quarter, Rosedale, Cibo is easier to get into at lunchtime. Bright and casual. L,D, daily. AE, D, MC, V.

Moderate

Bindi. 3241 Yonge St., north; 487–2881. About as close to new-wave Italian, in both food and décor, as you'll find north of Eglinton Avenue. Very good value, probably due in part to the lower-rent location. Excellent mussels in tomato broth. L, D, Monday–Friday; D, Saturday. AE, En Route, MC, V.

Carlevale's. 20 Grosvenor St. (upstairs at the new Toronto YMCA); 922–5663. The elegance of this pastel-colored eatery, with its graffiti paintings and fake columns, is one more testimony to the dramatic image change of the sweaty old Y. Where the old Y featured a sandwich bar, its male and female clients now demand spritzers and fresh pasta alfredo after a sauna and swim. The sausage dishes are particularly spicy, and kids brought here for the generous Sunday brunch sometimes object. Licensed, no smoking. Closed Saturdays. L, D, Monday–Friday; Sunday brunch 11–3:30. AE, MC, V.

La Bruschetta. 1325 St. Clair Avenue W.; 656–8622. This family restaurant is decorated with photos of the day Toronto's 400,000 Italians turned out to celebrate Italy's World Cup soccer victory. Dinner begins with a *bruschetta*— a thick piece of bread fried in olive oil and garlic and covered with a crushed tomato topping. The *padella* dinner consists of fresh clams, mussels, fish; the lamb is cooked delicately in rosemary and garlic. L,D, Monday–Saturday. AE, MC, V.

Trattoria Giancarlo. 41 Clinton St.; 533–9619. Another new-wave Italian eatery, Giancarlo's is dominated by black and white tile. Yet it still seems cozy, perhaps because it is small and the staff friendly. Pasta is homemade and the grilled shrimp and quail are particularly good. Outdoor tables in summer. Licensed. L, D, Tuesday–Saturday. V.

Moderate–Inexpensive

Carlevale's Café. 158 Avenue Rd., midtown; 922–4787. The first link in what has since become a New York and Toronto mini-chain (see Cafés and Coffeehouses: Bersani & Carlevale). The original Carlevale's, a converted greasy spoon, still looks the part. The kitchen experiments to mixed results, but it's a favorite with the local glitterati. L, D, Monday–Friday; L, Saturday–Sunday. AE, MC, V.

Inexpensive

Porretta's Pizza and Restaurant Ltd. 97 Harbord St.; 920–2186. A brightly lit, clean, cheerful hangout close to the university campus, its clientele is mainly students and profs. For them, Poretta's makes the thickest, richest, cheesiest pizza in town. One edition comes with a whole-wheat crust; all crusts are light and crisp. L,D, Tuesday–Sunday. AE, MC, V.

GREEK

Expensive–Moderate

Anesty's. 16 Church St., near Front Street.; 368–1881. Once the belly dancers get started it's a little awkward to make an exit from this airy, carpet-hung restaurant. Another complaint: the management is less than generous with pita to accompany the marvelous appetizers—sweetbreads, chicken livers grilled with bacon, *tzadziki, tarama,* chicken lemon soup. Desserts are huge. Retsina and regular wines. L, D, Monday–Friday; D, Saturday. AE, MC, V.

Moderate

Ellas. 702 Pape Ave., at Danforth; 463–0334. Dark and gaudy (fake caverns used to adorn one wall), this neighborhood restaurant caters to an enthusiastic Greek clientele and to anyone else who likes rich *moussaka,* greasy but savory vegetables (okra, spinach, eggplant), and slabs of lamb. L,D, daily. AE, D, MC, V.

Knossos. 433 Yonge St., Yonge and College; 598–2307. A bright, white-walled, tile-floored little Greek restaurant, surprisingly clean and cheery considering it is on the Yonge Street strip. *Tarama* (red caviar spread) and roast lamb are specialties. Some "Canadian" dishes, too. Patrons lingering over their wine are Yonge Street businessmen and journalists from the nearby CBC and Maclean-Hunter buildings. L,D, Monday–Friday; D, Saturday–Sunday. AE, C, MC, V.

CHINESE

Expensive–Moderate

Pink Pearl. 142 Dundas St. W., downtown; 977–3388; also 207 Queen's Quay, waterfront; 366–9162. Two upscale Chinese restaurants; portions are small but generally delectable. The Chinatown Pink Pearl is decorated with black bentwood chairs and Chinese brush paintings of the Toronto skyline. The Queen's Quay Terminal branch is pale, pastel, and overlooks the lake. Specialties: The Rainbow, a lettuce leaf wrapped around pork, shrimp, and crispy noodles, and a crispy-skinned chicken rising out of a sea of shrimp chips. The clientele is slightly more occidental than Chinese. L,D, daily. AE, MC, V.

Moderate

The Eating Counter. 41 Baldwin St., 977–7028. Slightly east of the Kensington Market shopping district, surrounded by old clothing and craft shops, this Chinese open kitchen offers much-praised fried squid and barbecue chicken and duck in resolutely plebian surroundings. Not licensed. Daily 11 A.M. to 11 P.M. No credit cards.

International. 421 Dundas St. W.; 593–0291. When officials from the People's Republic came to town, they were entertained here—perhaps simply because it's so big. Still, the crispy chicken (sporting a barbecued head) and other classics are well prepared. L,D, daily. AE, MC, V.

King Fook. 581–583 Markham St., west; 532–9111. A far reach from any of Toronto's several Chinatowns but conveniently at one end of the popular Markham Street row of bookstores and boutiques, King Fook serves some of the city's best Cantonese fare. By Chinese-restaurant standards, the rooms are uncommonly dressy. Intelligent service and fair prices. Very good for groups. A largish group can get a private room. L, D, Tuesday–Friday; D, Saturday–Sunday. AE, MC, V.

Taste of Sichuan. 950 Eglinton Ave. W.; 781–5669. A modest little Chinese restaurant in the middle of a bagel block. The food is inexpensive, especially considering the delicacy and care with which it's prepared, and the spicy shrimps are legendary. Good Szechuan beef, chicken, and bean curd dishes too. L, D, Monday–Saturday; D, Sunday. AE, MC, V.

Treasure Restaurant. 150 Dundas St. W.; 977–3778. In a basement, this popular gaudily decorated Chinese restaurant is patronized by the Chinese and city hall civil servants, for *dim sum* lunches or Cantonese and Pekinese dinners, featuring sweet-and-sour soup, corn soup, exotic mushrooms with chicken and shrimps. L,D, daily. AE, V.

Young Lok. 122 St. Patrick St.; 593–9819. The tile floors make this extremely popular place a bit clattery and noisy. But the Szechuan food is spicy and sensational—especially the spicy shrimps, the beef with garlic bean sauce, and the chicken with orange and hot peppers. The clientele is about equal parts Chinese, Jewish, and uptown. Count on long lines on weekends. L,D, daily. AE, MC, V.

Ho Yuen. 105 Elizabeth St.; 977–3449. A bare-looking place with white walls and Formica tables, but Toronto's Chinese community lines up here to enjoy Ho Yuen's legendary fresh lobster with garlic. Everything else is excellent, too. D, daily. No credit cards.

Inexpensive

Kowloon Dim Sum. 187 Dundas St. W., downtown; 977–3773. This may be the least-appealing *dim sum* joint in the city to look at, but the dumplings, in almost infinite variety, can't be beaten at any price. Try the *goun ton gow,* a delicate steamed-rice pastry envelope filled with soup. The thick, fluffy buns are called *bow;* the one filled with sweetish, delicious barbecued pork is a *char sin bow.* L, D, Monday–Tuesday, Thursday–Sunday. No credit cards.

THAI
Expensive

Bangkok Gardens. 18 Elm St., downtown; 977–6748. You enter through a bar redolent of sandalwood incense—or else via the lobby of an exclusive club for women, the Elmwood. The food is equally elegant. Carrots carved to look like lotuses adorn piles of spiced beef (*Laab*) and cucumber carved into boats (*Royal Barge Lum Naa).* The appetizer assortment is a good way to become acquainted with Thai food's spicy, pungent flavors. Some of your neighbors will be the Elmwood's well-heeled club women. L, D, Monday–Friday; D, Saturday. AE, D, En Route, MC, V.

INDONESIAN/MALAYSIAN
Moderate

Java. 105 Church St., downtown; 364–7666. High red louvered shutters keep this attractive restaurant in a kind of tropical gloom. It specializes in Indonesian *rijsttafel, saté* (grilled meat or shrimp on a stick with peanut sauce), and *gado-gado* (a salad with a hot peanut dressing). L, D, Monday–Friday; D, Saturday. AE, D, MC, V.

Ole Malacca. 886 St. Clair Ave. W.; 654–2111, and 67 Shuter St.; 364–2400. This Singaporean restaurant has become deservedly popular, so expect lines even on weeknights. It's family run; management delights in special touches, including advice about whether the shrimp in coconut sauce is good tonight and a flower for the women on Valentine's Day. The menu is predominantly seafood with hot chile, peanut, and coconut sauces. Try to avoid getting seated downstairs next to the garish turquoise wall. L, D, Monday–Friday; D, Saturday. AE, D, MC, V.

KOREAN
Moderate

Arirang House. 716 Bloor St. W., west; 532–2727. This Korean restaurant is beginning to climb in price, which is unfortunate—because once you're addicted to its hot cabbage relish and Korean barbecued beef you'll want to come back. The clientele includes local Koreans, which is a good sign of the restaurant's authenticity. No desserts. Licensed. D, daily. No credit cards.

JAPANESE
Expensive

Furusato. 401 Bloor St. E., midtown; 967–0180. From fairly humble origins —known chiefly for reliable *tempura*—Furusato has become one of the most ambitious Japanese restaurants in a city with more than its share. One of the few places on the continent to serve *fugu,* that notorious Japanese fish that's deadly poisonous unless a particular dorsal fin spine has been painstakingly removed. Less hazardous dishes are prepared with equal care. L, D, Monday–Friday; D, Saturday–Sunday. AE, D, MC, V.

Moderate

Bon Tei. 3345 Bloor St. W.; 231–7963. Way out in the west-end boondocks, this banner-hung, brightly lit *sushi* bar and restaurant is an oasis of delicate flavors and generous helpings. Japanese and occidental patrons sometimes take home some of their breaded pork in doggie bags, to leave room for green tea ice cream. L,D, Monday–Saturday; D, Sunday. AE, MC, V.

Masa. 195 Richmond St. W.; 977–9519. A path flanked by rocks leads guests to Japanese-style booths with bamboo mats. *Sushi* and *tempura* are available, as are less familiar, traditional Japanese noodle-and-broth dishes. Related to the uptown restaurant Michi, Masa also serves its admirable Mandarin orange pie. L,D, Monday–Friday; D, Saturday. AE, MC, V.

Michi. 459 Church St.; 924–1303. This place is a real bargain at lunch time, which is when the neighborhood's TV producers come here to take off their shoes, perch on bamboo mats, and relax with a bowl of miso soup. *Sushi* and *tempura* are available. The not-very-authentic Mandarin orange pie is delicious. L,D, Tuesday–Friday. AE, MC, V.

Inexpensive

Taiko-Sushi. 607-A Yonge St.; 921–6408. A modest, quiet little basement place hidden amid Yonge Street's trashy shops and boutiques, Taiko specializes in a wide choice of raw fresh fish and seafood, with hair-raising wasabi (green horseradish). Some tables are Japanese-style. Western clients may prefer the tables where you can keep your shoes on. L,D, Monday–Friday; D, Saturday–Sunday. AE, CB, D, En Route, MC, V.

SWISS

Expensive

Auberge Montreux. 1315 Bay St., midtown; 923–1005. A very quiet, rather romantic little Swiss restaurant that's near Yorkville, but not really *of* Yorkville. It hasn't got the requisite hype nor the larcenous prices. Just solid Swiss bourgeois cooking served with pride and consideration. For dessert, try the little canning jar of apple chunks put up a day or two before with cider and Calvados. L, D, Monday–Saturday. AE, MC, V.

Moderate

Mövenpick. 165 York St., downtown; 366–5234. Arguably the best all-round eating spot in the city, this is the first North American link in a Swiss chain long known and respected in Europe. There are countless niceties, like the lady who brings free small glasses of fresh-squeezed orange juice to latecomers in the lunchtime queue. Seasonal foods—the first local strawberries and so on—get special treatment. The Sunday brunches are a knockout. Very good before or after a concert at Thomson Hall. B, L, D, daily; brunch, Sunday. AE, MC, V.

SCANDINAVIAN
Expensive–Moderate

Copenhagen Room. 101 Bloor St. W., near Bay; 920–3287. This clean, comfortable, blue-and-white dining room is the sort of place to which great aunts in pillbox hats love to be taken. At lunch the open-faced sandwiches—including steak tartar with caviar, pork with cabbage, roast duck and shrimp with caviar —are a real bargain and a meal in themselves. Evening smörgasbords are magnificent but check ahead—they aren't presented every night. Good Danish beer and liqueurs. L, D, Monday–Saturday. AE, CB, D, En Route, MC, V.

OTHER EUROPEAN
Moderate

Old Viennese. 6 St. Joseph St., Midtown; 961–6683. *Austrian.* The ground floor is a cozy bar; upstairs is about as *gemütlich* a bit of Vienna as you're likely to find this far from the Danube, with familiar classics, such as *schnitzel,* and a large number of less familiar ones, too. L, D, Monday–Friday; D, Saturday. AE, CB, D, En Route, MC, V.

Sir Nicholas. 91 Roncesvalles, West Toronto; 535–4540. *Polish.* When representatives from the Polish Solidarity movement came to Toronto they are said to have wept with pleasure at the food here. It's heavy and very Polish, as is the dark, heavy hunting-lodge décor. Flavored vodkas, roast duck with red cabbage and *kasha,* pork and *pierogies.* In the evenings an accordion, drum, and fiddle dance band plays nostalgic polkas. L, D, daily. AE, MC, V.

Taragato. 553 Bloor St. W., midtown; 536–7566. *Hungarian.* Only in Toronto is it not a surprise to find a trilingual menu like Taragato's, printed in English, Hungarian, and Argentine Spanish. The food is resolutely Hungarian, with Taragato *schnitzel* (topped with cheese and strips of red paprika) carrying the flag. There is a large selection of Latin-American publications by the cash register. The prices attract graduate students and junior professors on tight budgets. L, D, daily. MC, V.

VEGETARIAN
Moderate

Queen Mother Café. 206 Queen St. W., downtown; 598–4719. This funky little Queen Street strip restaurant started off doing imaginative things with vegetarian ingredients—avocado and alfalfa sprouts. Now it occasionally does *boeuf Bourguignon,* too. Good desserts. Hip clientele. L, D, daily. V.

The Westend Vegetarian. 2849 Dundas St. W., Dundas and Keele; 762–1204.
The Vegetarian. 542 Yonge St., Yonge and Wellesley, midtown; 961–9522. The west-end place is remote, but dedicated vegetarians will travel for it. There's a takeout soy and bean-curd store next door. The restaurant is small and pleasant

with high chairs for kids, fresh flowers, and music. *Falafels,* soy burgers, and *ratatouilles* are among the entrées. Desserts are virtuous—carob instead of chocolate. The downtown restaurant is less attractive and a little more rushed. L, D, Monday–Saturday; brunch, D, Sunday. V.

Inexpensive

By the Way Café. 400 Bloor St. W.; 967–4295. Over this place there is a big red sign, from a previous tenant, reading "Chicken," but under it is a smaller sign, "Sorry, out of chicken." So you will understand the ambience of this student and aging hippie hangout that serves pita bread, falafels, salads, yogurts, and so on. L, D daily; brunch Saturday and Sunday. No credit cards.

CANADIAN

Moderate–Expensive

Babsi's. 1731 Lakehore Dr.; 823–3794. Herbert Sonzogni, the owner of this out-of-the-way restaurant, has worked with and trained some of Canada's best chefs. He concentrates here on fresh, local ingredients: barberries, pheasant, and Nova Scotia chanterelles. Says Sonzogni: "The motto is fresh." L, D, MC, V.

Moderate

Montreal Bistro. 65 Sherbourne St., at Adelaide; 363–0179. A comfy popular bar adjoins a French Canadian eatery specializing in Quebec cuisine: *Tourtière* (a pork and mince meat pie) and *fèves au lard* (pork and beans, sometimes made with maple syrup). Expatriate Montrealers mingle with downtown Toronto patrons. L, D, Monday–Saturday. AE, CB, D, MC, V.

The Newfoundlander Tavern. 185 Danforth Ave.; 469–1916. The décor is basic (paper table mats, formica tables). The food is authentic: cod fried with potato and onions, and variations thereof. Try some "screech," the potent Newfoundland rum. The clientele looks like the cast from the movie *Goin' Down The Road,* or *Deliverance,* perhaps. Entertainment on weekends. D, Tuesday–Sunday. No credit cards.

NORTH AMERICAN

Moderate

Bam Boo. 312 Queen St. W.; 593–5771. By night it is one of the city's liveliest clubs, frequented by out-of-town rock stars and reggae musicians. By day, it is a battered-looking, trendy eatery with a roof bar and patio. The menu is a weird mix of U.S. (barbecue chicken wings, key lime pie) with a dash of the South Pacific: Indonesian gado gado (a salad with a hot peanut sauce), chicken satay. Licensed. L, D, Tuesday–Saturday. V.

Hart's. 225 Church St., downtown; 368–5350. Downtown Toronto could use more restaurants like Hart's: a clean, pleasant, unpretentious place with a kitchen whose reach never exceeds its grasp. Fresh ingredients become nourishing soups, crisp salads, unambitious burgers and sandwiches, and one or two straightforward main-course specials per day. Regulars are the types who respect both their stomachs and their budgets. L, D, Monday–Saturday. AE, MC, V.

Underground Railroad. 225 King St. E., downtown; 869–1400. The décor is a barnboard-and-harness memorial to the escape route for runaway slaves, which for many ended in Canada. (Uncle Tom's *real* cabin is in Ontario.) The management and staff are black, and the menu features such rib-stickers as corn bread, fried chicken, ham hocks, and chitlins. The Anna Mae salad is like a Waldorf, but lots better. L, D, daily. AE, CB, D, En Route, MC, V.

Inexpensive

Mars Restaurant. 432 College St.; 921–6332. The Mars is just a greasy spoon, but one that everyone feels nostalgic about. Late at night one can see Mercedes Benzes bearing rich lawyers back to this near-campus haunt of their law-school days, to eat again the famous Mars rice pudding and bran muffins. Sandwiches are huge, and daily specials—such as cabbage rolls and liver and onions—are generally good. L, D, daily. No credit cards.

STEAKHOUSES AND BURGERS

Expensive

Barberian's. 7 Elm St., downtown; 597–0335. If you are going to patronize a Toronto steakhouse, it may as well be the best, and this is it. The food and service are beyond reproach. Many of the pictures are real museum-quality Canadian treasures. An after-theater stop here for the Austrian dessert soufflé called *Salzburger nockerl* is a must. L, D, Monday–Friday; D, Saturday–Sunday. AE, CB, D, MC, V.

Hy's. 73 Richmond St. W., near Bay St.; 364–3326. Hy's is a beloved of downtown lawyers. Its library bar, lined with remaindered volumes, is especially popular. The specialties of this Calgary-based chain of high-priced steak houses is, of course, high-quality steaks. L, D, Monday–Friday; D, Saturday. AE, CB, D, En Route, MC, V.

Moderate

Ed's Warehouse. 270 King St. W., downtown; 593–6676. The lavish furnishings (many of them for sale) inside this mammoth feeding factory demonstrate the proprietor's tendency to buy up entire antique shops when their owners go out of business. No jeans allowed, and "gentlemen over 12 are required to wear jackets." The very limited menu strongly urges diners towards mediocre roast beef with inferior Yorkshire pudding. Still, the antiques are a spectacle, and it's next door to the Royal Alex theater. L, D, Monday–Friday; D, Saturday–Sunday. AE, D, En Route, MC, V.

Fiesta. 838 Yonge, at Yorkville St.; 924–1990. Fiesta is a throwback to the 1950s: teen-hangout decor, neon colors, naugahyde seats, old-fashioned milkshakes, big delicious hamburgers, and great French fries. But there is also pâté, escargots, and more. Bar. L, D Monday–Saturday; Sunday D only. MC, V.

Hayloft Sirloin Pit. 39 Front St. E., downtown; 364–1974. Best in the steak-plus-salad-bar field, the Hayloft is one of the few places in town where the grill man knows how to broil the meat "Pittsburgh." A favorite for office and family parties, although the waiters no longer seem to sing their close-harmony choruses of "Happy Birthday," "Happy Anniversary," and "Happy Vasectomy" as often as they used to. L, D, daily. AE, En Route, MC, V.

The Keg. 515 Jarvis St.; 964–6609. Also at 2300 Yonge St., north; 482–0304. The downtown Keg is the flagship of the popular Keg chain, popular because it sells steaks, surf 'n' turf, and roast beef at affordable prices without too much attention to sissy things such as vegetables. But many who are not Keg fans still come here for the grand old building, a former mansion of Toronto's Massey family that is well preserved. The crowd is young, talks sports, and enjoys the cheerful and attentive service. Uptown branches feature the same food and service. D, daily. AE, D, En Route, MC, V.

Inexpensive

Toby's Goodeats. 725 Yonge St., midtown, 925–9908; Church and Wellesley, also midtown, 929–0411; and Eaton Centre, 591–6994. 93 Bloor St. W., midtown; 925–2171; 1502 Yonge St., north; 921–1062; 2293 Yonge St., north; 481–9183. Named after the all-time ugliest white bull terrier in town (now, alas, no longer with us), Toby's serves the city's best hamburgers in the funkiest surroundings, with Apple Brown Betty for dessert. The cheeseburger, topped with something resembling Welsh rarebit, is a pass, but the many other ground-beef variations are just fine. Licensed for beer and wine. L, D, daily.

FOR FAMILIES OR TOURISTS

Expensive

Top of Toronto (CN Tower). 301 Front St. W., downtown; 362–5411. Best for cocktail hour, when the drinks are pricey but the elevator ride is free, and you get to sit down for the view. L, D, daily; brunch, Sunday. Best to reserve. AE, CB, D, En Route, MC, V.

Inexpensive

Old Spaghetti Factory. 54 Esplanade St., downtown; 864–0761. Kids love the theatrical décor (including a retired Toronto streetcar refitted with tables) and the video games. The budget-priced menu generally pleases the average nondiscriminating 12-year-old, too. For the rest of us, the OSF's chief selling point is proximity to the O'Keefe and St. Lawrence centres. L, D, daily. AE, CB, En Route, MC, V. Right next door to the Factory is the **Organ Grinder** Restaurant, a cavernous place with interwired organ, player pianos, drums, mechanical bird whistles, and so forth, all for the benefit, mostly, of kids having birthday parties.

Swiss Chalet. 234 Bloor St. W.; 962–4570.
Swiss Chalet. 181 Eglinton Ave. E.; 485–1813.
Swiss Chalet. 950 Lawrence Ave. W.; 783–8262.
Swiss Chalet. 362 Yonge St.; 597–0101.
Swiss Chalet. 1415 Yonge St.; 922–0280.

Opinions on this chain are mixed. Some regard it as the best junk food around. Their fries are done in chicken fat and can be quite light and good. The chicken has spicy skin and is succulent. Buns are blah, but the barbecue sauce is savory, not sweet. The ribs are okay, too. Licensed. Good for kids. L, D, daily. AE, D, MC, V.

 NIGHTLIFE. If you can't find the style of music closest to your heart in Toronto, then it's been dead for more than 400 years. Toronto's musicians practice just about any style of popular music, while the more than fifty ethnic groups represented in the city have a regular calendar of musical events in as many different languages. The clubs run the gamut from quiet and classy to loud and seedy, with a wide variety of cover charges and drink prices.

Credit cards are generally not accepted for club entertainment, but tickets for high-profile events at some of the more important clubs can be purchased at BASS or Ticketron outlets and charged there. Door prices generally range between $2 and $6, although they can go higher for weightier acts. Information about the acts and scheduled showtimes should be double-checked by phoning sometime around 6:00 or 7:00 P.M. If nothing else, it will cut down the amount of time spent sipping expensive beer waiting for the music to start. Finally, be mindful of Toronto's grim licensed hours; although you can boogie until sun up, the bar goes dry after 1:00 A.M. You can not drink on Sunday unless you also eat. After hours and on Sundays, blind pigs flourish, but this guidebook can not say where.

CLASS ACTS

Imperial Room. In The Royal York Hotel, 100 Front St.; 368–2511. The fare runs from Las Vegas-style floor shows with scantily clad dancers to hard-core rhythm-and-blues from the likes of Tina Turner, in an elegant dinner-club environment. Dinner and a show runs more than $30 a head. Major credit cards.

JAZZ CLUBS

Basin Street. 180 Queen St. W.; 598–3013. An upscale spot, with live cabaret upstairs in Basin Street and first-rate live music, with a focus on local and imported jazz stars downstairs in **Bourbon Street.** There's dining in both spots. Major credit cards.

Molson Jazz Club. 235 Queen's Quay W., Harbourfront; 364–5665. Like so many of the attractions at Harbourfront, it's free. Drink up your Molson's Golden and celebrate.

The Brunswick House. 481 Bloor St. W.; 924–3884. The only Toronto asylum where they let all the patients go home at night. Lunacy reigns downstairs, where just about anything can happen on stage, with a bizarre crew of regulars who sling beer as well. Upstairs in Albert's Hall there's fine blues, jazz, and dixieland in a (relatively) more restrained atmosphere.

Café des Copains. 48 Wellington East; 869–0898. A basement bar and bistro with chanteuses, jazz pianists, and a well-clad, laid-back clientele.

Meyer's Deli, 69 Yorkville Ave.; 960–4780. Traditional jazz and wilder stuff, good pastrami too. Also good for jazz is **The Chick'n'Deli,** 744 Mount Pleasant Rd.; 486–1900.

SINGLES BARS

Brandy's. 58 Esplanade; 364–6671. Young, well-dressed single men and women are the denizens of this shiny chrome-and-glass establishment. A dee-jay puts out the dancing sounds every night. There's a dining room, with some food surprises. Major credit cards.

Thank Goodness It's Friday (TGIF). 204 Eglinton Ave. E.; 485–1222. Another singles bar, this one a bit toney, with a no-jeans rule between Thursday and Saturday. Loud dee-jay music, with dancing more than encouraged. Dining as well. Major credit cards.

POP, ROCK, AND SOUL CLUBS

Albert's Hall, 481 Bloor W.; 964–2242. The best blues and R&B is arguably heard here.

Bam-Boo Club. 180 Queen St. W.; 593–5771. The home of intellectual punkism and the regular meeting spot for faddists in music and clothing. Sip slowly and watch the passing parade.

Blondie's. 767 Dovercourt Rd.; 532–8665. A refurbished neighborhood bar, now a live venue with a rock and rhythm-and-blues bias. Best on weekends.

Club Blue Note. 128 Pears Ave.; 921–1109. A Toronto landmark of the 1960s revived in the 1980s. The fare is rhythm and blues, both local and international, with a soft spot for great names (Martha Reeves and the Vandellas and Junior Walker and the Allstars) of the past.

The El Mocambo Tavern. 464 Spadina Ave.; 961–2558. The premier rock club, still resting on its laurels as the only small club the Rolling Stones have played since 1968. It's hooked into the best of the Toronto dance bands, such as the local reggae favorite, Messenjah, which play nightly downstairs. Upstairs international talent runs the gamut from blues to new wave. A little pricey, a little rough and smoky. At the corner of College and Spadina. Take the Carlton car west from College station or the Spadina bus south from Spadina station.

Grossman's Tavern. 379 Spadina Ave.; 977–7000. Just down the street from the El Mocambo, it's special flavor comes from the mix of regular customers and newcomers drawn by a changing lineup of local acts. Good proletarian food at the snack bar.

Horseshoe Tavern. 368 Queen St. W.; 598–4753. Once the home of country music in Toronto, it has gone through many changes and is now a venue for standard local rock. A large room with a good snack bar.

Isabella Hotel. 556 Sherbourne St.; 921–4167. Two floors of entertainment, some local, some international, in a very friendly environment. To get there, take the Sherbourne Street bus south from Sherbourne station, or walk the three blocks.

Larry's Hideaway. 121 Carlton St.; 924–5791. A rough-and-tumble basement club, the sort of place The Beatles would have started in if they were in Toronto in 1983. It has a bias toward fresh, relatively untried new-wave and visiting stars from the British pop scene, plus hard rock.

Nags Head North. 7170 Woodbine Ave.; 475–6405. Dancing is encouraged, with local acts that play good stomping music. In the northwest corner of Toronto. Take Highway 401 west to Highway 404, go north and keep going when the highway proper ends.

Rivoli. 334 Queen St. W.; 596–1908. Consciously new wave, it has a little bit of everything: live music, taped music, video, and comedy. Another good spot to keep tabs on the latest fashions.

The Rondun Tavern. 2238 Dundas St. W.; 531–9941. A west-end bar with a working-class flavor, with medium-core rock and roll and heavy metal as the standard fare. Videos, too. Take the subway to Dundas West station and take either the 504 or 505 trolley south three blocks (counting on the right-hand side of the trolley).

SPECIAL

Free Times Cafe, 320 College St.; 967–1078, is a licensed restaurant with folk acts and poetry readings.

Newfoundlander Tavern. 185 Danforth Ave.; 469–1916. Good steaks—and traditional Newfie cod-and-potatoes fry-up—are the eating fare here, with live country music and Newfoundland-flavored traditional music to eat by. An overtly friendly spot; be prepared to meet and talk with people.

Tiger's Coconut Grove. 12 Kensington Ave.; 593–8872. Tiger is one of Toronto's most beloved characters. He likes his reggae music loud and he hustles up delicious piña-colada shakes, beef patties, and sundry Caribbean delicacies. Periodically Tiger hosts all-night dance parties in his back room. A good spot to relax after a survey of the Kensington Market area. Tiger's is now licensed.

Trojan Horse. 179 Danforth Ave.; 461–8367. They rarely answer. An interesting one, this. Run in part by refugees from a number of dictatorships from around the globe, it features Greek and Latin-American folk and traditional music and is hotly political. Take the subway to Broadview Station and walk east.

DANCING

The Diamond. 410 Sherbourne St.; 927–9010. Weeknights this art-deco restaurant features live rock, including some well-known international acts; weekends, dancing and video watching.

The Copa. 21 Scollard; 922–6500. Very expensive. During film festival season, the site of galas.

Heaven. 2 Bloor St. E.; 968–2711. It's pricey, due to its classy location in the Bay Centre at Yonge and Bloor. It's all glitter inside and attracts an upwardly mobile singles crowd. The music is loud and the dancing non-stop.

Igwana Lounge. 138 Pears Ave.; 961–2000. The latest in electro-beat and black dance music. They're determined to stay a few beats ahead of mass taste. Trendy and a little bit expensive. Open seven days a week until the small hours.

Nuts and Bolts. 277 Victoria St.; 977–1356. Dance and video every night but Sunday. It used to be punkier than it is now. On Friday and Saturday night the music blasts until 4:00 A.M.

COMEDY

Garbo's. 429 Queen St W.; 593–9870. Moderately priced French entrées are followed by comedy and sitcom veterans, such as Audrey Meadows (*The Honeymooners*). Dinner and a show costs around $20.

Yuk-Yuk's. 1280 Bay St.; 967–6425. When drug pioneer Dr. Timothy Leary last came to Toronto he appeared here, so it's clear that Yuk-Yuk's has a very broad view of comedy. Toronto's funniest comedians can generally be found here. Licensed. All major credit cards. Open Monday through Saturday. Showtime at 9:00 P.M. weeknights, 8:30 P.M. and 11:00 P.M. weekends.

SUPPER CLUBS AND DINNER THEATER

Basin St. Cabaret. 180 Queen St. W.; 598–3013. The Italian food is fine, but the revues are better. Some of Toronto's longest-running and most risque hits have called this place home—including Indigo, a musical history of the Blues, and the sex comedy *Let My People Come.*

Harper's East Side Restaurant and Dinner Theatre. 38 Lombard St; 863–6223. After feeding you its palatable versions of Yankee and Deep South cuisine, Harper's turns the spotlight on comedy revues. Dinner and a show cost about $27; the show alone is $10 weekdays, $14 weekends. Major credit cards.

Other dinner theaters are: *Firehall Theatre* (home of the Second City comedy troupe [see the *Theater* section above]), 110 Lombard St., 863–1111; *His Majesty's Feast,* 1926 Lakeshore Blvd., 769–1165; *Limelight Dinner Theatre,* 2026 Yonge St., 482–5200; *Old Angelo's,* 45 Elm St., 597–0155; *The Teller's Cage,* Commerce Ct. South, 862–1434; *Theatre in the Dell,* 300 Simcoe St., 598–4802.

 BARS. In the bad old days when the city was known— but not widely admired—as "Toronto the Good," its watering holes were almost as scarce and uncomfortable as those of the Sahara: a handful of grim beer halls, a few garish licensed lounges, and an assortment of stuffy hotel dining rooms. People drank—but they weren't supposed to take much pleasure from it. Booziness was next to godlessness, and the Protestant work ethic dominated the city's politics and press. Governments severely limited the number and business hours of establishments selling alcoholic beverages, and the city's largest newspaper (*The*

Toronto Star) refused to carry advertising for beer, wines, or spirits as it waged editorial campaigns against the evils of alcohol.

No more. Since the mid-1960s, when the *brio* and *gemütlichkeit* of the city's burgeoning immigrant population began to dispel the guilt and prissiness of the Anglo-Saxon majority, Toronto has evolved into a major-league good-times town. There are now hundreds of licensed outlets offering the potables of the world in almost every conceivable atmosphere: mock-British pubs, Paris-style sidewalk cafés (in the warm-weather months), Italian *trattorias,* New York-style saloons, California-inspired fern bars, strip-tease joints, singles bars, and a few solid and subdued rooms where serious drinkers can pursue their avocation without having to listen to music or babble. Visitors are welcome in all of the above. Prices vary, but not by very much. Food is usually available, and it ranges from the ordinary to the superb. Service is usually friendly, sometimes fawning, occasionally nonexistent. But fun is more or less ubiquitous, even on Sundays (which used to be bone-dry and gave the nation's stand-up comics a wealth of anti-Toronto jokes; Kris Kristofferson used to sing of being "sick of spendin' Sundays, wishin' they was Mondays, sittin' in the park alone").

Where are the bars? Everywhere, but visitors to the city are well advised to dine and drink within walking distance of the main drag (Yonge Street), not for safety reasons but for convenience. Yonge Street is like a spinal column with ribs attached, the ribs being major cross streets, which in turn are the principal arteries of a series of neighborhoods. Toronto is proud of its neighborhoods—their preservation was one of the dominant issues in civic politics during the 1970s—and there are many of them scattered throughout the city, often being dominated by one ethnic group or another (Little Italy, Chinatown, the Greek community, etc.). But stretched along Yonge Street there are "drinkers' neighborhoods" as well, starting in North Toronto at the intersection of Eglinton Avenue and hopping a few blocks at a time south to Lake Ontario. Each of these drinkers' neighborhoods offers a variety of styles, at least one of which ought to please the fussiest visitor.

YONGE-EGLINTON

Charley's. 44 Eglinton Ave. W.; 486–6665. A big, busy street-level saloon with stained wood, adventurous menu featuring trendy youth-oriented dishes, live bands on some weekend nights, and a seemingly endless program of special events and/or parties to attract patrons. The food is good, drinks are reasonable, the clientele is young, and the proprietors (Johnnie Vaughan and John MacDonald) are acceptably crazy.

Cheaters. 2087 Yonge St.; 481–8772. A down-and-dirty strip joint (the girls retain their G-strings), featuring expensive beer, a few pretty barmaids, and a coin-operated pool table, which is the scene of most of the action. Spouses welcome, but they ought to be broad-minded and not very hungry.

The Chick 'n Deli. 744 Mount Pleasant Rd.; 489–4161. Bright, cheery, and featuring some of the best jazz in North America. Big-name groups appear regularly every evening, plus Sunday matinees. Dynamite chicken wings in a variety of styles. Reasonable drinks, especially when you can hear good musicians live for the price of a beer. Owner Jackie Brewer, a former hockey player who once coached in Norway, is almost always on hand. So is the hard core of Toronto jazz aficionados.

The Duke of Kent. 2315 Yonge St.; 485–9507. A perfect imitation of a tarted-up West End London pub, complete with English beers on draught and a menu leaning to bangers-and-mash and shepherd's pie. Noisy in the evenings, full of rugby players on weekend afternoons. Friendly barmaids, melancholy Scots, a few would-be Irish terrorists, passing Aussies, and the occasional native Torontonian.

Friday's. 204 Eglinton Ave. E.; 485–1222. One of Toronto's first swingles/fern bars. Noisy, busy, and patronized by a crowd growing uncomfortably close to middle age. The last divorced man in Toronto to wear a turtle neck and a medallion will be leaning over the bar at Friday's. Food above saloon average. The owners keep the staff on their toes, the patrons content. Fun at lunch, when customers can see one another.

Hector's. 49 Eglinton Ave. E.; 483–1048. A popular and noisy local hangout, featuring modestly priced drinks and good burgers, but an otherwise limited menu. After dark a singles crowd predominates, but it's not really a pickup joint. Jocks galore, including gigantic co-owner Tom Lennox, who buys patrons almost as many drinks as he sells them. Very friendly, if inexperienced, waitresses.

Paddy's. 2409 Yonge St.; 484–1455. A curious Irish saloon, tucked away in a mini-mall called Broadway Lanes. Good all-day breakfasts (bacon, sausage, eggs as you like them, baked beans, mushrooms, toast). Safe in the extreme (it's a favorite of the police, who have a station across the street).

ST. CLAIR-YONGE

The Guv'nor. 1240 Yonge St.; 922–9310. Another example of an English pub, this time a few steps below street level. The Guv'nor, part of a chain owned by the convivial Stan Anderson (formerly celebrity hairdresser Mr. Ivan), features a full range of British beers plus solid pub fare. Best value: the daily lunchtime specials, including prime rib and a variety of meat pies.

Jingles Too. 1378 Yonge St.; 960–1500. The second bar in singer-songwriter Tommy Ambrose's empire. A small, cozy, and moderately priced saloon, much favored by neighborhood ad men and radio types. Friendly staff, a piano anyone can bash away at, hearty food leaning to pasta dishes. Excellent value.

Rhodes. 1496 Yonge St., 968–9315. A first-rate bar with restaurant attached. Part of the Chrysalis chain, owned by master-host Tom Kristenbrun, Rhodes' front room features a lot of blonde wood, marble counters, and one of the best cheeseburgers in the country. The rest of the menu is first-rate. Beverages and nibbles are expensive, but probably worth it. The clientele is mixed, but determinedly trendy. Busy at lunch, mobbed in the evenings.

Rooney's. 1365 Yonge St., 924–2923. A luxurious disco/bar/eatery with surprisingly good food, costly drinks, and some of the best-looking young people in town. Noisy and crowded, especially Thursday through Saturday. Patrons tend to drive Mercedes roadsters acquired from daddies, both natural and sugar. Rooney's sells a lot of Champagne, usually *Dom Perignon* (or, as some of the heavier clientele refer to it, "Donnie P.").

DOWNTOWN

The Barristers Lounge. Westin Hotel, 145 Richmond St. W.; 869–3456. A barrister of any era would feel comfortable in this wood-paneled room. The bookshelves lining the walls hold real books, not jacketed slabs of plywood. You may find yourself ensconced in a big leather wing-backed chair reaching for a tome to read quietly by the lamp at your side, or sitting at the square bar or standing at another to order a three-ounce Grand Slam—martini, Rob Roy, or Manhattan. The kitchen serves up chicken fingers and top sirloin on a roll and such from 11:30 A.M. to 1:00 A.M. If you come in around the lunch hour you will be joined by well-to-do businessmen, stockbrokers, and lawyers. In the evening, listening to the piano player, you'll be joined by the returning business crowd and hotel guests.

Buddy's. 370 Church St.; 977–9955. Well-established middle-classers and young collegians gather around the big U-shaped bar at Buddy's, keeping the place crowded from 10:30 P.M. on, and jumping Sunday afternoons. Not quite a gays and singles bar, it is more of a meeting place. When not "meeting," the crowd gets into the pinball and video games or shoots a little pool. Besides shots and beers, you can order seven days a week from the fine Crispin's kitchen next door, with its full menu of seafoods, steaks, and soups.

Dewey, Secombe and Howe. Holiday Inn Downtown, 89 Chestnut St.; 977–0707. You can grab a stool at the bar, sidle up to one of two long bars, take a comfy winged-back chair or sofa seat around a low table, sit in front of the gas fireplace, or gather with friends in the small room around the coffee table. Wherever you settle in at Dewey etc., the mahogany-and-brass décor and friendly service will make you forget that you're in a hotel bar. Lawyers and judges from the close-by Provincial Court Houses have decreed it a haunt and partake of the libations and country casserole and potato skins stuffed with meat sauce at lunch. In the evening, 30-and-over professionals gather to sample the specials that the bartenders concoct in friendly competition, and listen to the live entertainment—usually a keyboard artist and vocalist. The two eight-foot brass palm trees may cause a bit of a start at first, but they seem to blend in just about the time that you do.

Gimlet's. 74 Victoria St. (one block north of King St., near Jarvis); 864–1441. This place was the model for the dance joint in the movie *Flashdance.* At both lunch and dinner times, very attractive and skilled female dancers bring stripping to some sort of near perfection; each one could be in a *Playboy* centerfold. The place may look a little sleazy, but it isn't, and is in fact quite friendly, patronized largely by the business-suited crowd from the nearby offices. A fair step above Cheaters in class. The food is burgers, French fries, etc., L and D

Monday–Friday; D only Saturday. The prices, given the entertainment, are not expensive. Major credit cards.

Hy's. 73 Richmond St. W.; 364–3326. The wood paneling, European murals, and beautiful upholstered chairs tell the visitor at a glance that those gathered at the tables or sitting at the stools at the bar can afford to be there. This is the watering hole of City Hall and stock market power brokers and bottom-line walkers who have the final say. Chris, Gus, Tom, and Angelo serve the drinks, which do not include anything so crass as a "special." The dining area would never be described as a family restaurant, with entrées ranging from $15.25 to $36.75. But you never know. A finance community tidbit overheard at the bar may well be worth the $3.75 plus tax for your shot of Chivas.

Joe Allen. 86 John St.; 593–9404. The Toronto edition of a successful New York-based chain catering to show-biz types, this second-story walkup features some of the strongest and best mixed drinks in town. The manager is a New York expatriate, the meals are huge, and the atmosphere is lively.

The Keg Mansion. 515 Jarvis St.; 964–6609. Situated in an immense and magnificent old mansion, Keg Mansion features pretty good food for dinner (only)—steaks, seafood, burgers—downstairs for a more established crowd, and upstairs a number of very comfortable bars (complete with old sofas, easy chairs, wing-back chairs, chessboards, etc.) to provide a club-like atmosphere for the Young Urban Professionals. Finger food provided upstairs. Major credit cards.

The New Windsor House. 124 Church St.; 364–9698. If you're Irish or simply wish you were, there's no finer place to stop in for a jar. This is an Irish joint; in March its walls sport enough shamrocks to festoon a New York St. Paddy's Day parade. The accents lilting from the patrons at the bar are not feigned, but may be Fenian. The Guinness on draught is lovingly tapped, so don't expect it in a hurry. It will arrive at your table or stool at the bar in good time, with a perfect creamy head. A shot of Jameson is served straight away, but order a glass of Guinness if you're having a delicious plate of Irish stew or a helping of farmer's sausage of Black Forest ham. Traditional Irish folk bands play Saturday afternoons, and weeknights you may be treated to rebel songs or the sounds of some tight young band. There will be enough burly lads with broken noses holding court each afternoon and evening to give the place a taste of home. Steer clear of the two dart boards at the end of the bar unless you've been practicing; newcomers have been known to be given expensive, if friendly, lessons.

The Silver Rail. 225 Yonge St.; 368–8697. When it opened on April 2, 1947, Toronto's finest had to be called out to direct the traffic and control the crowds. The crowds aren't the same now; in fact, they're not the same as they were a few years ago, when Massey Hall just down Shuter Street was still the city's principal concert hall. But befitting such a historic joint in the annuals of Ontario boozing, the clientele is considerable, and more importantly, loyal. The regulars still sidle up to the 100-foot-long bar, one of the longest in the province, and quaff their beers and shots. The faces are the same most days. The civil servants come over from nearby City Hall and the nurses come over from even nearer-by St. Michael's Hospital. They revel in the nostalgia, put their feet on the rail, and look around the art-deco bar that can accommodate 160 fellow drinkers, and think of the nights when many more than that elbowed their way in. The 130-seat dining room downstairs, once renowned for its lobster, is now patronized for its other seafood, steaks, and roast beef. But it's the grand old bar upstairs that now hosts and absorbs the cheer of its fourth decade of revelers.

Trader Vic's. Westin Hotel, 145 Richmond St. W.; 869–3456. Ever since Vic Bergeron met Don the Beachcomer and sampled his rum and fruit juice concoctions in the late 1920s, patrons of the twenty-four Trader Vic's worldwide have been stirring their drinks with little umbrellas. Vic's spot in Toronto is no exception. Afternoon, evening, and night, Mai Tais, Rum Gigglers, Navy Grogs, Scorpions, and the like are passed out amid the wicker, the authentic war and fertility God Tiki carvings, and the hemp wall hangings. Once you attain your Vitamin C and booze quota, you can buy a bottle of Vic's secret Mai Tai mix to take home. But before you go, you'll rub shoulders with secretaries and a cross section of the city's and nation's corporate elite and fellow travelers. And before departing, you'll be sorely tempted by eighty entrées in the dining room and the aromas from the wood-burning Bar B Que grill. But if you plan on dining and lingering over a *café diable,* make a reservation, or the bar will be as close as you get to the Polynesian taste treats.

The Wheat Sheaf. 667 King St. W., corner Bathurst; 364–3996. Toronto's oldest bar, founded in 1847, is still famous for chicken wings and fist fights. You would have to travel to McSorley's in New York City or small-town pubs in eastern Ontario to encounter the Sheaf's special atmosphere of mysogyny and guilt—of men sitting in semi-gloom, undistracted by women patrons, getting down to serious beer drinking.

MIDTOWN

The Bellair Cafe. 100 Cumberland St.; 964–2222. When a new trend hits town, it has shown up the day before at the Bellair, amid marble tables, through the ferns and plants and modern art. The pasta bar and lounge upstairs, where hot jazz licks are laid out each night, is high voltage. It has become almost mandatory that movie stars filming in town make at least one stop at the Bellair. If you want to see who is on the town wanting to be seen, this is the place. But if the glancing and staring and alternating currents at the upstairs lounge or at the stand-up bar downstairs get to be too much, you may take a break at the rather elegant dining area. Patrons may be entertained by or attempt to match the pretensions, or simply enjoy a superb meal and pleasant evening.

Bemelman's. 83 Bloor St. W.; 960–0306. Bemelman's long bar, stretching virtually the length of the room, is regularly elbow-to-elbow, the huge mirrors reflecting the fashions, styles, and various sexual proclivities of the patrons—many of whom are artists and musicians—and the dark woods, glass, and ferns that define this bar/restaurant as "New York style." Even its favorite winter drink, a mix of Bacardi and hot cider with a cinnamon stick, is called the "Big Apple." Indeed, the bar specializes in hot winter drinks and cool summer cocktails that feature fruits in season. The quaffers jostle to good, loud, rocking music, while in the rear restaurant orders pour in for the popular orange-ginger chicken, a sort of Chinese-style pasta served on a bed of green fettuccine, or add further endorsements to Bemelman's claim to the best eggs Benedict in town. And at the bar or in the restaurant, the international coffee collection should be sampled. The house coffee isn't exactly Sanka: a concoction of whipped cream, chocolate, Kalua, Glayva, Madeira, and Napoleon brandy. Cheers.

Carlyle and **Southside Charlie's.** 119 Yorkville St.; 929–0316. Carlyle, downstairs, features good food at good prices to a busy lunch crowd, but is a bit quieter at night. The contemporary-design bar is very popular during those cold winter evenings, though. Southside Charlie's is upstairs, with a patio out front, perfect for watching the passing Yorkville parade in good weather. Even more pleasant is the busy garden bar out back, reached from the Old York Lane walkway between Cumberland and Yorkville Sts. Brunch Saturday, Sunday. Major credit cards.

Hemingway's. 142 Cumberland, near the Bloor–Avenue Rd. intersection, Yorkville District; 968–2828. This bar-restaurant was the original big draw for Yuppies (Young Urban Professionals) in the regentrified Yorkville. It is always crowded, with singles at the bar up front and tables for good burgers and more upscale food in back. A country breakfast-brunch all day Saturdays and Sundays. Major credit cards.

The 22. 22 St. Thomas St.; 979–2341. Deep green carpets and off-white comfortable chairs bespeak understated luxury and successful regular clients. For its regulars, The 22 is something of a private club for the finance and film communities. But outsiders call it Toronto's answer to the Polo Lounge in Los Angeles, where movie deals are made and broken—hence the bar's other name, "the Pole Lounge." Camillo, The 22's bar manager, dispenses the bar special, the Treasure Key, a combination of lemon and orange juices (fresh), liberally enhanced with rum, triple sec, and anisette.

EAST END

Newfoundlander Tavern. 185 Danforth Ave.; 469–1916. Definitely Canadiana. Where else could you drink Screech, the notorious overproof Newfie rum, stare at a paper placemat that identifies fish species, and get an earful of foot-stomping country music about Labrador Lil?

NIAGARA FALLS

And Niagara-on-the-Lake

by
PAUL MCGRATH

Paul McGrath is a freelance writer and broadcaster who has lived in Toronto most of his life. He is a regular contributor to The Globe and Mail, *Canada's national newspaper, and is often heard on the Canadian Broadcasting Corporation radio network.*

It's good fortune that the City of Niagara Falls (Canada) sits astride one of the nation's most productive sources of hydroelectric power: the energy required to light this city at night, with its miles of neon tubing and its full illumination of the Canadian falls, could surely illuminate any city twice its size (which is 72,000). But then, Niagara Falls depends on catching the eye of 14 million visitors every year.

Niagara Falls has been a developed tourist attraction for more than a century. It has appeared to be somewhat cocky and garish; any place that advertises itself as "The World's Most Famous Address" must surely take first prize for bravado, even in this era of promotional hyperbole. The postwar development boom has made it more than just a city with a tourist industry. The city *is* the industry, with a large percentage of its population engaged in the business of giving the visitors exactly what they want and sending them home with a few knick-knacks they hadn't even considered.

It's possible to find just about any amusement or pastime here, packed into an area roughly equal to the size of Toronto's downtown core, and one can find levels of extravagance unattainable in a city of comparable size anywhere else in Canada. The city is, of course, made for people with plenty of cash to spend. Yet the best things, the falls themselves and the surrounding twenty-five miles of parkland, are free. With or without money, if you have an affection for crowds packed with children suffering volubly from too much of a good thing, it's a decided asset.

The city is a crescent laid out from the curve of the Niagara River on the east to the straight line of the Queen Elizabeth Way on the west. Clifton Hill is smack in the middle of the river-side strip, and from there the city view spreads out to the north and south up and down the length of the river. A ride to the top of The Skylon close by is a good, if somewhat expensive, way to discover the lay of the land. Clifton Hill itself is one of the main tourist concentrations, with the luxurious setting of Queen Victoria Park providing an oasis in the middle of sometimes furious commerce. From here many of the boat and bus tours depart. The bus tours cover the entire 60-kilometer (36-mile) stretch of the Niagara Parks System, from Fort Erie on the south to Queenston on the north. Slightly to the north, along Robert Street, you will find the Carillon Tower and the Niagara Falls Museum —much more seriously historical than any of the other "theme" museums, it is also North America's oldest museum; tourists have been gawking at its Egyptian mummies for a century. But it is in tune within the city's attention-grabbing spirit. Here too you will find the region's Daredevil Hall of Fame. Just behind the museum stands one of the gaudier Falls enterprises, Maple Leaf Village, with over 80 shops, restaurants, and games arcades topped by an octagonal tower that casts an eerie glow at night.

Continue north, now along Victoria Avenue. The downtown commercial core along Robert Street (which has by this time curved east) reminds visitors that there is indeed a resident community here; the

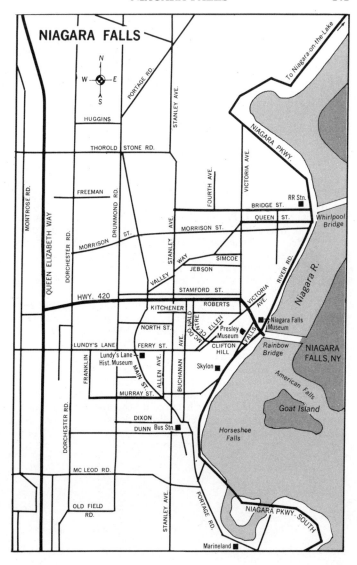

prices for everyday goods are not much out of line with Canadian standards, although American visitors may find things a little pricey— keep in mind that Canadians often travel across the border to buy clothing in the United States at significant savings. Past Robert Street to the north lies the transportation hub, the Via rail station, and the specialized tour attractions, such as the Spanish Aero Car, the Great Gorge Trip, and the helicopter tours.

Circling back from Robert Street south on MacDonald Centre brings you back to Clifton Hill. Walking west from there along Ferry Street: a cluster of good restaurants appears at Ferry and Buchanan streets, all with standard American cuisine—the hamburger in its many disguises will always be king of foods here—complemented by a variety of European cuisines. Farther west along Ferry Street, the Lundy's Lane area features the Lundy's Lane Historical Museum, which sits at the beginning of the country's longest hotel-motel strip. At its end are the area's camping and trailer parks.

Keep an eye on The Panasonic Tower—the name is spelled out and visible from at least half a mile away—and move back toward it along Stanley Street. A left turn on Murray Street leads back to the falls and the Falls View area, with knick-knack shops containing the words "Niagara Falls" printed, embossed, painted, or burned onto any conceivable object, from statues of Mounties to rock candy. The gleam of shiny, gaudy objects, glass or metal, can be blinding on a sunny day. To the south beyond Falls View lies the sprawling Marineland complex, certainly the area's most famous, most all-inclusive amusement, renowned for its trained dolphins and killer whales—the latter, the friendliest mammals on fins, are quite inappropriately named.

Head back again toward the river. The bottom end of Queen Victoria Park, with its Greenhouse and par-3 golf course, is much appreciated after this relentless tour of amusements and souvenirs. Not far from here is the reason for it all, the point where 200,000 cubic feet of Great Lakes water drops 182 feet each second to the lower Niagara River. Watch your step at the water's edge. People do fall in, and once in it's a race against time to get them out. Keep an eye on the kids at all times.

PRACTICAL INFORMATION FOR
NIAGARA FALLS

 HOW TO GET THERE. Niagara Falls is 131 kilometers (80 miles) from Toronto. By car, take the Gardiner Expressway–Queen Elizabeth Way west and south and exit at Highway 420, which goes directly into downtown.

By train. Via Rail runs three trains a day, morning, afternoon, and evening. In Toronto, call 366–8411 for schedules and fares.

By bus. Gray Coach Lines has three morning departures from the Bay Street terminal, at 8:30 A.M., 10:00 A.M., 11:30 A.M., and then every hour on the hour from 2:00 P.M. until 7:00 P.M. It's a two-hour trip, $12.30 either way, with no roundtrip discount. Call 979–3511.

 TELEPHONES. The area code for Niagara Falls, Canada, and the entire Niagara Peninsula is 416, the same as Toronto's. Directory assistance is free from Toronto by dialing 1–555–1212 or from inside the Falls area by dialing 411. Calls from pay phones are 25¢.

 HOTELS AND MOTELS. Niagara Falls has more motel rooms per square block than any other spot in Canada. The competition is fierce; thus the variety of services and the variation in price are quite remarkable. Specialties that have become more or less standard are sightseeing packages, babysitting, bridal suites, waterbeds and, of course, heart-shaped bathtubs. Prices based on double occupancy, categories determined by price, are as follows: *Deluxe:* $100 and up; *Expensive,* $75–$100; *Moderate* $50–$75; *Inexpensive,* less than $50. Major credit cards are accepted at all listings below. Rates drop significantly in the off-season, most markedly between December and February.

DELUXE

Americ-Cana Motor Inn. 8444 Lundy's Lane L2H 1H4; (416) 356–8444. A moderately sized motel with outdoor pool; recommended for its honeymoon suites.

Brock Sheraton Hotel. 5685 Falls Ave. L2E 6W7; (416) 357–3090. A great view of the falls costs more; city-side rooms are significantly less expensive. Close to Maple Leaf Village, with dining and babysitting. Prices range from *Moderate* to *Deluxe.*

Michael's Inn. 5599 River Rd. L2E 3H3; (416) 354–2727. A pleasure palace, with whirlpool spa, waterbeds with stereo, heart-shaped tubs. Falls view on half of the balconies; no pets.

Sheraton Inn. 5875 Falls Ave. L2E 6W7; (416) 357–3090. Another hotel with a dramatic view from the pricier rooms. A short walk to the nicest scenery.

EXPENSIVE

Holiday Inn By The Falls. 5339 Murray St. L2G 2J3; (416) 356–1333. It's by the falls, but you can't see it from the hotel. Usual Holiday Inn standards.

Inn By The Falls Motel. 5525 Victoria Ave. L2G 3L3; (416) 357–2011. An eye-pleasing arrangement with iron fences and plenty of trees.

Park Hotel. 4960 Clifton Hill L2E 6S8; (416) 358–3293. 180 rooms within a block of the river, with sightseeing arranged at the front desk.

MODERATE

Canuck Motel. 5334 Kitchener St. L2G 1B5; (416) 358–8221. A clean, friendly spot on the outskirts, with a full range of dining and activities.

Carriage House Motor Lodge. 8004 Lundy's Lane L2H 1H1; (416) 356–7799. Close to the Queen Elizabeth Way at the end of the Lundy's Lane strip. No pets.

Park Lane Motel. 7797 Lundy's Lane L2H 1H3; (416) 356–5070. There's no dining here, but it's close to a dozen other establishments that do have a variety of food choices. Outdoor pool, pets welcome.

Quality Inn–Modern-Aire. 6663 Stanley Ave. L2G 3Y9; (416) 354–2322. 58 rooms set back from the falls but still in the thick of the action. A refreshing change: no waterbeds.

INEXPENSIVE

A1 Motel. 7895 Lundy's Lane L2H 1H3; (416) 354–6038. Small, quiet spot, no dining, on the motel strip. Sightseeing arranged, pets welcome.

Caravan Motel. 8511 Lundy's Lane L2H 1H5; (416) 357–1104. Close to golf and tennis, just in from the Queen Elizabeth Way.

Econo Lodge. 5781 Victoria Ave. L2G 3L6; (416) 356–2034. Well-appointed with indoor and outdoor pools.

Mayside Motel. 5450 Kitchener St. L2G 1B8; (416) 358–7844. Bargain basement, but quite neat and comfortable. A few minutes in three directions gets you to a theme park.

GETTING AROUND. The Niagara Transit Commission (356–1179) runs buses throughout the city and the surrounding areas. Niagara Falls Taxi (357–4000) runs the local cab service. The city can be covered on foot (provided you have a sturdy pair of walking shoes), but don't try it all at once.

TOURIST INFORMATION. The Niagara Falls Visitors and Convention Bureau runs one of the most efficient enterprises in the country. It's at 4610 Ontario Ave.; 356–6061. During the tourist season Travel Ontario operates an information center at the corner of Highway 420 and Stanley Avenue.

SEASONAL EVENTS. Spring. *The Blossom Festival.* The Niagara Parks do indeed blossom magnificently in the spring. Local celebrations include tours, a parade, sports, and the coronation of a Blossom Queen. Usually in the first two weeks of May.

Summer. *The Rainbow Carillon Tower.* During the summer this fifty-five-bell carillon plays daily. The best place to hear it is in the Rainbow Gardens.

Winter. *Festival of Lights.* The city goes all out during the winter months with this special illumination of the falls at night.

TOURS. *Double Deck Tours Ltd.* (3957 Bossert Rd.; 295–3051) operates tours of the Falls and surrounding areas. The route takes about one-and-a-half hours to cover, but it's possible to stop at any point along the way, dawdle, and wait for the next bus to come along twenty minutes later. It visits all major attractions. Adults, $8.95; children, $4.50.

Table Rock Scenic Tunnels. Equipped with raincoats and boots, you are taken through tunnels cut in the rock to the foot of the Horseshoe Falls. Watching the water hit the bottom can be terrifying in a nice, safe way. Starts at Table Rock House in Queen Victoria Park. Open daily all year, except holidays.

Jack McLaren Tours and Tour Guides (3824 Bridgewater St.; 295–4936) operates fully guided tours of all attractions. Air-conditioned limousines for those who so desire.

Maid of The Mist Tours. 5920 River Rd.; 358–5781. The boats depart at the foot of Clifton Hill and take you right to the foot of the falls. A wet ride, raincoats provided.

Bright's Wine Tours. 4887 Dorchester Rd., off Highway 420. A one-and-a-half-hour guided walk through vineyards, followed by a wine tasting. Open Monday through Saturday. Call (416) 357–2400 for tour times.

Niagara Helicopters. Victoria Ave. and River Rd.; 357–5672. The most expensive, but without a doubt the most exciting, way to see the falls. Regular departures from 9:00 A.M. to sunset, daily, March through mid-November.

PARKS. The area surrounding the falls itself is one long park, twenty-five miles long, to be exact. *Queen Victoria Park* has a wide variety of tree and plant life, and is a relaxing place to spend the afternoon in sight of the Falls. *Queenston Heights,* 10 kilometers (6 miles) north of Niagara Falls on the Niagara Parkway, is a huge picnic and recreational area overlooking the Niagara River. The summit is dominated by a monument to General Sir Isaac Brock, the Upper Canadian hero of the war of 1812. He died leading an implausible charge uphill against the Yankees, who held the top.

 GARDENS. The Niagara Parks Commission Conservatory (less than 1 kilometer—½ mile—south on the Niagara Parkway) has an abundance of smells, colors, and textures from around the world captured inside, in a controlled environment. Admission is free. At *Niagara Glen Nature Area* (about 7 kilometers—4 miles)—north of the falls on the Niagara Parkway) you climb down to the Niagara Gorge to survey the plant life that exists in this fragile environment and to pick your way among the water-sculpted rocks. North of Niagara Glen is the School of Horticulture, the workhouse of the area's botanic breeders and cloners. Phone 356–2241 for information.

 THEME PARKS. Marineland, at 7657 Portage Rd. (356–8250), is billed as "Another World," and it's at least big enough to be called another town. It's the city's most famous amusement, with an impossibly long roller coaster, its own buffalo and deer herds, midway-style rides, and an aquarium show featuring dolphins and killer whales. In the summer the gates are open from 10:00 A.M. to 6:00 P.M., and the park closes at 10:00 P.M. Off-season hours are 10:00 A.M. to 4:30 P.M. Admission, which includes everything inside, is $13.95, adults; $8.95, seniors; $8.95, children between 3 and 11; under 3, free. Off-season admission is lower.

 THEME MUSEUMS. *Criminal's Hall of Fame Wax Museum.* 5751 Victoria Ave.; 356–6137. A celebration of all things criminal. Mass murderers, bank robbers, and other nasty people line the hallways. Open 9:00 A.M. to midnight, seven days a week. Admission: adults, $3.75; children, $1.75; children under 6, free.

Elvis Presley Museum. 5705 Falls Ave.; 357–0008. Everything anybody could want to know about the King of Rock and Roll, minus all the bad rumors. Open 9:00 A.M. to midnight, seven days a week. Admission: adults, $3.95; children, $2.50; children under 7, free.

Guinness Museum of World Records. 4943 Clifton Hill; 356–2299. From the people who started the books, exhibits relating to famous and obscure deeds, right down to Volkswagen-stuffing and pole-sitting. Hours: 9:00 A.M. to midnight, seven days a week. Admission: adults, $3.50; children, $2.50; children under 6, free.

Movieland Wax Museum. 4950 Clifton Hill; 358–3061. Hollywood greats, including Clark Gable, Mae West, Marilyn Monroe, Ronald Reagan, and Clint Eastwood, in costumes from their movie roles. Daily, 9:00 A.M. to 11:00 P.M. (July and August, 1:00 A.M.). Admission: adults, $3.95; students, $3.50; children, $2.50 (under 7 free).

CAMPING. *Miller's Creek Park.* Niagara Parkway, just south of the city. Fifty-four sites on ten acres, with fireplaces, store, beach, and boat launch.

Niagara Falls KOA Kampground. 8625 Lundy's Lane; 354–6472. 500 sites on 24 acres, with a pool, fireplaces, store, and showers. Close to the Queen Elizabeth Way.

PARTICIPANT SPORTS. There is a wide variety of activities at *Dufferin Creek Park* (just south of the city on the Niagara Parkway).

The Niagara Parks Commission operates the 18-hole *Whirlpool Golf Course,* situated 7 kilometers (4 miles) north of the falls, just off the Niagara Parkway.

HISTORICAL SITES. The Brock Monument in Queenston (10 kilometers—6 miles—north of the falls on the Niagara Parkway) is a tower commemorating the death of General Sir Isaac Brock at the Battle of Queenston Heights during the War of 1812. A healthy walk up the inside staircase leads to one of the best views of the entire Niagara area. Free.

MUSEUMS. *The Niagara Falls Museum* (5651 River Rd.; 356–2151) is a scholarly collection relating to local history, with more than 700,000 exhibits. But real Egyptian mummies are the stars of the show.

SHOPPING. *Dansk Factory Outlet.* 5395 Ferry St.; 357–0808. Household items and dinnerware from this famous manufacturer at substantial savings. Major credit cards. *Minolta Towers Gift Shops.* 6732 Oakes Dr.; 356–1852. Perhaps the city's widest selection of souvenirs, with a strong suit in electronic gadgets. *Maple Leaf Village,* Rainbow Bridge, 5685 Falls Ave. A massive shopping center with giant ferris wheel and observation tower to give you a break from all the tourist-industry souvenir shops and restaurants.

DINING OUT. American food reigns supreme here, with the inevitable conglomeration of fast-food outlets. There is good, moderately priced dining in an array of national styles. Prices are for an average three-course meal, excluding alcohol, tips, and extras. Categories based on price are as follows: *Expensive,* more than $25; *Moderate,* $18–$25; *Inexpensive,* less than $18. Unless otherwise stated, all of the restaurants listed below accept major credit cards.

AMERICAN

Expensive

The Casa D'Oro. 5875 Victoria Ave.; 356–5646. Pasta is the specialty, but prime rib and lobster tails are also featured. Somewhat baroque décor, with a fireplace. Lunch and dinner.

The Rainbow Room. In The Brock Sheraton Hotel, 5685 Falls Ave.; 354–7441. Sky-high dining here, with beef Wellington and prime rib the favorites. Delicious cherries jubilee tops it all off.

Moderate

Carlos O'Brien's Dining Lounge. 5645 Victoria Ave.; 357–1283. Exposed wooden beams and Tiffany lamps complement the favorite dish: "Oink, Peep and Moo," a little pork, a little chicken, and a little beef. Lunch and dinner, seven days a week.

Open Hearth. In Michael's Inn, 5599 River Rd.; 354–2727. Steaks, prime rib, and filet mignon make this one of the most unapologetically meaty restaurants in town. Cuts cooked on an open hearth in full view. Lunch and dinner, seven days a week.

Minolta Tower Dining Room. 6732 Oakes Dr.; 356–1568. The veal Oskar is a good bet here, with changing daily features. The dining room is at the top of the tower, with a gorgeous falls view. Lunch and dinner, seven days a week.

CONTINENTAL

Happy Wanderer. *Moderate.* 6405 Stanley St.; 354–9825. Hilde Mercnik has been in business since 1963 with solid Bavarian food in a building reminiscent of a Alpine retreat.

Hungarian Tavern. *Moderate.* 5329 Ferry St.; 356–2429. In business since 1939, it features *schnitzels,* veal goulash, and other Eastern European dishes. A gypsy trio entertains. Lunch and dinner, seven days a week.

ITALIAN

Capri Restaurant. *Moderate.* 5438 Ferry St.; 354–7519. The chef is particularly proud of his veal Parmigiana, but there are also decent steaks. Lunch and dinner, seven days a week.

JAPANESE

Suisha Gardens. *Moderate.* 5705 Falls Ave.; 357–2660. Tempura, teriyaki, and other traditional Japanese dishes, in a lush, serene atmosphere.

NIAGARA-ON-THE-LAKE

It's not hard to imagine why this tiny time capsule of a town was once of strategic importance in early Ontario history. Placed handily at the point where the Niagara River reaches Lake Ontario—the last of the Great Lakes chain—it was at the meeting point of the British and American Empires. Once the capital of Upper Canada, Niagara-on-the-Lake was also, for 80 years after the American Revolution, full of soldiers, spies, and border intrigues. Cannonballs and armed raiders crossed the river going both ways until the last of the Fenian raids in 1867 marked an end to Canadian-American border hostilities.

For 100 years thereafter artists and shipbuilders gave the town a special character—until 1962, when the nascent Shaw Festival dragged it into the orbit of Toronto. Now the town is a regular feature of summer outings for thousands of Ontario and American theater-goers, drawn as much by the picturesque serenity of the surroundings as by the drama festival. Ringed by parklands and historical sites, with scores of gorgeously preserved Georgian and Victorian homes, it seems to exist for nothing but pleasure and quiet contemplation.

It's possible to roll a bowling ball down the main street of Niagara-on-the-Lake with enough momentum to carry it all the way through town and on to Queenston. It's a tiny town and can easily be covered on foot.

Queen Street is the commercial core and has become, over the last dozen years, a showcase of by-and-large tasteful gifts and souvenirs. Walking east to west takes visitors past glasswork, art, fine china, antiques, and beautiful old furniture that would be perfectly appropriate inside some of the finer old houses. Don't miss McClelland's, which has been purveying good local cheeses and jams since 1835. The Royal George Theater sits almost exactly in the middle of town at Queen and Victoria streets, a beautifully restored building that is the major showpiece of the street. The intersection of Queen and King streets is dominated by a clock tower. Nearby is Simcoe Park, with a huge wading pool for kids, lawns, trees, picnic tables, and flowers.

At the western end of Queen Street is the main festival theater and, beyond it, Fort George, once the British stronghold for this part of the Niagara River. Turning right at King Street takes visitors into the loveliest part of town, where the streets are lined with old homes given new life with paint, shingles, and shutters. Some of the nicest buildings are along John Street all the way to the south end of town, and along the way is the Niagara Historical Society Museum, Ontario's second-oldest collection of local artifacts and documents. Some of the smaller houses along Johnson and Gage streets were once home to runaway American slaves (Canada abolished slavery two generations before the United States). A quiet knock at the door and a pleasant introduction at some of the nicer homes will, more often than not, produce a friendly response and a good look at the insides of places that were already in adolescence when Toronto was still York. Visitors might be surprised, delightfully so, at the modernizations of homes which, on the outside, have escaped trendy modernity.

A left turn from Queen at the corner of King, instead of a right, leads to the river. Here is a paddling beach, a view of Lake Ontario, and a good view of Fort Niagara across the river, the American fortress whence flew the cannonballs that so inconvenienced the town from time to time. Boats do cross the river from the Ricardo Street dock, but take along a passport or equally official document for the customs people on the other side. If you walk west along the river, you'll be out of town within minutes into peaceful parkland, a perfect resting spot at the upper end of the Niagara Parks system.

PRACTICAL INFORMATION FOR

NIAGARA-ON-THE-LAKE

 HOW TO GET THERE. Niagara-on-the-Lake is 125 kilometers (75 miles) from Toronto and is a little hard to get at. **By car.** Take the Queen Elizabeth Way from Toronto, through St. Catherines. Take the first exit past the Garden City Skyway (this is the second bridge on your route, not to be confused with the Burlington Bay Skyway around Hamilton) and double back approximately 4 kilometers (2.5 miles) to Highway 55, then turn right and travel 11 kilometers (7 miles) into town.

By bus. Connections from Toronto require a change of buses in St. Catherines, and can be time-consuming. Call Gray Coach information in Toronto at 979–3511, and they will happily find the best and quickest connection to avoid waiting in an unappealing bus terminal.

Theater-goers pressed for time but not for cash have been known to take a cab from downtown Toronto. One-way fare is approximately $100.

TELEPHONES. The area code for Niagara-on-the-Lake and the area is 416, the same as Toronto. Directory assistance is free from Toronto by dialing 1–555–1212 and from inside Niagara-on-the-Lake by dialing 411. Calls from pay phones are $.25.

HOTELS AND MOTELS. There isn't a lot, but what's there is of the utmost charm. In the height of the season the town has to rely on St. Catherines, Queenston, and Niagara Falls (see the *Niagara Falls* section, above) to take up the slack. Those listed below are often booked solidly in advance for much of the festival season. All accept major credit cards. Room rates based on double occupancy, categories determined by price as follows: *Expensive,* $85 and over; *Moderate,* $65–$85; *Inexpensive,* less than $60.

The Pillar and Post Inn. *Expensive.* 48 John St. at King, Box 1011, L0S 1J0; 468–2123; in Toronto, 361–1931. A pleasing mixture of old and new décor, with pool, sauna, and tri-level lounge. As with just about everything here, it's about five minutes' walk from any of the theaters.

Prince of Wales Hotel. *Expensive.* 6 Picton St. L0S 1J0; 468–3246. One of the Princes of Wales did indeed sleep here, but it's not clear which—there are about eight to choose from. The newest addition to the original 1864 building offers bigger rooms at a higher price. Pool, sauna, and a tasteful nineteenth-century dining room.

Moffat Inn. *Moderate.* 60 Picton St., Box 158, L0S 1J0; 416–468–4116. Built in 1835, its 12 rooms have been lovingly renovated.

The Oban Inn. *Moderate.* 160 Front St., Box 94, L0S 1J0; 468–2165. More than 150 years old, it owns one of the nicest views in town. Comfortable and English-flavored, with a first-class Sunday buffet in the dining room.

The Angel Inn. *Inexpensive.* 224 Regent St. L0S 1J0; 468–3411. Named for the wife of the man who restored it after the War of 1812, it's filled with museum pieces and canopy beds.

Royal Anchorage Motor Hotel. *Inexpensive.* 186 Ricardo St. L0S 1J0; 468–2141. Right on the river, close to Fort George, and only minutes from the theaters. Not quite as classically antique as the others, but very respectable.

TOURIST INFORMATION. The Niagara-on-the-Lake Chamber of Commerce has a full line of tourist and theater information at the Court House Theatre (Queen and Victoria streets). Call 468–2326.

TOURS. The Niagara Foundation tour of local homes and gardens happens only once a year, on a Saturday in late May or early June. Check with the Chamber of Commerce for the date, 416–468–2326. It's the definitive tour of the old and stately homes.

Inniskillin Wines, one of the first companies to convince Canadians that domestic wines can be more than just tolerable, offers free pre-arranged tours (call 468–2187) May 1 through December 25, Tuesday through Saturday,10:00 A.M. to 4:00 P.M. The winery is located just south of town on the Niagara Parkway.

 PARKS. Almost the entire length of the river through town is public parkland, and the sleepiest part of the entire Niagara Parks System lies just south of town on the way to Queenston. Here the Niagara is tame and idyllic, a perfect spot for a picnic. Simcoe Park at King and Queen streets is good for children. It has a wading pool and swings, as well as picnic tables and flowers.

 HISTORICAL SITES. *Fort George.* The fort was the focal point of armed activity between the United States and Canada in the last century. It was leveled by American guns during the War of 1812 and restored in bits and pieces from 1930 onwards. Now a fully operative tourist attraction, it is open seven days a week, from 10:00 A.M. to 6:00 P.M. during the summer and by appointment only between Labour Day and October 31. Adult admission is $2, children 16 years and under, $1 with a $6 family rate. Phone 468–4257 for information.

Niagara Historical Museum. 43 Castlereagh Ave.; 468–3912. The area is rich in military and heroic history, and much of it is revealed here in over 20,000 artifacts, including mementos of the deeds of Laura Secord (1812 war hero, later made famous by a candy maker); John Graves Simcoe (the first lieutenant-governor of Upper Canada); and Sir Isaac Brock (who would have claimed the British-Canadian victory at the Battle of Queenston Heights had he not perished by unwisely charging uphill during it). Open daily from 10:00 A.M. to 6:00 P.M. from mid-May through mid-October; at other times open daily from 1:00 P.M. to 5:00 P.M., except Monday.

McFarland House. 2 kilometers (1 mile) south of the Niagara Parkway. A refurbished Georgian house, built circa 1800, with period furniture. A picnic pavilion and snack bar make it a good lunching spot. Open Saturday through Wednesday, 11:00 A.M. to 6:00 P.M., from July 1 to September 13; weekends only from mid-May through the end of June. Adults, $.75; accompanied children under 12, free.

 THEATER. The Shaw Festival. The drama of Shaw and his contemporaries brings the majority of summer visitors to the town. Starting humbly in 1962 with a performance of *Don Juan in Hell,* it now runs a full May–October season with more than half-a-dozen plays in three locations. Alternately adored and criticized, it is always taken seriously and provides high-quality productions of famous and obscure dramas and comedies.

Rush seats are available for weekday performances only at $16 a seat, on the day of the performance. The sale starts at 10:00 A.M. at the box office in the Festival Theater. Not available for Sat. or Sun. matinee or Sat. evening. Ticket information is available by writing to the Shaw Festival Box Office, P.O. Box 774, Niagara-on-the-Lake, Ont. LOS 1JO. Phone 468–3201 from town or toll-free from Toronto, 361–1544.

The main Festival Theater (corner, Queen and Wellington streets), is open the entire season. Tickets are $12 to $26.50 during the week, $20 to $32.50 on weekends. Evening performances every day but Monday, with Wednesday, Saturday, and Sunday matinees.

The Royal George Theatre, restored to Georgian primness, runs from mid-May through early October. Prices are $5.50 to $17.50 on weekdays, $17.50 to $22.50 on weekends. Dates and times same as Festival Theater above.

The Court House Theater is open only during the July through September height of the season, with prices, dates, and times the same as the Royal George Theater above.

DINING OUT. The food fare is as classy as the accommodation in Niagara-on-the-Lake. There's not a wide variety of cuisines, but the standards are lovingly treated in some beautiful surroundings. Prices are based on an average three-course meal for one, excluding alcohol, tips, and extras. Categories defined by price are as follows: *Expensive:* $20 and up; *Moderate,* $10–$20; *Inexpensive,* under $10. All of the restaurants listed below accept major credit cards.

The Luis House. *Expensive.* 245 King St.; 468–4038. A conservative, unpretentious eatery opened in 1979. A family place, it serves beef, ribs, crab, sole, salmon. L, D.

The Oban Inn. *Expensive.* 160 Front St.; 468–7811. Steak, roast beef, lobster, and duck are the standards here. Splendid view of the lake and decor accented by foliage. A hearty Sunday buffet is first-class.

The Prince of Wales Hotel. *Expensive.* 6 Picton St.; 468–3246. Ambitiously rich and often successful European and Continental cuisine in nineteenth-century surroundings. Rack of lamb is a specialty. Lunch, dinner, and after-theater snacks.

Angel Inn. *Moderate.* 224 Regent St.; 468–3411. A friendly and extremely well-fed ghost haunts this, the oldest extant building in town. Steak, seafood, and duck are the standards, with the "Catholic Cake" a dessert feature. It's been blessed, with all the calories taken out, says the owner. Lunch and dinner, with after-theater fare until 1:00 A.M.

The Buttery. *Moderate.* 19 Queen St.; 468–2564. A regular menu is buttressed by a weekend "Henry VIII" feast that will cause the belts to be loosened. In The Tavern, an array of snacks are perfect for after-theater hunger. Lunch and dinner.

George III. *Moderate.* 61 Melville St.; 468–4207. Prime rib is the specialty, but the alternate Chinese menu offers Kwang Tong Chow Mein, with everything but the kitchen sink in it.

STRATFORD

A Theatrical Experience

by
PAUL MCGRATH

There are few Ontario pastimes that are more civilized than polishing off a picnic lunch on the expansive front lawn of the Stratford Festival Theatre while waiting for the theater's trumpeters to play a fanfare announcing the start of the day's performance. The swans drift by on the Avon River, the willows shimmer on the small Avon islands, and a lazy crowd of theater-goers make their way up the incline to the theater. This has been the Stratford summer lifestyle for the past thirty years and is likely to remain so.

When artistic director Tyrone Guthrie started his bold experiment of bringing Shakespeare to the Ontario countryside three decades ago, he set in motion an enterprise that has transformed this rural town of 26,000 into a major showcase of English and Canadian theater. Few people thought it would succeed, and no one in 1953 would have bet it would still be alive even ten years later.

Stratford is a dainty little town, not quite so self-consciously preserved as Niagara-on-the-Lake (which, with Stratford and London, is the third of Ontario's world-famous theatrical-festival trio) but with enough pleasant refurbishing and restoration to give it a historic air befitting the Shakespearean bias of the annual drama festival.

Like Niagara-on-the-Lake (see the previous chapter), the city can be covered comfortably on foot in a morning's walk. The festival theater is at the eastern end of the city, and surrounding it is pretty parkland that stretches down to the river, where paddle boats and canoes move as lazily as the swans, and two islands provide lush tree cover for afternoon meals or, to be more in the proper spirit of things, play readings.

Lakeside Drive is a lovely street that leads from the theater to downtown, no more than fifteen minutes away on foot. To the south along the way, on Nile and Front streets, there are beautiful homes lost in trees, some of them offering bed-and-breakfast accommodation. As well, Lakeside Drive is where you'll find canoe and paddle-boat rentals. The Waterloo Street bridge to the right leads to even more serene surroundings on the north side of the river, where fewer people tend to go.

Lakeside Drive becomes Erie Street when it reaches downtown, and at the corner of Erie and Ontario streets you're in the thick of the commercial section, with establishments such as Gallery 96 on York Lane, a co-op run to display works by regional artists, and Village Studios, 69 Ontario Street; art galleries, china, glassware, and linens shops, such as The Linen Shop, 13 Market Place; records, books (with a strong suit in things dramatic), antiques, children's dolls, and just plain souvenirs are there in profusion. Many of the wares are quite tasteful, if not a little expensive. The tourist information outlets are close at hand at 38 Albert Street and at the intersection of Lakeside Drive and Ontario Street. The material you get here can be perused in a leisurely manner in the Shakespearean Gardens, one block west at the foot of the Huron-Street bridge. Close at hand, on Downie Street, the restored City Hall is the centerpiece of a classic town square, little changed from the Stratford of the last century.

Heading back in the direction of the theater, east along Ontario Street, a mini-downtown presents itself, starting at Front Street, with jewelry by Aylesworth, the city's resident goldsmith, on sale at The Carriage House Works, and fine food at The Church Restaurant, so revered that it is often booked solid for weeks on end during the height

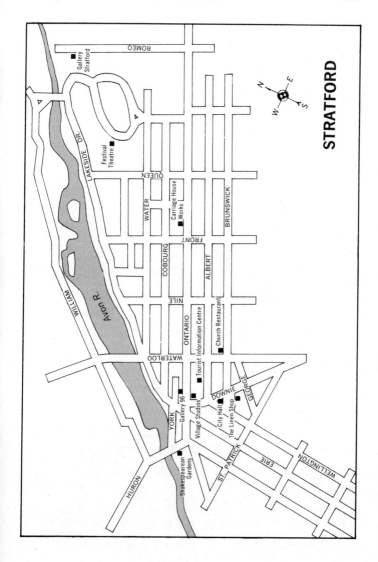

STRATFORD

of the season. If you're late for the theater, turn left on Queen Street. If not, keep going until you get to Romeo Street and turn left. A five-minute detour left down Romeo Street will bring you to The Gallery Stratford, at 54 Romeo Street North. Open all year, but with special seasonal shows, it is set in a small pine woods and sculpture garden. A small gallery, it is blessed with imaginative administration. Here you might catch an exhibition of theatrical costumes next door to a display of contemporary French tapestries or American photography. It is worth the detour.

PRACTICAL INFORMATION FOR STRATFORD

HOW TO GET THERE. Stratford is 157 kilometers (90 miles) from Toronto. **By car,** take Highway 401 west to interchange 35, then go north on Highway 8 and west on Highways 7 and 8 (combined).

By bus. Gray Coach runs bus service to Stratford six times a day, starting at 6:30 A.M. from the Toronto terminal at Dundas and Bay streets. The trip takes between two-and-a-half and three hours. Phone 979–3511 in Toronto.

By train. Via Rail runs from Union Station five times a day. Phone 366–8411 for fares and exact times.

TELEPHONES. The area code for Stratford and surrounding areas is 519. Directory assistance from Toronto is free by dialing 1–519–555–1212 and from inside Stratford by dialing 411.

HOTELS AND MOTELS. It can be tough finding accommodations during the festival season. The city does not have an abundance of rooms, and what's available is pricier during the summer than at other times. Bed-and-breakfast accommodations are often the cheapest and most pleasant way to get around the problem; contact the Stratford and Area Visitor and Convention Bureau, 38 Albert St. (271–5140) for a list of B & Bs. Hotel rates are based on double occupancy; categories determined by price are as follows: *Expensive,* $80 and up; *Moderate,* $60–$80; *Inexpensive,* under $60.

The Festival Motor Inn. *Expensive.* 1144 Ontario St. N5A 6W1; (519) 273–1150. A semi-rural setting on acres of land at the east-end outskirts of the city. A quick drive to the theater.

The Jester Arms, *Expensive.* 107 Ontario St. N5A 3H1; (519) 271–1121. Only 13 suites, with an English pub and dining room.

The Victorian Inn. *Expensive.* 10 Romeo St. N. N5A 5M7; (519) 271–4650. Standard modern accommodations with pool, sauna, dining, and the pleasant Library Bar. Just a cork's pop from the main theater. All major credit cards.

The Raj House. *Moderate to Expensive.* 123 Church St. N5A 2R3; (519) 271–7129. An elegant bed-and-breakfast, with 14 rooms furnished with antiques and curios.

Swan Motel. *Inexpensive.* 1482 Downie St. S. N5A 6S3; (519) 271–6376. Nineteen rooms at the south end of Stratford, most of the way out of town into the pleasant surrounding countryside. No credit cards.

Traveller's Motel. *Inexpensive.* 784 Ontario St. N5A 3K1; (519) 271–3830. Only 22 rooms, close to the downtown, and they'll babysit children during performances. MasterCard and Visa; no AE.

HOW TO GET AROUND. Stratford is eminently walkable, but for short hops in a hurry call Radio Cab at 271–4242.

 TOURIST INFORMATION. The Stratford and Area Visitor's and Convention Bureau operates year round and has a full range of information at 38 Albert St.; phone 271–5140. During festival season there is a tourist information booth at the corner of Lakeside Drive and Ontario Street, as well as a special theater information phone service at 271–7080.

 SEASONAL EVENTS. May. *Festival City Days.* A parade, dance, and pancake breakfast kick off the season.

July. The *Festival of Arts and Crafts* is the highlight of the summer-long Art-in-the-Park exhibition.

Blyth Summer Festival. 70 kilometers (42 miles) northwest of Stratford is the tiny town of Blyth, which annually holds a modest but theatrically inventive alternative to the Stratford gala. Plays relating to the lives of the local inhabitants highlight this festival. To get to Blyth, take Highway 8 west to Clinton, then Highway 4 north to Blyth. From Stratford, call 1–523–9300 for tickets and performance information.

July–August. *Stratford Summer Music.* Daily except Mondays, an ongoing concert program of jazz, classics, and pop at City Hall Auditorium and Knox Presbyterian Church.

 TOURS. Local dining and theater performances are wound into tours of the city run by *Stratford Tours Inc.* They'll take both individuals and groups. Phone 271–8181 or write to P.O. Box 45, Stratford, Ont. N5A 6S8.

The *Avon Historical Society* conducts one-hour tours of historic Stratford, Monday through Saturday, at 9:30 A.M. from July 1 through Labour Day. They start at the tourist information booth at Lakeside Drive and Ontario Street (on nice days only).

PARKS. Some 175 acres of parkland run the length of the Avon River through Stratford on both sides of the river. Picnicking in small or large groups is not only permitted but encouraged. Keep in mind that the only good swan is one that's at least three feet away—they can cause extremely nasty bruises with their wings and beaks.

GARDENS. The *Shakespearean Gardens* (near the bridge at the beginning of Huron St.) features formal arrangements of most of the flowers that Shakespeare mentioned in his sonnets and plays. The essence of botanic serenity.

CAMPING. There are accommodations for tents and recreational vehicles at *Wildwood Conservation Area,* ten miles south of Stratford on Highway 7. Activities include sailing, swimming, and fishing.

PARTICIPANT SPORTS. In St. Mary's, 16 kilometers (10 miles) south of Stratford on Highway 7, there is swimming in the stone quarry, referred to locally as "Canada's largest outdoor swimming pool." It's free.

MUSEUMS AND ART GALLERIES. *The Gallery Stratford.* 54 Romeo St.; 271–5271. Open all year, but special summer shows featuring contemporary art and sculpture are the attraction. Admission: adults, $2.00; students (12–16), $1.00; accompanied children free.

Village Studio. 69 Ontario St.; 271–7371. It features a collection of crafts from more than 50 Canadian artisans. Admission free.

The *St. Marys District Museum* in the nearby town of St. Marys is located in a large stone house on a hill. The museum features pioneer artifacts. Open afternoons, May to October. Closed Mondays

MUSIC. *Stratford Summer Music* runs in conjunction with the drama festival and features jazz, classical, light pop, and folk. Main venues are City Hall Auditorium and Knox Presbyterian Church. Times fluctuate. Call 273–2117, or write to Stratford Summer Music, 38 Albert St., Stratford, Ont. N5A 6T3.

THEATER. At the height of the season there is a choice of three different plays on many nights. Tickets for all three venues can be ordered by writing The Festival Theatre, Stratford N5A 6V2, or by phoning 271–4040. The **Festival Theater** (55 Queen St.) is the stellar, Shakespearean venue, with an unusual thrust stage set in a billowing, fan-shaped example of 1950s architecture. It's open the entire length of the season, from early June through mid-October. Nightly performances Tuesday through Sunday, with Wednesday and Saturday matinees. Ticket prices range from $7.50 to $30.00, the high end applying only on weekends in summer. Weekday and fall prices are lower.

The **Avon Theatre,** downtown at 99 Downie St., is the site for the non-Shakespearean drama offered during the season, including the now-customary Gilbert and Sullivan operettas. The last two G & S productions have gone on to become national television hits. Its season length and performance schedule, as well as ticket prices, are the same as the Festival Theater above, early June to mid-October.

The Third Stage, on Lakeshore Drive close to downtown, is the newest addition to the Stratford lineup, and is home of the Festival's *Young Company.* Its season is shorter than that at the other venues, but there are evening and matinee performances at the height of the season in July and August. General admission for all productions is $15. Get there early.

SHOPPING. Good taste is standard in specialty shops in the downtown area, and prices are not particularly out of line.

Fanfare Books, 30 Waterloo St. S.; 273–1010. Canadian authors, children's literature, and things Shakespearean are the strengths here in a thoughtful, serious collection of books. *Festival Gift Shop,* in Conestoga College opposite the Festival Theater lobby; 271–4040. A good range of souvenirs, sketches, reproductions, and posters relating to the festival.

DINING OUT. Stratford has a few restaurants of the type that would not ordinarily be found in a town this size. High-class English and Continental cuisine is favored in the more expensive spots, but there is an ample supply of more standard fare. Ratings based on the price of an average three-course meal for one person, excluding alcohol and tips are as follows: *Expensive,* over $25; *Moderate,* $15–$25; *Inexpensive,* under $15. Unless stated otherwise, major credit cards are accepted..

The Church. *Expensive.* Corner of Waterloo and Brunswick streets; 273–3424. Owner John Mandel runs the city's most acclaimed restaurant amid the pews of a renovated church. A luncheon buffet features exotic salads, cold beef and salmon, and daily hot dishes. Dinner is a *prix fixe* menu, while after-dinner eating revolves around a dazzling buffet. The décor is true to the name: very inspiring. Reservations are advised during the height of the season. All major credit cards, except American Express. Closed Monday, except when music concerts fall on that day during the season.

Rundles. *Expensive.* 9 Cobourg St.; 271–6442. Caspian caviar and ragout of lobster and red snapper are the temptations here. Summer dining on a terrace overlooking the water. Reservations are required in the thick of the season. Lunch and dinner.

The Old Prune. *Expensive–Moderate.* 151 Albert St.; 271–5052. Traditional Canadian cuisine with a Quebec accent. Dining on a peaceful garden patio in summer or in three pleasant rooms when the weather gets nippy. Lunch and dinner.

Mothers. *Inexpensive.* 988 Ontario St.; 273–3131. Standard Italian fare, perfect for when the kids are screaming for pizza. No credit cards.

NIGHTLIFE. The Jester's Arms. 107 Ontario St.; 271–1121. Cabaret performances during the drama season, with good, standard English pub food to munch on. There are also rooms available.

INDEX

The index contains four sections. The first section includes general information for Toronto and nearby attractions. The second section includes practical information for Toronto and its attractions. The third section includes geographical information for Toronto. The last section includes both geographical and practical information for nearby attractions which are: Niagara Falls, Niagara-on-the-Lake, and Stratford.

General Information

Practical Information for Toronto

Geographical information for Toronto

Nearby Attractions

Speak a foreign language in seconds.

Now an amazing space age device makes it possible to speak a foreign language *without* having to learn a foreign language.

Speak French, German, or Spanish.

With the incredible Translator 8000—world's first pocket-size electronic translation machines —you're never at a loss for words in France, Germany, or Spain.

8,000-word brain.

Just punch in the foreign word or phrase, and English appears on the LED display. Or punch in English, and read the foreign equivalent instantly.

Only 4¾" x 2¾", it possesses a fluent 8,000-word vocabulary (4,000 English, 4,000 foreign). A memory key stores up to 16 words; a practice key randomly calls up words for study, self-

testing, or game use. And it's also a full-function calculator.

150,000 sold in 18 months.

Manufactured for Langenscheidt by Sharp/Japan, the Translator 8000 comes with a 6-month warranty. It's a valuable aid for business and pleasure travelers, and students. It comes in a handsome leatherette case, and makes a super gift.

Order now with the information below.